Paul Wood is a doctor of psychology, motivational speaker, leadership and personal development specialist, media personality, husband and father. At 18, he was in prison and his life was completely off the rails. In his work today, Paul uses his subsequent journey from delinquent to doctor to illustrate the process of transformational change and how we can strive to be the best possible versions of ourselves. In his work today, Paul assists others pursue excellence, have more meaningful lives, and flourish through adversity by enhancing their capacity to cope effectively under stress and recover and grow afterwards. He does this through his deep knowledge of psychology, the insights he gained through his own journey from delinquent to doctor, and his experience of working with elite performers across industries and occupations. He wrote about his own journey in the instant bestseller *How to Escape from Prison* (2019). Paul contributes regularly to the media and works with a number of charities that focus on helping young men avoid prison or reintegrate effectively on release. He lives in Wellington, New Zealand.

www.paulwood.com

Dr. PAUL WOOD

MENTAL FITNESS

HarperCollins*Publishers*

IMPORTANT INFORMATION
While this book is intended as a general information resource and all care has been taken in compiling the contents, this book does not take account of individual circumstances and this book is not in any way a substitute for medical advice. To ensure safe practice, before starting any new exercise, diet or weight-loss program, please consult with a qualified medical practitioner as well as a qualified personal trainer and nutritionist or dietitian to ensure the recommendations meet your specific needs, especially if you have a pre-existing medical condition. The author and the publisher cannot be held responsible for any claim or action that may arise from reliance on the information contained in this book.

HarperCollins*Publishers*
Australia • Brazil • Canada • France • Germany • Holland • India
Italy • Japan • Mexico • New Zealand • Poland • Spain • Sweden
Switzerland • United Kingdom • United States of America

First published in 2021
by HarperCollins*Publishers* (New Zealand) Limited
Unit D1, 63 Apollo Drive, Rosedale, Auckland 0632, New Zealand
harpercollins.co.nz

A catalogue record for this book is available from the National Library of New Zealand.

ISBN 978 1 7755 4167 7 (pbk)
ISBN 978 1 7754 9198 9 (ebook)
ISBX 978 1 4607 8647 5 (audiobook)

Cover design by Jack Smyth
Front cover image by Nora Carol Photography / Getty Images
Typeset in Sabon LT Std by Kirby Jones

For my wife Mary-Ann and our sons Braxton and Gordy.
You give my life meaning.

CONTENTS

PROLOGUE

My name is Paul Wood.

My story to date is relatively well known. I was born in Wellington and grew up in Karori, a fairly average New Zealand suburb. I was lucky enough to come from a good home, with two parents, and while we weren't wealthy, we never went hungry or wanted for any of the basics. I have three brothers, and I was on good — if often robust — terms with all of them. I went to a good college, until we parted company on mutually agreed terms.

But I was what psychologists call a 'high sensation-seeker'. I was attracted to physical risk and wasn't too fussed about which side of the law I found it on. I was already involved in petty crime by the time I was 12, and within a couple of years of that I was no stranger to substance abuse.

I also had a tragically mistaken view of what it was to be a man. I was conditioned by my upbringing and by prevailing social attitudes to believe that to be masculine was to be physically, mentally and emotionally invulnerable. Anything short of these ideals — physical weakness, or mental or emotional vulnerability — was contemptible. I now realise that real strength comes through managing such oh so human vulnerabilities, not in denying them. I wasn't the biggest kid at school, but from as early as I can remember I wanted to be the toughest, and I was drawn to sports that featured lots of physical confrontation: I got involved in martial arts and I played rugby league. When I thought of the future (which wasn't that often), I dreamed of a career in the Army — definitely infantry, probably Special Forces.

By the time I was in my mid-teens, I was veering off the rails. I was fighting a lot in order to prove myself to myself and win the respect of my mates, and was on the fringes of gang culture. I was doing more and harder drugs, particularly opiates. And my criminal activity was escalating as I chose the company of antisocial associates.

My mother had been diagnosed with breast cancer, and my parents were wholly absorbed with her treatment and recovery at precisely the time I probably needed reining in — which is not in any way laying the blame at their doorstep, but rather a recognition of the fact that probably the only chance that anyone had of pulling me back into line was missed. Even then, it was only a slim chance. I was a teenage boy, after all: cocky, bulletproof and attracted to chaos.

I had a girlfriend around then, and when I was finally dragged into court on burglary charges, her parents saw enough potential in me to attempt an intervention. They were leaving New Zealand for their native Chile, and by offering to take me with them, they helped me dodge the sentence that was otherwise inevitable. I was 14. I lived with them in Chile for the best part of a year before Dad called to tell me that Mum's cancer had returned and this time it was terminal. It was time to come home.

Back in New Zealand, I wasted little time in reconnecting with the same old group of dodgy mates and falling back into drug abuse and criminality. Meanwhile, Mum's condition deteriorated. She lived longer than expected, and died when I was 18.

Three days later, I found myself in a situation with which I was woefully ill-equipped to deal. The man from whom I had been buying drugs engineered an excuse to be alone with me in my flat, then made a forceful sexual advance on me when I was high on morphine. I had been sexually abused when I was 13, and had repressed rather than come to terms with that experience. All of the anger, pain and confusion arising from that life event, the intensity of the grief I felt at my mother's death, a million other frustrations and disappointments ... these all contributed to what happened next. I reacted violently, and by the time I had finished, I had beaten a man to death. There was a point where I had defended myself, but instead of then letting him leave, I chose to take actions that ended his life.

I was arrested, charged, tried and sentenced to life imprisonment. Over the next 11 years, I spent time in some of New Zealand's toughest prisons. For well over half of my sentence, I was far from a model prisoner: I spent my entire time doing drugs to avoid contemplating my situation, and planning to escape so that I could resume the life of crime, drug-taking and mayhem for which it seemed I was destined. For this reason, I was regularly in trouble, and spent lots of time in solitary confinement.

Nothing about my story to this point is that different to the stories of many of those with whom I was in prison and shared cells (apart, perhaps, from the fact that my home life gave me less reason to be in prison). And I could so easily have shared the future of most of them, too: the dismal cycle of release, recidivist offending, re-imprisonment. But through luck as much as through anything else, my path crossed those of some people who encouraged me to begin to look at my life and prospects in a different light.

One of these men asked me to predict whether, if he dropped them from the same height, a heavier or a lighter object would hit the floor first. He held out a scrunched-up ball of paper in one hand and a tennis ball in the other.

Well, any moron knew that the heavier object would fall faster, didn't they?

He had to perform the experiment twice, and I had to perform it for myself to ensure there was no trick, before I could believe the evidence of my eyes, which flatly contradicted what I had believed. I had just been introduced to the Galilean principle of gravity — it is not the weight of the objects that determined how fast they fell, but rather the equally experienced gravitational pull of the earth. And that was the start of it, really. If I could be so profoundly wrong about something of which I was so staunchly convinced, which other deep-rooted beliefs did I hold that were also wrong? Perhaps some of my beliefs about myself and my potential were wrong, too.

With the encouragement of several of the positive influences who were around me at the time, I enrolled in a university course. I wasn't thinking noble thoughts of rehabilitation or anything like that; my original plan was to do a legal executive course so that I could more effectively argue my own case in my many grievance and disciplinary hearings against the prison authorities. Nor did I have high expectations: I had put little effort in at school and had failed to achieve; many of my teachers had assured me I was useless, and that had reinforced my belief that there was no point in trying. It was what psychologists call a 'vicious cycle' or a 'negative feedback loop', and it's a common enough example of one, too.

But the first assignment I did for my extramural university course — ignorant, naïve and chaotic as it seems to me now — got a pass mark, and that was a revelation. That little dose of affirmation left me craving more, and I began to put more effort into my reading and thinking. More than that, I found myself actually *enjoying* reading and thinking in their own right. It was what's called a 'virtuous cycle' or a 'positive feedback loop': the more I enjoyed the work, the more effort I put in, and the better my marks became, which encouraged me to put more effort in. The fact that your outcomes are directly related to the work you put in is going to be a key theme of the book you are about to read.

The subject that captivated me was psychology. By now, I had turned away from the firm conviction that I was a career criminal, and that everything I did — including university study — was only worth doing if it made me a better criminal, and a more resourceful inmate. By the time I graduated with a Bachelor of Arts degree in Psychology, I had begun to imagine other futures for myself. I had kicked my drug habit, as I had realised dope was getting in the way of my study, which I had come to value above everything else. And I had made the conscious decision to make life-affirming, pro-social choices from now on. I didn't always succeed, but I was on the right path.

By the time I became eligible for parole, I had finished my master's degree in psychology and was a year into my doctorate. When I was finally released, I was two years into my PhD and had a job with a psychology consultancy. I stepped out into the sunshine on the day of my release and vowed that I would never do anything that might result in my recall to prison. And in fact, I have done such a good job of living my way into the future I imagined for myself that after 14 years of release, the parole board recently took the almost unprecedented step of extinguishing my obligation to periodically report to my parole officer.

My present has turned out to be even better than the future I hoped I would have. I married an amazing woman and have two lovely children. These days, I have my own business doing what I love, helping others to recognise and realise their potential. And I am involved in a number of charities and programmes that support those in prison who want to turn their lives around.

Of course, my story has a dark flipside. All I have become, all of the opportunities that have come my way and got me where I am, I denied to the victim of my crime. He was a villain. But so was I, and I managed to turn my life around: I denied him the chance to do the same. I have, as the phrase goes, 'paid my debt to society', but I will never be able to undo the wrong that I did to my victim or his family.

I have used this to motivate myself. I owe it to myself and everyone that was hurt by my actions to be the best person I can be, and to do the most good in the world that I can in the precious time that is left to me. In life we can choose to be the villain, the hero or the coward. Often our choice is heavily influenced by the cards we are dealt, the role models we see, and the experiences we have had. Yet we can always choose to play a different role. That choice is always in our control, and it is never too late. This book will ensure that you can develop and maintain the psychological and emotional capacity you need to make the right choice.

*

In my work, in some of the workshops that I facilitate, in the public talks that I do, I use the story I've just told you to illustrate much of what I'm seeking to teach. When you boil it down, it's a story of how powerful the human mind can be to work change in our lives.

Like most powers, the mind can work for or against you. It was my mind that held me back, that made me blind to my own potential, in my early years. It was my mind that ultimately enabled me to change my situation for the better. And what I learned along the way is that your mind is like a muscle. The more you use it, the better it gets, just like any other muscle. It's possible to become mentally tougher and more resilient, just as it's possible to become physically fitter. All it takes in either case is effort.

In this book, I'll explore the concept of what we'll call mental fitness — mental toughness, strength and resilience. In psychology, mental toughness focuses on the ability to remain effective under pressure, while resilience relates to flourishing through adversity and then recovering afterwards. Mental fitness is what allows you to unlock your potential, to feel mentally strong, be happier with your life on a day-to-day basis, to imagine better futures for yourself and to live your way into them. It's also what helps you get through times of crisis and bounce back afterwards, or even come out better off as a result of the adversity.

We'll start by looking at you, the human animal. We'll look at how you've been equipped by nature to deal with life, because it's only once you understand how your mind interacts with reality that you can begin to understand some of the more baffling aspects of your existence, such as the way you think, feel and behave in different situations. At the same time, we'll bust some of the less helpful myths that we in the developed world labour under, most notably the myth of eternal happiness. We'll try to change some of the mental models you have about both happiness and stress.

Next, we'll look at the steps that you can take to proactively increase your capacity to feel positive and optimistic, to realise your potential, to flourish as a human being.

Then we'll have a look at how a combination of a decent level of mental fitness and a few simple tricks used by the Special Forces and others can help you when, as always happens sooner or later, the shit hits the fan. One of my favourite sayings is attributed to the Roman philosopher Seneca: 'Luck is what happens when preparation meets opportunity.' Life can be relied upon to provide you with opportunities to cope in a crisis. I'll be encouraging you to take a warrior's approach to the battles ahead, by beginning your preparation right now.

And lastly, we'll look at ways in which you can turn what you've learned in this book to good use, by embedding some of the behaviours as habits. Just like physical fitness, the benefits of mental fitness come not from what you know or the effort you put in on any one occasion, but rather from what you do on a regular and consistent basis. In both cases, it is the small daily disciplines that put a bounce in your step over time and equip you for whatever the future may hold.

1

The Monkey in the Mirror

You're driving on the motorway at 100 km/h when the brake lights of the car in front of you go on. What happens next depends on the distance you've allowed between your car and that car, for precisely this contingency.

Your eyes register the brake lights. The information is relayed to your brain, where it is processed and a decision is relayed to your muscles, which perform the various operations required: to step off the accelerator and apply pressure to the brake pedal. After that, it's all a matter of simple physics — driving conditions and what shape your brakes, tyres and suspension are in. Suppose everything's average, you'll come to a stop within 56 metres from the point that those brake lights first went on, before you plough into the rear of the car in front. That's because you're a prudent driver, and you've been repeating, 'Only a fool breaks the two-second rule' to yourself each time the car in front passed a stationary object beside the road. Whenever you've passed the same object before you've finished saying the sentence, you've eased off to open the gap a bit. The sentence takes roughly two seconds to say, and an object travelling at 100 km/h — you and your car — covers roughly 56 metres in that two-second interval.

Human reaction times — the time that elapses between a sensory stimulus and a motor response — were the very first brain operations to be scientifically measured, in a series of experiments performed by an Austrian named Franciscus Donders in the 1860s. They vary from individual to individual, and they get longer as you age (which you can verify by chucking a tennis ball at your granddad). Young men can react to a visual stimulus in as little as 180 microseconds (thousandths of a second). By the time you're in your 80s, it might take you as long as 800 microseconds to react. The average human reaction time is reckoned to be a little under 300 microseconds. This being the case (and amazing as it seems), your car will hurtle along at 100 km/h for fully 8 metres before you even react to the brake lights in front of you. (By the way, we humans are pretty slow. Other animals, if they could drive a car, wouldn't need a two-second rule. Dogs wouldn't need a one-second rule. Cats wouldn't even need a half-second rule.)

Our reaction times evolved to keep us alive. They're a function of how sharp our senses are and the speed at which we can move. The fastest human being of all time (Usain Bolt) has been recorded running at a shade under 45 km/h between the 60- and 80-metre marks of a 100-metre sprint. But thanks to technology, Usain Bolt and Usain Bolt's granddad can drive at 100 km/h, or more. We are simply not adapted to moving at the kinds of speeds that we can now reach. Hence, the two-second rule was invented, to try to keep us safe.

It's when you consider, like this, the mismatch that exists

between the world which we evolved to live in and the world we *actually* live in that you begin to understand why modern life can be such a challenge. We have brains that evolved to help us survive a hunter-gatherer lifestyle on the African savannah, which are not that well-suited to coping with the demands of life in the developed world. To continue the motoring metaphor, we evolved into off-road vehicles but now we're asking them to tackle a Formula One racecourse. No wonder we get untidy on the corners!

What's the time, Mr Wolf?

There's a meme — you may well have seen it — comprising two frames, one above the other. In the top frame, there's a picture of a staring timber wolf, all apex-predator intensity. The caption reads something like: 'I'm cold and hungry. I see humans around a campfire. Maybe I could ask for some food ... what's the worst that could happen?' The frame beneath features a pug wearing a crocheted bonnet in the shape of a birthday cake with three candles. Its wet, buggy eyes stare out at us in mute, miserable appeal. It's captioned: '30,000 years later'.

You'd be hard-pressed believing that squashed-faced little lapdogs like pugs share a common ancestor not all that very far back with Siberian huskies, say, or Great Danes. But it's true. All breeds of dogs, from the Mexican hairless to the Rhodesian ridgeback, can interbreed. They're the same species, after all. And for dogs, the differences in their appearance, so striking to us, is pretty trivial to them. In dog world, it's the inner dog that counts. That's why you'll sometimes see a Great Dane cringing in submission to a pug or a chihuahua. They share a common language — the same language, most probably, that their wolf ancestors spoke.

Being social animals, dogs are adroit communicators. As soon as one dog comes into view of another, they start sending each another signals. Ears prick, noses twitch, tails tentatively wag. A negotiation has begun to determine where each belongs in the Great Chain of Dog Being, so that they can work out how they're going to share space with one another. One dog will usually signal submission — putting its ears back, crouching a bit lower to the ground, flicking its tail between its legs. The other, meanwhile, will raise its ears, tail and hackles and walk stiffly, as tall as it can make itself. As they come into proximity, depending on how satisfactorily they have worked out their respective statuses, they will either relax and greet, or escalate things. The dominant dog might growl and show its teeth. The submissive dog will sit on its haunches or roll over on its back, even urinate (total don't-kill-me submission). If all of this fails to establish who's boss dog with sufficient clarity, the matter will be sorted out with a fight.

Our best friend is a timber wolf at heart, 30,000 years of domestication and selective breeding notwithstanding. A pug and a timber wolf would likely have little difficulty understanding one another, despite being, to the human eye, completely different animals. In other words, you can take the dog out of the wolf pack, but you can't take the wolf pack out of the dog.

Meet your rellies

There's no agreement on when our remote ancestors first became 'human'. Millions of years back, definitely in Africa but quite possibly in other parts of the world as well, there were populations of human-like creatures. Around 3.6 million years ago, at a place now called Laetoli, in northern Tanzania, a volcano erupted, strewing the surrounding countryside with ash. A few weeks later, it did it again. But between these eruptions, a group of ape-like creatures picked their way cautiously across the plain. Their feet left clearly defined prints in the first layer of ash, exactly as your cat leaves its prints in freshly laid concrete. Then the second layer of ash blanketed it and preserved it, pristine, until 1978, when the first few prints were uncovered.

The remarkable thing about the so-called 'Laetoli footprints' is that the creature that made them walked almost exactly like us — the heel struck first, then weight was transferred to the ball of the foot before the walker pushed off with the toes. This indicated the walker, like us, walked upright on two legs most, if not all of the time. This was a remarkable conclusion, because it helped to disprove the theory that the ability to walk upright, which freed the hands for carrying and using tools, was a distinguishing feature of emerging humanity. The Laetoli walkers weren't much like us at all. They belonged to a species named *Australopithecus afarensis* (literally, 'southern African ape') and, as the name suggests, they looked far more like modern apes or monkeys than like *Homo sapiens* (us). There is no evidence that they used tools.

A million years or so later, a recognisably more human-like creature lived nearby in the vicinity of the Olduvai Gorge, also in Tanzania. The oldest fossilised remains of *Homo habilis* (literally, 'handy man') that have been found date to around 2.8 million years ago, and the species was so named because the remains were consistently associated with stones that had been deliberately shaped and used as tools.

This is one signifier of human-like intelligence; another is that Handy Man's skull seems designed for a brain that was larger than those of apes or other early human-like creatures. The regions of the brain that were notably larger were also those that — in modern humans, at least — are responsible for language. But *Homo habilis* wasn't exactly made for basketball — they were only about 1.2 metres high when fully grown — and with their low, flat skulls, prominent eyebrow ridges and long, chimpanzee-like arms, they too would have looked far more like apes than modern humans.

You have to come forward to *Homo erectus* ('upright man'), who seems to have appeared around two million years ago, to find a species which looked more like us than our primate predecessors. From Africa, *Homo erectus* spread widely throughout the rest of the world, and is therefore the species most likely to have been our direct ancestor (whether the others were truly ancestral, or whether they were simply dead-end branches on the human family tree, is the matter of much debate).

Homo erectus was almost certainly capable of complex speech, strategic hunting, making not only sophisticated tools but also fire, and perhaps even creating art and performing funerary rituals. All of the early human-like creatures were social animals, living in groups beyond a family unit, and *Homo erectus* societies may well have resembled much smaller versions of our own. There is considerable argument over whether *Homo habilis* had a similar reproductive strategy to modern humans (i.e. primarily monogamous, rather than the one dominant male to a harem of females set-up more typical of apes), but there is a fun fact that indicates that affection, perhaps even something like love, was known to even the earliest of our ancestors. It has been conjectured that two of the sets of prints in the Laetoli ashfall, being parallel and so close together, were made by a large individual and a smaller one — a male and a female, perhaps, or a female and a child — walking at a leisurely pace, hand and hand.

Don't give me culture

So much for ancient history — and, let's face it, human history doesn't get much more ancient than this. But just as you can't take the wolf pack out of the dog, you can't do much about how we are built, either. Because most of what separates us from even our most remote ancestors isn't evolution: it's culture. If we accept that what makes us human is our capacity for language and complex social organisation, then we haven't really evolved much beyond *Homo erectus* two million years ago. We're physiologically almost identical. Sure, we're on average taller, far, far smarter and with better fashion sense, but we are essentially the same animal.

In the seventeenth century, as Europeans began to travel widely and observe other cultures, they became convinced that theirs was superior to others. By the nineteenth century, in the wake of Charles Darwin's theory of evolution by natural selection, it became popularly believed that some *races* were superior to others. Needless to say, because this idea originated in Europe, it placed European culture on top of the heap. It explained European superiority simply by arguing that Europeans were superior — somehow more evolved — than other races. In fact, as Jared Diamond showed in his awesome book *Guns, Germs and Steel*, the differences in technological achievement from continent to continent were largely the result of happy accident — the availability of resources chief amongst them — rather than any racial difference.

And here's another fun fact: back when the West was being won and Europeans were first coming into contact with Native Americans, there were lots of instances of Europeans abandoning their way of life and taking up with various tribes. (Sometimes Europeans were initially captured and then, when rescue was on

15

offer, choose to stay with their captors; the most famous of these was Cynthia Ann Parker, who was kidnapped at the age of 10 and lived with the Comanche for 24 years. After being 'rescued', she repeatedly tried to return to the Comanche.) There were very few examples of this happening the other way around. Similarly, it was common for Pakeha to choose to live among Maori in the early days of contact in New Zealand, but while Maori adopted European technologies (and religion), they were far less willing to abandon their own social structures. It's almost as though the largely hunter-gatherer culture called to the souls of European defectors.

Regardless of differences in appearance, the various ethnic races of *Homo sapiens* have more in common with one another than different breeds of dogs have. And when you scratch the surface, we are identical. Take away culture (of which technology is a part) and there is no meaningful difference between a Kalahari bushman, an Inuit, a Swede, a tribesman from the Papua New Guinea highlands, a Japanese salaryman or a Polynesian. And none of us, no matter what we drive or what model of iPhone we've got, is essentially biologically different from anyone who was walking the Earth two million years ago, let alone 10,000 years ago when modern culture — 'civilisation', as it's often called — began with the agricultural revolution.

This, of course, is not to downplay the spectacular cultural advances *Homo sapiens* has made. If you look at the lifestyle of a middle-class family in an affluent part of the developed world today, it doesn't bear much resemblance to the nasty, brutish and short existence of the Neanderthals, for example.

Our remote ancestors were hunter-gatherers and, as such, spent most of their waking hours getting food. As the name suggests, they either hunted or gathered, or both, for much of the day (although it is worth noting that many scholars now believe that people in hunter-gatherer societies worked fewer hours in the day than us modern folk do!). It was a physically demanding and quite often very risky enterprise, as seeking wild food meant you spent a lot of time presenting yourself as a target for other creatures out to get a feed. And quite apart from not being quite at the top of the food chain, very often hunting and gathering failed to produce enough food: for most populations, hunger was a constant, and starvation never far away.

Today, in the developed world, we live longer and are generally healthier than most of our species throughout most of its history. Partly, this is due to nutrition. Our shelters are also (largely) warm and dry and, thanks to technology and our societal arrangements, relatively safe from marauders. Modern medicine protects us from many of the diseases that once devastated human populations, and cures us of a great many ills and injuries that would have been a death sentence only two centuries ago. We have even devised ways of sparing ourselves the need to deal with our own waste. Modern sanitation means we come no closer to the products of excretion than the occasional need to clean the toilet — and some of us hire other people to do that for us.

When we do productive work — thanks to industrialisation and labour unions — we only work a proportion of the hours in each day, and many of us do it indoors and sitting down all day. Our lives are more or less disconnected from the cycles of night and day by our ability to produce artificial light. We buy processed foods at the supermarket that bear little resemblance to the natural products from which they were created. Even when foods are relatively unprocessed, we are still removed from the process by which they were produced: meat is already butchered, trimmed of fat, bone and gristle. It's in little plastic trays covered in cling film, with an absorbent pad underneath it to mop up any blood that might have oozed. We don't have to expose ourselves to the unpleasantness, let alone the dangers of catching, slaughtering and butchering animals. Similarly, we buy fruit and vegetables without the need to climb trees, dig and till the soil or even get our hands dirty.

Our remote ancestors were confronted with what evolutionary psychologists call 'immediate return' challenges. They were constantly reacting to stimuli that required an immediate response, and those responses produced an immediate effect on their survival prospects. This is the kind of world to which the human species has adapted, and nothing much has changed: our bodies and our minds are still finely tuned to an immediate-returns environment.

By contrast, today we live in a 'delayed-return environment', which means that we are not under the relentless pressure to act in order to survive that our ancestors were. Things we do have a delayed effect: we work for money, which we might spend several days later at the supermarket. Then the food we buy at that supermarket gets stored in the fridge or the freezer for days — even weeks — before we consume it.

It's really important for what follows to understand this point: in evolutionary terms, we are still nomadic tribespeople. Evolution is slow, and plays out over millions of years, whereas technological change has been rapid (especially in the last 200 years), transforming our lives from one generation to the next, or even within the timespan of a single generation.

But I've got news for you. No matter how fancy your house, your car, your clothes, you're a caveman or cavewoman underneath it all. Many of the emotional and psychological problems that we suffer from in the twenty-first century have arisen because we have lost sight of this fact. Once you understand that you are using a Stone Age brain to try to make sense of the modern world, a whole lot of what you think and feel begins to make sense.

2

A User's Guide to You

Mental fitness, as we've mentioned, is what we need to cope in times of crisis, and to flourish the rest of the time. A key component of such fitness is emotional self-regulation — what used to be called 'self-control'. The distinction may seem subtle, but it's important. The difference is that the first reflects a positive view of the self, which allows that emotions happen and that they are a normal and often useful part of human experience, while the second is a negative view, where the self and its emotions, particularly unpleasant ones, are necessarily negative and have to be denied, ignored or ruled with an iron fist. Let's keep it positive.

So let's have a look at emotions: what they are and, first of all, what they aren't.

Human beings have probably always wondered and mused about what's what. We date the dawn of Western philosophy (literally 'the love of knowledge') to the time of the ancient Greeks, but only because we have decent written records from that period of who thought what. The ancient Greek philosophers were often profoundly insightful, so they have cast a long shadow over Western thought. Much of what we know about the natural world arose from the observations of philosophers such as Aristotle. And much of the way we have traditionally conceptualised the relationship of the mind to the body is owed to Aristotle's teacher, Plato.

Plato taught that we are a kind of hybrid being, comprising a soul and a body. The human body was much like that of any other animal, made of perishable flesh and bone. But the soul was very different. Plato believed that it was immortal, and housed in the body only temporarily. It possessed knowledge that it couldn't have derived simply from observing the world about it (maths and geometry, for example): this proved, as he saw it, that our souls had communed with perfection in some previous phase of their existence. Therefore, if the soul pre-existed the body and didn't depend on the body to survive, then it was reasonable to suppose that it would persist after the death of the body.

Plato ascribed the functions of what we today call the mind to the soul, most notably the faculty of reason (the ability to think). Our word for the study of the mind (psychology) derives from the Greek word for the soul (*psyche*). The job of the soul/mind was to be the boss of the body, from which arose impulses that were called 'passions'.

For the most part, and probably because they were a warrior race, the Greeks were big on discipline and self-control (*enkratia*). They believed people were in control when they were thinking rationally; people were out of control when they 'gave in' to their passions, their emotions, their animal impulses.

You may never have heard of Plato, but this will all sound pretty familiar. That's because Plato's theory of the duality of mind and body dovetailed nicely with the Christian notion of human beings as immortal souls more or less imprisoned in a mortal body. (Christianity inherited this idea from certain sects of Judaism, which may well have influenced Plato himself … but that's another story.) In the fourth century, a theologian named Augustine of Hippo explicitly bolted biblical Christianity to Platonism, and this became the ruling notion of how the mind/soul related to the body for the next thousand years.

You can see examples of mind/body dualism throughout Western history, language and literature. Some legal systems allowed for diminished responsibility when a person committed 'a crime of passion' — when they were so overcome with emotion that they couldn't think straight. Some jurisdictions still do! Throughout history, women were thought to be less adept at mastering their emotions. (Aristotle couldn't decide whether women were rational — fully human — at all.) Emotions arising from the womb were thought to be particularly powerful, and when women surrendered rational control to passions arising from the womb (*hystera* in Greek), they were said to be 'hysterical'.

Even the way we commonly talk about our feelings today is full of the loaded notion that to experience an emotion is somehow to surrender to it. We tend not to say 'I feel angry.' We tend to say 'I am angry.' We have 'given in' to anger and, in the moment, we're consumed by it, defined by it. See the difference? It is far more accurate to say 'I feel angry' — that anger is something I am experiencing. We'll return to this important distinction in Chapter 5.

For a time, around the Middle Ages, emotions were supposed to have arisen from the relative balance or imbalance of four liquids (humours) in the body, and people were considered to be disposed by nature to one set of emotions over another. If you were choleric (that is, had a natural abundance of yellow bile, a humour named choler), you were cranky and irritable. If you were melancholic (melancholy was black bile: *melan* meaning dark or black), you were a misery-guts. If you were phlegmatic (your character was dominated by phlegm), you were calm to the point of being apathetic. And if you were sanguine (ruled by blood), you were extroverted and energetic. But humourism was a mere refinement on the basic model: the ruling element in a properly ordered individual was still considered to be the rational soul.

Even though scientific enquiry has advanced our knowledge of anatomy, physiology and psychology a long way from the theory of humours, the notion that the mind rules the body in the way that the rider controls a horse has persisted. What do you say to someone who's losing their shit? 'Get a grip!' It's as though we're appealing to one part of them that has lost its grip on another, unruly part of them. And most of us still tend to see it in those terms even though the current view of how emotions are formed has changed.

All the feels

In the 1960s, psychologists firmly believed that emotions were universal. It didn't matter where you went in the world, or who you tested, regardless of whether they lived in a Western city or a remote tribal village, people seemed to recognise the emotions being portrayed in photographs depicting people wearing expressions of anger, surprise, joy, fear, sadness and disgust. If we could recognise these expressions, the suggestion was that we must all feel something similar to one another, too.

In the 1980s, an American researcher named Lisa Feldman Barrett found herself confused that her attempts to induce feelings of anxiety and depression in a group of test subjects were failing. She was especially confused because she wasn't trying anything new: she was merely trying to replicate the findings of older experiments.

After eight failed attempts, she was about ready to abandon her ambitions to become a clinical psychologist, because she thought she must just be useless at science. But reviewing her results, she discovered that while the pattern she had been expecting to find was absent, there was a pattern there, after all. When she looked with an open mind, she found she had discovered that people aren't necessarily very good at distinguishing between anxiety and depression. Some couldn't even really identify that what they were feeling was anxiety or depression: all they could report was that they were 'feeling crappy'.

At first, Feldman Barrett continued to accept the conventional view that there were universal emotions, but that some of us were more accurate in our identification of them than others. She wondered whether it would be possible to help people sharpen up in this area. In order to do so, it would be necessary to find an objective means of determining what people were feeling, so that you could teach them to recognise the different emotions. If there were universal emotions, she reasoned, there must be certain regions of our brain that are responsible for producing our experience of each category of emotion.

But when she enlisted the help of neuroscientists to produce images of the brain activity corresponding to each emotion — its 'fingerprint' — she found that there was, in fact, no distinct pattern of activity that could be attributed to any one emotion. Even anger, something that you might suppose to be completely universal, seemed to be represented by a wide range of patterns of brain activity, indicating that the experience of anger varied widely from individual to individual. This, she points out, makes sense when you consider the various ways that people act when they're feeling angry: some might shout, some might cry, some might laugh and some might pace around while others will sit and quietly seethe.

Similarly, whereas the classical experiments designed to test recognition of emotions used photographs of people wearing exaggerated expressions of emotions, Feldman Barrett found that there are no universal expressions of emotions. Her own experiments showed that 'reading' the facial arrangements of others is just *one* of the information streams that we use to determine what they are feeling. In fact, she went so far as to decide that there weren't universal facial expressions *arising* from emotions, either. What we infer from another person's facial expression is heavily influenced by context and by our expectations of what they will be feeling.

Feldman Barrett began to realise that there is a wide variation in the way people feel things, and that for any given emotion for which we have a name, there is a vast difference in the way people experience them. This was the beginning of a journey of discovery that has redefined our understanding of how emotions are made (the title of her book on the subject). As you've probably begun to guess, by the time she had gone a few years down this track, Feldman Barrett had decided that pretty much everything we thought we knew about emotions was wrong.

So what happens when the heat is on?

First, we sense it. Sensory information is collected by our faculties of vision, smell, hearing, taste and touch, and it's relayed to our brain and central nervous system.

Next, it is perceived. That is, the mind ascribes significance to it. Those Stone Age minds of ours are designed to detect threats first and foremost: three times as many neurons (connections in the brain) are devoted to recognising something that will do us harm as are tasked with identifying good things. You probably know this about yourself already: we tend to fear the worst in uncertain situations until we have firm evidence to the contrary.

After we've triaged what we've sensed into potential threat, opportunity or neutral, we experience emotion. As we've touched upon, it's not as easy as it was once believed to be to describe what emotions we might feel. But the point of emotions is that they exist to get us to choose a course of action — simply put, either to stay in the situation we're experiencing, or to leave or change it.

We can broadly categorise emotions into positive and negative. If we feel good, we're inclined to choose courses of action that will see us remain in the situation we're experiencing in order to benefit from it. If we feel bad, we'll choose a course of action to change our situation. For this reason, you'll more often hear psychologists talk about positive and negative 'affect' (*aff*-ect) these days than about emotions.

An even more useful and accurate way to categorise emotions is as 'pleasant' or 'unpleasant'. And the *most* useful way to categorise them is as 'helpful' and 'unhelpful' according to the situation we are in, what we do with them, and the outcomes we get. This completely moves us away from the incredibly unhelpful and generally irrelevant judgements associated with whether they are good or bad, or whether or not they are nice to feel. More on this later.

After emotion comes thought, or 'cognition'. This is what the classical definition called 'reason' or 'rational thought'. It's the deliberative function of our brain, where we can weigh different courses of action and choose which one to take.

In the course of her research, Feldman Barrett discovered that there is no particular pattern of brain activity associated with 'rational' thought, just as there is no particular pattern associated with any given emotion. In Feldman Barrett's model, rational thought isn't some kind of superior, separate faculty: it's just the next stop along the line in our reaction to a sensory event. As we'll see later in the book, this is a highly useful distinction.

The classical, dualistic notion of emotions cast our capacity for rational thought as the rider and our emotions as the horse. One of my favourite psychologists, Jonathan Haidt, prefers to cast the emotional self as an elephant, to put the relative scales and power of the rational mind and the emotional self in perspective. For Haidt, self-mastery is like a rational rider directing the far stronger and more powerful impulses of the elephant. Feldman Barrett's model takes a more holistic view, as though beast and rider are the same being, sort of like a mythical centaur. She sees no meaningful distinction between emotion and rational thought: they are equally part of human experience, and emotional self-regulation is best achieved through understanding what each is for.

Later in this book, we'll see that the better we get at identifying our emotional experiences in all their many and varied forms, the better we get at understanding what information they have for us, and the more adept we become at managing them. Just pause for a minute here to consider the implications of this: your emotions are not something that happen to you; problems to be managed. Your emotions are you. They're like your arms and legs. Like your memories of yourself and your sense of smell. They are an integral part of your experience rather than something to repress or deny.

We'll return to this in Chapter 12.

What else is going on?

Our senses give us a window on the world, but they are not the only information stream that is being constantly fed to our brain. While we're looking through the window, there's plenty going on in the building. We're not conscious of most of the workings of our body — the pumping of our heart, the inflation and deflation of our lungs, the peristaltic rhythms of our digestion, the straining of our blood through our kidneys and liver, the secretion of hormones into our bloodstream — but all of these systems and more are delivering information to our brain all of the time.

Ever found yourself being cranky with friends, family or workmates for no real reason? Your youngest child asks you for the seventeenth time in five minutes when you're going to take her to the pool and you feel a surge of anger. Whoa, you think. Where did that come from? Even as you feel it, you recognise your emotional response as out of proportion to what provoked it.

Here's an interesting thing. If you're a parent, you'll be adept at recognising the reasons that underlie your children's temper tantrums: when the shouting and the tears come, it's almost always because they're hungry, or tired, or need to go to the toilet. Or they're trying to get attention and/or some show of affection from you. Perhaps they want to be noticed, or to get you to stop a sibling from deliberately annoying them. They are, in other words, experiencing negative affect, and their outburst is a natural reaction, calculated to get you to relieve it for them. Your child might be articulate and fully self-expressed, shouting and ranting about something entirely different — 'You're so unfair! Why can't we have an elephant?' — but you, the seasoned parent, will reflexively run through a checklist of possible sources of physical or emotional discomfort: they've had dinner (can't be hungry), they went to the toilet ten minutes ago (doesn't need wees or poos) ... they must be tired. So you don't buy them an elephant, or even try to argue the practicalities. You give them a hug and put them to bed.

We often do that effortlessly with our kids, but we're not very good at doing it for ourselves. We might not be conscious of the subtle signals that our brain is receiving from our body: we might be tired, we might be hungry, we might have unmet social needs (discussed in Chapter 4), we might even need to go to the toilet. That nagging signal combines with the irritation you feel when your child demands to go to the pool. Five minutes ago, when she first asked, it was irksome but easily shrugged off. Now, you're enraged. Time to employ your powers of emotional self-regulation (which we'll talk about shortly): take a deep breath, ask yourself what unconsidered item has entered the picture to produce this disproportionate reaction, and address that.

Of course, you don't have to be a toddler or a parent for mild physical or psychic discomfort to distort your perception. Our brain, as Feldman Barrett sees it, is like the chief financial officer of a large corporation, constantly receiving information about income and expenditure and seeking always to match resources to demands and to balance the budget. A demand upon our resources — or the anticipation of a demand — is experienced as negative affect: we feel bad. We'll see this clearly when we come to look at what it is to feel stress shortly.

Our brains are meaning-making machines: that's how they operate. They make meaning from beliefs (which arise from experience) applied to the data that they receive from the senses and from our many and varied bodily systems.

When we're born, we're pretty much a blank slate. Some aspects of our brain are already configured: we know to seek our mum's nipple for food without having to be taught, for example, and we know to cry when we are feeling unpleasant. That stuff is like a computer's firmware or operating system. But the rest is just waiting to be wired, and that happens through experience, driven by the combination of genetic predisposition and environment. And from the moment we are born, our experience tends to be heavily modulated by our culture. We learn our emotional vocabulary just as we learn language itself: from those around us.

You're sitting in your highchair and you've just filled your nappy. Feels bad. You screw up your face and start bawling. Your mum's face swims into view and says, 'Don't be angry.' A few dozen repetitions of this and you come to associate the bad feeling you had with anger. A belief has been instilled that arose not from your DNA or your physiology, but from your culture. Far from being universal, 'anger' is cultural.

That can take a lot of getting your head around, because we are so accustomed to considering emotions to be something innate (literally in-born). We're also accustomed to assuming that our picture of reality, constructed of our thoughts and our emotions, corresponds exactly with objective reality, as though our senses give us direct access to reality.

Interestingly, given he formulated the whole unhelpful notion of duality, Plato had a clear sense of how incompletely our senses represent reality to us. He wrote of human souls as being like prisoners in a cave. People passing to and fro in front of a fire cast shadows on the wall of the cave: these shadows are all that our soul can perceive, and perception is to reality what the flickering, shifting, ever-changing shadows are to the real beings that cast them. Both emotion and cognitive (that is, deliberate) thought are mediated by perception, which is to say our beliefs.

You might know the basic story of Shakespeare's *Othello*: Othello marries the beautiful and innocent Desdemona, but he comes to mistrust, suspect and ultimately murder her because he hears reports of her words and deeds from Iago, who is determined to poison Othello against her. Because he trusts Iago implicitly, Othello forms a completely distorted picture of Desdemona's character (even while the audience sits there muttering: 'Have a long, hard look at that Iago, mate!'). Our thoughts are not necessarily so bent on bringing about our self-destruction as the malicious Iago, but they do stand between us and reality, as Iago does between Othello and Desdemona. They mediate our experience.

When you realise this, you can begin to assert control over what you think and feel by interrogating or giving less weight to the beliefs that are standing between you and reality. That is, we can choose what to do with the signals that our body and our senses are sending us.

It's like a modern car: when you open the bonnet, most of the componentry that makes the thing go is sealed off from you with forbidding-looking, bolted-down cowling. The bits that you can manipulate — mostly fluid levels — are brightly coloured and accessible. Well, that's you under the bonnet. You can't control much of the machine that you are, but there are bits you most certainly can fiddle with. Perception — your set of beliefs that colour your reactions to experiences — is one of these. When you experience intense affect, as Feldman Barrett puts it, it's a clue that one of your deeply held beliefs is engaged. Examining what it is that you believe that is so colouring your perception can be highly useful in dialling down the intensity.

Survival of the fittest

So much for affect. The other component of emotional experience is arousal — the biological system by which the body is readied for action — and its opposite, calm. Let's have a look at how those work, and what they were originally for.

Look closely in the mirror. There you are, a nomadic tribesman, finely adapted to a hostile world in which survival — yours and that of your tribe — crucially depends upon your ability to make rapid decisions in challenging situations. Your survival prospects aren't so precarious these days, but that doesn't change who or what you are. When challenges arise in your modern world, as trivial as these may be on the wider scale of things, your response to them is exactly what it would have been 100,000 years ago, when you were confronted by something of a far more primal nature. What you experience is stress.

We'll go into stress — what it is, what it feels like, what makes stress good or bad for you — shortly. But right now, let's look at what stress is *for*.

Imagine you're crossing a plain of rippling long grass, sparsely studded with trees. You're on foot and carrying a spear. You're not alone: members of your tribe are all around you. You're all alert, highly tuned to the most minute details of your environment. You have to be. If it rains, you'll need shelter. If you come across edible plants or prey animals, you'll have to exploit them as efficiently as you can. If a dangerous animal — a mammoth, a sabre-toothed cat — suddenly appears, you and the rest of your tribe will have to take appropriate action and either fight, flee or freeze and hope you are not noticed.

Nervous? Well, that's natural. This kind of low-level stress is what's needed to keep you in the state of arousal that you need to be in to detect threats and opportunities and to respond to them. You can be pretty sure that your ancestors were well accustomed to this level of alertness, because they survived in order to *become* your ancestors. However, they probably didn't have the vocabulary to define this emotional experience as nervousness, let alone consider it a negative emotion. Had you asked them, their best and completely accurate response might have been that they felt 'ready'.

This is something I can relate to myself. When I was a 20-year-old knuckle-dragger in maximum-security prison, I was constantly on the lookout for attack, constantly vigilant to threats. Yet I didn't have the emotional self-awareness and vocabulary to recognise the specific emotions I was feeling. Had I been asked, I would have said that I felt ready for whatever was coming. In later chapters, we'll look at the benefit of both increasing your emotional vocabulary and your self-awareness, and also the value of recognising, as Feldman Barrett discovered, that our labels for emotional experience are socially constructed. We'll see how this means you can learn to reinterpret the signals your brain and body are sending you to increase your effectiveness in challenging circumstances.

But back to the savannah.

Imagine there's a sudden ripple in the grass. There's something large there. It could be food. *You* could be food. Scared? Well, you should be, because fear is nature's way of drawing on your body's reserves in order to meet the challenge of an unusually demanding situation. Fear is natural, and no one whose fear has saved their bacon would ever call it a bad thing.

Then shit gets real. There's a sudden, decisive movement in the grass. With a swift, muscular movement, an animal springs into view. It's a sabre-toothed cat! It's a ferocious predator, and while not really a cat — it's more like a bear — those really are sabre-shaped teeth. The fact that this creature is adapted to hunting and killing much larger animals than you is unlikely to occur to you at this point. I'm pretty sure those teeth will have your full attention.

As challenges go, this is ... significant. But you're adapted to such situations. You're mentally tough, so you're capable of making decisions under the kind of pressure that you now find yourself facing. And it's not just you: the rest of your tribe is responding as well, each according to their roles.

The adult males mount an aggressive response with whatever weapons are to hand. The females gather the juveniles and prepare to defend them. Everyone could be described as stressed at this point. But afterwards — once the creature is successfully beaten off — it won't occur to anyone to say, 'Oh, man, I was so stressed back there.'

Without stress — the anxiety that produced the alertness, the fear that brought everyone to the level of physical and mental arousal needed to deal with the problem — some of you definitely wouldn't have survived. Given that the strength of the tribe is in numbers, you can't afford to lose any contributing member. And besides, there's no time to reflect, really, because where there is one sabre-toothed cat, there are usually more: like you, these are social animals. And nor are sabre-toothed cats the only things you have to worry about. There's still the far-from-trivial matter of finding enough food and a safe place to shelter from the elements and from animal menaces. You come down off the adrenaline rush, but you can't exactly be called relaxed. You're still tense, alert and ready to do it all again.

As mentioned, evolution is the process of natural selection for the fittest individuals in a species, and the fittest species in an environment. We're not just talking about physical fitness: there's far more to survival than being able to press twice your weight on the bench or recording an impressive time in a beep test. Mental toughness and resilience were essential qualities for our ancient ancestors. And the same qualities are there within us, too. To a large extent, they lie latent unless we choose to exercise them.

At some point, every personal trainer in the history of the world will have assured their client that there can be no gain if there is no pain. The same applies to mental fitness. We don't become, or stay, mentally tough or resilient without experiencing stress. Just as stress — ranging from nervousness and anxiety through to full-on fear — was vital to our ancestors in their struggle to survive in a hostile world, stress is what arms us to deal with the challenges of our modern world. We still feel what our ancestors felt — nerves, unease, anxiety, fear, even (at times) panic. It's the nature of the challenges that have changed.

Viewed in this way, stress is not necessarily a bad thing. It's what we feel as we build mental toughness and resilience. It's the mechanism by which we become mentally fit. It is this knowledge that has led the Special Forces and the broader military to specifically focus on 'stress exposure training', which will be outlined in Chapter 12.

Once you have an understanding of where stress comes from and what it's for, you're in a better position to judge whether you're feeling appropriate levels of discomfort (called eustress, or good stress) or unhealthy levels (dys-stress, or bad stress). This judgement is key to becoming and remaining mentally fit. As one of my favourite psychology theorists, Karen Horney, has put it, 'Life provides the right therapy, as long as you're listening to the feedback.'

Stress is that feedback. Let's have a look at how to listen to what it's trying to tell you.

Evolution, stress and you: the facts

We are, to all intents and purposes, no more evolved than our remote ancestors — we have a Stone Age brain in a modern world.

We are social animals, and much of our capacity to cope with life challenges lies in our ability to form connections, and to function as part of a group.

Our brains have evolved for us to experience lots of unpleasant emotions, as those were useful to the survival of our ancestors.

Rather than judging our emotions as 'good' or 'bad' based on whether they feel pleasant or unpleasant, it is more useful to think of our emotions as 'helpful' or 'unhelpful' according to our situation and what we do with them.

We have the capacity to become mentally tough and resilient. The way in which we accomplish this is by experiencing stress.

A first step in becoming mentally fit is learning to listen to what our stress levels are telling us.

3

Stress — What is it Good For?

Although I am from Wellington, I served part of my prison sentence in New Zealand's toughest facility, Paremoremo Prison in Auckland. Eventually, I discovered that I had been transferred there in contravention of a regulation that stipulates that inmates should do their time in a facility close to their family. When I pointed out the breach, I was transferred back to Rimutaka Prison near Wellington.

Initially this came as an enormous relief, but it was short-lived. It seemed that no sooner had the door to my cell at Rimutaka been locked than it was pounded with heavy kicks. Three faces covered with gang tattoos loomed in the inspection hatch.

'Wait till unlock!' a voice yelled. 'We're gonna fuck you up!'

Cue: stress!

I spent the night planning how to tactically defend myself against multiple, determined, possibly armed attackers. I focused on thinking about the exact tactics I would employ to use their numbers against them, inflict maximum damage and survive. I would mount my defence in the doorway, which would act as a bottleneck, and use a ballpoint pen to stab them in the eyes.

I now know that the approach I used intuitively to cope with the anticipation of this attack is called 'instructional visualisation'. It is one of the 'big four' mental skills Special Forces and other soldiers are trained to use in order to remain effective under stress and pressure. (More on these in Chapter 13.)

As you can imagine, despite the instructional visualisation, it wasn't the most restful night I've had!

You may not have experienced anything quite like this, but you'll know the feeling. You might be sitting in the noisy, cramped interior of a small aircraft, fiddling with the chin strap of your helmet, when a light goes on, indicating that you're five minutes from the drop zone on your first skydive …

You're third from point as your patrol makes its way through light jungle. The man in front raises a hand to signal a halt. His next hand signal indicates that he has eyes on the enemy …

You're taken aside by the coach at the end of training. You were brought into the national squad as injury cover, and now the coach is telling you that the injured player has failed a fitness test. You're in the starting line-up for Friday night's must-win game …

No, no, no, you're saying. That's not me. I've never been skydiving, or in a combat situation. I'm not an elite athlete, and I've never lain awake in a prison cell expecting an assault. I wouldn't have a clue what any of those situations would feel like.

Well, try these instead.

You're startled awake at three in the morning. The phone's ringing. Your teenage daughter borrowed the car the night before to go to a party …

The phone rings at nine in the morning, just after you arrive at the office. It's the CEO of a company to which you applied for a job. You believe you're way underqualified for the role, but you allowed your friends to convince you to put your hand up on the nothing-ventured, nothing-gained principle. It takes you a few moments to realise that you're being offered the position ...

You're sitting in a hall with a couple of hundred other people. There's an exam script face-down on the desk in front of you. The examiner glances at her watch and says: 'You may turn over your papers and begin' ...

You and your girlfriend arrive at the beach just before sunset. It's exactly the kind of evening you were hoping for, and you've got a picnic hamper and a blanket. There's a small box burning a hole in your pocket, and in that box there's an engagement ring ...

You're standing beside the chairperson as she nears the end of her introduction. There are a hundred people in the auditorium. You've spent your life avoiding public speaking, but the chairperson, in her wisdom, has decided that you are the best person to speak to the issue ...

In all of the above scenarios you will feel the same things, to a greater or lesser degree. The reluctant public speaker will experience exactly the same response as a soldier in combat, or the exam candidate, or the netballer about to play above her grade, or the skydiver about to make their first jump. And in every case, the response is exactly the same as the one our remote ancestors would have experienced when confronted by challenges in their long-ago world.

What you're experiencing is stress.

Interestingly, no one experienced 'stress' before the 1930s, when the term was coined by Hungarian scientist Hans Selye.

He borrowed the word from physics, where 'stress' is the internal process that a material undergoes when external forces act upon it. Selye was building on a field of research into what is known as homeostasis — the tendency of organisms to exist in a kind of 'systems-normal' state, and to seek to return to it if disturbed. You can think of homeostasis as your mental and bodily comfort zone.

Biological homeostasis involves physiological factors such as body temperature and hydration, and there are mechanisms by which the body tells us what it needs so that we can take the appropriate action to return them to balance. We all know how these work, as the signals are fairly unambiguous. If our hydration is less than optimal, we feel thirsty: we drink, and our thirst is quenched. If our energy reserves drop, we feel hungry: we eat, and we feel full and energised.

But there's also a psychological component to homeostasis, and we're less adept at interpreting these signals. Partly, this is because psychological stress is complicated, as I'll show you. Partly, it's because we're not evolved to cope with many of the stressors to which we're exposed in modern life. But partly it's also because we have become conditioned to believe that psychological discomfort is necessarily bad.

Put simply, stress is the mechanism by which our bodies and minds respond to a challenge. The sensation of psychological stress is no different to thirst or hunger: it's there to encourage you to take the action that's necessary to respond to the challenge, prevail and then return to your comfort zone.

Your body's reaction to stress

Before we go on to look at the various different kinds of psychological stress, let's have a look at what happens when you experience psychological stress of any kind. As with hunger or thirst, the human response is the same in any normally functioning individual. The difference is only in the degree to which it is experienced.

You know the feeling; you may even have felt it in a mild form simply imagining the moments of stress described above. Your mouth goes dry. Your scalp prickles. The palms of your hands go sweaty. You feel your heart pounding and your breathing accelerate. Your stomach tightens and you feel a fluttering sensation, perhaps even to the point where you feel sick ... It's nerves, butterflies — it's your biological response to a challenge.

When you perceive a challenge, two major physiological systems are engaged. One is what is known as the HPA, or hypothalamic-pituitary-adrenal axis. (You can forget all about this in a moment, but bear with me for now. Knowing the mechanisms at work can help you to identify the kind of stress you're experiencing, and actually help you to cope with it.) The HPA involves several components of your endocrine (chemical messenger) system, but three main ones: the hypothalamus (a gland around the size of an almond buried deep at the base of your brain), your pituitary gland (a pea-sized nodule on the hypothalamus) and your adrenal glands (pyramid-shaped structures perched one on top of each of your kidneys). Like the rest of the endocrine system, these glands all exist to release chemical messengers named hormones.

When a challenge presents itself to you, it is interpreted as such by the central nervous system — your brain, responding to stimuli from your senses — and the hypothalamus is stimulated. This triggers a cascading release of hormones, beginning in the hypothalamus and ending in the adrenal glands, which release another lot of hormones known as glucocorticoids.

The most important of the glucocorticoids is cortisol. Just about every cell in the human body has receptors for cortisol, so when it circulates in the bloodstream, it has a message for practically every biological system. Think of it as a fire alarm, or an all-points bulletin. Among the many, many systems that cortisol affects are your metabolism, your cardiovascular system and your immune system. Elevated levels of cortisol cause your liver to release more glucose, which is your body's fuel, and increase the body's energy in times of stress. High cortisol also raises your blood pressure, suspends bone growth and suppresses your immune response, sending more blood to your vital organs and muscles and directing resources away from processes that aren't deemed necessary to meet the immediate challenge.

Meanwhile, and particularly in moments of acute stress — especially where the threat is perceived to be life-threatening — the adrenal glands are also releasing another hormone: adrenaline. This hormone is chiefly responsible for setting in motion the 'fight or flight' reaction, as it was termed by the man who first described it, American physiologist Walter Cannon, in 1926. Today we tend to call it the fight/flight/freeze reaction, to cover the full range of responses (although it is also interesting to note that psychologist and combat expert Lieutenant Colonel Dave Grossman adds 'posturing' and 'submission' to the mix). As the name suggests, this reaction swiftly sets the body on a war footing, preparing us either to battle the threat, escape it, or try to evade its attention. It's not just human beings that exhibit fight/flight/freeze: practically every higher animal has its own version of the reaction.

Fight/flight/freeze involves the engagement of what is known as the autonomic nervous system, which mostly comprises the major nerves of the spinal column. It's known as 'autonomic' as its functions are outside our conscious control. There are two sets of autonomic nervous system functions: crudely put, they're the fire-up system and the calm-down system; the sympathetic nervous system (SNS) and the parasympathetic nervous system (PNS) respectively. The SNS is all about supercharging our physiology to meet a threat, while the PNS is all about trying to restore us to homeostasis.

The two chemicals released when the SNS is engaged are adrenaline and noradrenaline (adrenaline released within the brain), and they have a number of immediate effects. They cause our pupils to dilate, which admits more light into our eyes and sharpens our vision. They dilate our airways, which increases the amount of oxygen we can inhale.

Anyone who understands how the carburettor in an internal combustion engine works will know that a functioning engine needs a precise balance between fuel and oxygen. If you increase the amount of fuel you're supplying to the engine, which is what you do when you press the accelerator, the engine needs to increase the amount of oxygen being taken in to maintain the balance. The body's fuel-burning system works on exactly the same principle. Adrenaline and noradrenaline cause our heart rate to accelerate and our blood vessels to constrict. Our rapidly beating heart gets fuel and oxygen to tissues. The constricted blood vessels raise blood pressure, pumping muscles and organs full of blood.

Between them, adrenaline and noradrenaline also inhibit activities such as digestion and salivation — both unnecessary processes in a crisis. And although the stimulation of the SNS is referred to as 'arousal', your ability to get an erection is inhibited: that's not going to get you out of trouble and, in a life-threatening situation, it's a bad use of perfectly good blood!

In a state of arousal, you sweat more and your body hairs stand on end. It's not entirely clear why this happens, although looking at the rest of the animal kingdom, it's likely that they are vestigial (that is, evolutionary leftovers) versions of the kind of threat signals common in hairier animals with a better sense of smell — handy if you're going to fight rather than flee. Soldiers before battle and players before a big game also often yawn, which is thought to be a human version of the teeth-baring that most other mammals do when threatened.

Once the crisis is perceived to have passed, the PNS kicks in. The PNS has the opposite effect to the SNS: it controls the conservation of energy and re-activates the bodily processes that are suspended when we're in a state of arousal. We begin to produce saliva again; our stomach and intestines resume rumbling away, digesting food; and we're again capable of sexual arousal. Under the effects of the PNS, we resume bodily business as usual, our systems restored to their comfortable homeostatic balance.

GOOD STRESS AND BAD STRESS

So what is stress actually for? Well, think about the kind of challenges we were evolved to face — the short-lived, urgent challenges our hunter-gatherer ancestors were continually confronted by in the immediate-returns environment in which they lived. The state of arousal we enter when our SNS is engaged is the state you need to be in to rise to a challenge. It might feel unpleasant — remember, your whole system wants to return to its balanced state (homeostasis) as soon as it possibly can. The stress you feel when confronted with a challenge is the tool with which nature has equipped you to unlock extra physical and mental resources in case of emergency. And it's a good thing, because it's both necessary and useful.

Stress performance curve

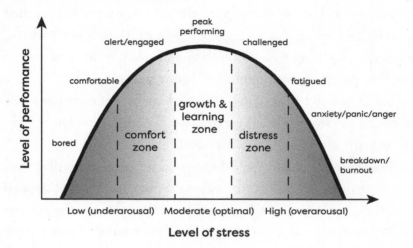

As mentioned earlier, the kind of stress that you experience when you're confronted with a challenge is called 'eustress' (the prefix 'eu' in Greek means 'good'). When you're experiencing eustress, you're right up there at the peak of the performance curve.

The conventional wisdom is that you should strive to lead a stress-free life all of the time — down there on the left-hand side of the curve, untroubled by challenges. But even if we could achieve this, as paradoxical as it sounds, we wouldn't flourish, because as humans we are evolved to face challenges and experience stress.

It's like physical exertion. In our modern, sedentary lifestyles, we don't get much opportunity to really use, let alone extend, our physical capabilities. Because this feels wrong for our bodies — and plainly is less than ideal for our physical wellbeing — we've invented ways of artificially incorporating physical exertion into our routines: organised sport, ocean swimming, mountain biking, jogging and gym memberships. We're conscious that we must use or lose our physical resources.

Our psychological resources are exactly the same. Because our species evolved to survive on a hostile planet, we are finely tuned to a life of meeting challenges. We're like a climbing plant which, without something to lean on, will fall over, or at least fail to flourish. Adversity, you might say, is our trellis.

But not all stress is good. There are long lists of different kinds of stress, but in the end, there are two kinds that are bad for us: chronic stress and excessive stress.

Sudden events requiring a fight-or-flight response will put us in a state of hyper-arousal for as long as they last: you've stepped into the road and a car has come speeding around the corner; you're swimming at a surf beach and find yourself further from shore than you had intended … We react to these situations pretty much as any other mammal would. Once the immediate danger has passed, our parasympathetic nervous system kicks in and we return to a calmer, more relaxed state.

But sometimes stress isn't just an immediate, momentary thing. It could be that it's just one thing after another, or it could be that the thing that is causing stress just doesn't go away. This is called chronic stress.

When I was in B Block at Paremoremo — the toughest block in the toughest prison, dominated as it was by the gangs — I managed to fall foul of a Black Power member through some perceived slight (I had been smoking a joint with a mate and had failed to offer the gang guy a toke). From that moment, I was a marked man. I spent almost every waking hour in a state of hyper-vigilance. Whenever I was unlocked, even (especially) when I was on the toilet or coming out of the shower, I had to keep an eye out for him or anyone affiliated with him, in case I got attacked. I lived this way, in fear of imminent danger for months. The stress ramped up when my mates and I decided that we needed to be proactive and take the guy out before he took us out; fortunately, for both him and me, I was transferred out of the prison before we could implement our plot.

While they're equipped to deal with it, most animals struggle when stress is prolonged, and we're no different. Most of us have, at one time or another, experienced stress arising from an on-going cause or set of causes. Money worries, relationship worries, our unrealistic expectations or those of others, our own failing health or that of a loved one, whether we are professionally successful ... each might not amount to an imminent crisis provoking a flat-out, fight-or-flight alarm, but there's a feeling of constant, nagging dread that represents elevated cortisol in our bloodstream.

Human beings are prone to stress to which most — if not all — other animals are blissfully immune, due to our capacity for making stuff up. Most of us spend time 'stressing' about — experiencing a stress response to — things that haven't happened yet and may never happen at all. We call these distant stressors, and they're not just real things that are distant from us, either in time or space. They can also include things that are only possibilities, even remote possibilities, or outright fantasies. This chronic stress is bad because we're just not designed for it.

The other kind of bad stress is excessive stress. This occurs once we shift to the right of the performance curve above, and move past the point where we're coping to where, to a greater or lesser extent, we're not just stretched, we're overwhelmed. The point at which this happens depends on a whole lot of things, because not only is susceptibility to stress highly individual, but it is highly variable for any given individual as well.

Sink or swim

People's reactions to stressors may vary with the time of day, their age, their social situation, even their gender: some of the chemicals we've been talking about are circadian, which means their levels go up and down according to the time of day. Some of them also interact with other chemicals in our bodies — both naturally occurring and artificially introduced — varying our natural stress levels.

The stress hormones — adrenaline, noradrenaline and cortisol — all have complicated relationships with dopamine and seratonin (brain chemicals that both play a role in mood) and the principal sex hormones, oestrogen and testosterone. This means that men will often react differently to stressors than women, and that a woman's reaction will often be determined (or at least modulated) by where she is at in her menstrual cycle, and whether or not she is pregnant.

There is also a huge range of variation between people in how susceptible to stress we are. You've probably noticed that one person's reaction to a stressor is different from another's. Some people just seem to be wired differently, and are able to relax and function normally when everyone else is screaming and running for the hills.

When that five-minutes-to-drop-zone light comes on in an aircraft, those ready to jump out will react with different levels of stress. The jumpmaster, with several hundred jumps behind them, will be pretty calm and relaxed. One novice will be bordering on fight-or-flight panic. Another may be calmer, because he has studied the design of parachutes and the mechanism of tethered release and the statistics of successful jumps versus failures, and he likes his odds of survival. Another novice may well be calm not because he has faith in man and machine, or is an adrenaline junkie, but simply because he is taking cues from the others around him: they seem calm, so he sees no need to be stressed himself. We are, after all, social animals, and whether we're fully conscious of it or not — mostly not — a very large part of our perception of stress and danger is drawn from our sense of what the group is feeling. Yet another novice may be cool, calm and collected simply because that's the way she is: for reasons that are as mysterious to herself as to everyone else, she has a high threshold for physical risk ...

Since the 1960s, the kind of person who is drawn to seek out new experiences or ever greater intensities of experience, has been called a 'high sensation-seeker'. This personality type came to be recognised, ironically enough, in the course of research into how different people react to being *deprived* of sensation.

The subjects of the experiment were placed in darkened, soundproof rooms and made to just sit there. Some were capable of sitting for hours; others fairly quickly became bored and fidgety. The second group of people — those who got bored easily — were more likely to be high sensation-seekers out in the real world, constantly in search of experiences which evoked in them a sense of awe. Most of these people were highly tolerant of risk, and some (of course) seemed to actively seek out riskier activities.

I have a mate who served two tours in Afghanistan with the SAS, who has told me a bit about his training to become an elite special forces soldier. Once he described the swim assault course he had to do, where they were required to swim underwater using rebreather apparatus for two hours at night. If you think nighttime is dark, wait till you're in the ocean, where it's just about impossible to tell up from down, let alone one direction from another.

Our brains are designed to deal with lots of information flooding in from all our senses at once, so it's a special sort of disorientation to be both out of your element and deprived of pretty much all sensory information. I'm a physically large man with a black belt in judo and a lot of experience of violence, but I still find myself more aware and emotionally engaged in situations like dark alleys or carparks. I can only imagine how hypersensitive to threat detection and stressed by uncertainty we become when alone in the pitch black of the ocean.

An extreme example of a high sensation-seeker is Alex Honnold, the craziest solo climber in the crazy world of solo climbing. In case it hasn't crossed your radar, free or solo climbing is the sport in which people climb without the kind of protection — ropes, harnesses, anchors — that ordinary climbers use to give themselves a safety margin. In a National Geographic documentary called *Free Solo* (watch it, if you dare: it's the scariest thing you'll ever see another person doing), Honnold is wired up to a CT scanner to measure his brain activity while he is presented with 'aversive stimuli' (things that cause most people distress or anxiety to look at, such as pictures of extreme injuries, car crashes and physical confrontations). In anyone else, such stimuli would produce a burst of activity in the amygdala (sometimes called 'the lizard brain' — the brain's first responder, which controls primitive, deep-seated, hard-wired reflex responses to danger). In Honnold ... not so much. Partly, this will be because of his experience of scary situations, and because he stares down danger for fun. But partly, perhaps even mostly, it is because he is starting from a different place from the rest of us. He simply doesn't feel as much fear, or he feels fear differently, from everyone else.

A colleague and friend of mine, Dr Elliot Bell from Otago University, captures the individual variation in susceptibility to stress beautifully in explaining the 'vulnerability-stress model' when applied to psychological conditions. You're swimming, comfortably within your depth. A wave comes along. Whether or not you can keep your head above water when you're standing on the bottom depends not only upon how high the wave is, but also upon how tall you are. Suppose it's a 1.8 metre wave and you're 1.9 metres. No problem. But suppose you're 1.6 metres. You'll go under.

The point is, of course, that there's no point in making value judgements about someone's tendency to be overwhelmed, any more than there is in attaching moral significance to the height you were born to be. Learning to swim confers a greater advantage than genetics, as sooner or later a wave will come that could overwhelm even the tallest person amongst us.

The idea of this model is that coping (drowning or swimming) is a function of the magnitude of the stressor (wave size/water height), genetic risk factors (nature — height) and coping skills (nurture — swimming ability). We can even extend the metaphor to consider the contribution of social environments to mental fitness — e.g. swimming with family and friends, or between the flags where help is available if you get into trouble. (More on the role of such social factors in Chapter 9.) So your die is not cast — even with a strong family history to contend with, you are not powerless to change the ways in which you cope with stress. And a big part of what determines how vulnerable you are to stress is your *perception* of stress.

The eye of the beholder

There is an enormous component in the whole mechanism of stress that is modulated by perception. Whether or not an object, an event or a set of conditions triggers a stress response is dependent upon whether you consider it to be something to get stressed about. And, of course, our individual perceptions are as many and as varied as we are.

Some things that cause stress — mostly those that trigger our acute, fight-or-flight response — are plain and obvious. You step off the kerb and a car comes around the corner really fast: you jump back on the kerb without having to think about it. You are on the point of nodding off when driving, then you start awake with a jerk. In these types of situations, the business of perception is largely bypassed. This is your amygdala at work. It's capable of initiating fight-or-flight without recourse to all the higher functions of the brain that involve rational thought and the weighing up of options.

You can clearly see this at work when you see someone with a simple, genuine phobia (an extreme and irrational fear) react to the thing that triggers them. You're with a mate walking along the street and you see someone dressed as a clown, doing what clowns do. You notice your mate hesitating. You study him with interest. He's actually scared of the clown! You've heard of this condition, but try as you might, and even though you've read Stephen King's *It* and seen both movie versions, you don't find anything remotely scary about clowns. But your mate is in fight-or-flight in the twinkling of a dilated pupil. This whole sequence of events seems like a hilarious overreaction to you.

When a group of people are told that they will each shortly be called upon to address a large auditorium full of people, their reactions will likely range from blind panic to a nod and a shrug, depending upon how this information is processed. If you've never done any public speaking, you'll likely be nervous at the very least. If you're an introvert, or even if you just have fairly normal concerns about how others might judge your appearance or the sound of your voice or the quality of your address, this news will be highly stressful, and you'll be on the edge of panic. If, on the other hand, you're an experienced public speaker, with a well-organised set of notes and a precisely rehearsed presentation to speak to, and you're comfortable with how you're groomed, all you might get is a mild case of butterflies — a sure sign your sympathetic nervous system is engaged to help you perform to your best.

Using stress to help you flourish

Which brings me to my last point in this chapter. You know the feeling: when you've been faced with a crisis that has really tested you, stretched you to the limit of your resources, and you come out the other side with a sense of empowerment, satisfaction and exhilaration. You may even feel some of these emotions while the crisis is unfolding and you find you're equal to the challenge: you feel alive in a way that you never did sitting, yawning in your La-Z-Boy, free from all cares and worries.

And it's not only the feeling it gives you. Each time you are tested like this, you become that much more adept at coping, just as each time you push yourself up to and beyond the point where you're physically comfortable in training, you find you can run further and faster. The stress you feel as you cope in a crisis is the psychic equivalent to that burn in your muscles and your lungs. It's good for you, and you know it.

This is the kind of stress we're going to call eustress. You need more of this in your life. You don't need to go about courting disaster, actively seeking life-or-death crises: you can exercise your capacity for dealing with stress simply by trying new things or new ways of doing things you're already doing. You can also do it by identifying and eliminating the strategies you have developed for avoiding stress — we'll look at these in Chapter 4.

The more you grow accustomed to experiencing eustress, the better you will get at coping when stressed (in the sense of dealing with a real crisis), and the faster and more completely you will recover from stressful episodes. We had names for this, remember? We called the ability to cope 'mental toughness'. We called the ability to recover fast and fully to higher levels of general satisfaction with your life 'resilience'. Together, they comprise mental fitness. And when you're mentally fit, you not only have the resources to perform in your everyday life, but you will be up for whatever comes your way.

What we now know about stress

Stress is a biological response to a challenge.

There is good stress (eustress) and bad stress (dys-stress).

We need a certain level of stress to raise our performance to meet challenges and perform at a high level.

There is a cognitive component to stress: that is, if we can control our perception of a stressor, we can control how stressed we become by it.

In order to build our mental toughness and resilience, we need to maximise our exposure to eustress.

4

Stress — What is it Bad For?

Your child has a mild fever and a sore throat. It's plain you can't send her to school today.

You are leading a major project at work. The reporting deadline is looming, and you're well behind schedule.

You changed jobs six weeks ago, taking a minor pay cut.

You're going on a three-week overseas holiday in a fortnight's time.

The car won't start.

The landlord has given you notice.

You and your partner argued last night, and the possibility of a trial separation was raised.

Any of the above situations are stressors. Indeed, they come from a list of stressors called the Holmes-Rahe Stress Inventory, a tool designed to help people to calculate their stress levels. Some of you will read an item in this list and shrug, thinking 'no big deal' — for example, what's stressful about going on a nice overseas holiday? Others will blanch and feel a catch in their breath when they read some scenarios. But most of you will regard pretty much any item in the list, taken in isolation, as something you'd back yourself to cope with.

Now think about this:

You changed jobs about six weeks ago, taking a minor pay cut. With timing so awful that it almost looked like someone planned it, your landlord has told you he's retiring and he and his wife want to sell their big house and move into their smaller one — that you're renting. Aw, man! You're supposed to be going on an overseas holiday in two weeks' time, for heaven's sake! You and your partner argued last night and the possibility of a trial separation was raised. You kissed and made up, but then you lay awake worrying about what might lie behind the argument, and the fact that the major project you are leading at work is well behind schedule and the deadline is only eight days away. You wake up feeling tired and grumpy, then your daughter complains that she's not feeling well. She has a temperature, and is complaining of a sore throat: you certainly can't send her to school, so you'll have to stay home to look after her. You'd better take her to the doctor to have her throat checked. But wouldn't you know it? The car won't start!

*

When the report into the catastrophe that destroyed the American space shuttle *Challenger* in 1986 was released, it detailed what is popularly known as a 'systems failure' — a cascade of events, each of which *individually* did not account for the disastrous outcome but contributed to it. For example, the shuttle had sat on its launch pad in extremely cold temperatures, which caused a rubber O-ring that was supposed to seal a joint in one of the solid-fuel rocket boosters to become brittle and fail to stretch as it was designed to when it was subjected to the extreme loading of the launch. Instead, it pretty much burned completely away. The powdery exhaust from the booster temporarily blocked the gap, but as it rose, the shuttle experienced high wind-shear (layers of wind moving in different directions), which in turn caused the defective joint to flex and the fortuitous temporary seal to fail. A jet of flame began to burn a hole in the side of the rocket booster, and the lateral thrust produced caused it to partially detach from the rest of the shuttle assembly. It crashed into the huge liquid-hydrogen tank mounted beneath the shuttle itself, and this in turn crashed into the liquid-oxygen tank. The combination of events resulted in a huge explosion. The entire assembly — shuttle, twin rocket-boosters and external tank — was subjected to aerodynamic forces that it couldn't survive, and it disintegrated. The crew compartment was fired like a bullet into the upper atmosphere, reaching a peak altitude of 20,000 metres before falling into the sea. It is not known how long the seven-member crew were alive after the explosion — there was some evidence that they survived the initial blast — but the final impact was not survivable.

Stress can be just like this. It's not a single thing: it's an accumulation of single things, each of them sapping your ability to cope. It is not dealing with a single fatigue factor that consumes our psychological and emotional energy, but a collection of fatigue factors that create a cumulative effect. Even things which ought to be positive — your upcoming overseas holiday, for example — place a demand on your resources that, taken with everything else, is just another straw on the poor old camel's back.

Of course, as mentioned above, some people seem to be able to cope with all sorts of shocking adversity; others fly apart pretty early on. Some camels can presumably carry a lot more straw than other camels. Whatever your breaking point happens to be, however, we all know the feeling when things get too much. It's like when you're swimming and you duck under a wave. You surface, and there's another wave, breaking right on top of you. You snatch what breath you can and duck under that one too, but would you believe it? As you surface, gasping, there's another wave already rearing high over your head.

As we noted in the previous chapter, stress can be excessive: one thing after another, so that you never quite get the chance to gain your breath. And stress can be chronic — always there, in the background, nagging away at you, such as when you live in poverty, say, or you're the inmate of a maximum-security prison. We're evolved to cope with immediate challenges. And we're adapted to deal with challenges that can be resolved immediately by taking action. We're not designed to cope with on-going, distant stressors, or with too much stress at one time — especially when we can't get the recovery time that we need and can't hit the reset button that refreshes our ability to cope.

Here's an analogy to help you conceptualise your stress load. Fill a glass with water. Literally do this now! OK, now hold it at arm's length, and stand there. At first, you don't even notice its weight. You're coping just fine. But as you keep standing there, the glass seems to be growing heavier bit by bit. After a while, your arm starts to shake and you will have to put the glass down or you'll drop it.

It doesn't matter how strong you are: there will be a point where the glass feels heavy and the demand of holding it in place consumes all of your energy and focus, until it just becomes too much. When we approach this point, we no longer have the discretionary energy to be that best, most tolerant, values-driven version of ourselves. All our energy is focused on the demand of the glass.

Have you ever noticed that when you have been under prolonged stress and pressure, the politeness slips from your personal relationships? There's just a little less patience and assuming the best of each other? That's because you lack the discretionary energy required to be that better version of yourself.

Remember the performance curve from the last chapter? You didn't function to your potential when you were bored and idle — you weren't holding a glass. You were at your best when you were experiencing good stress and managing to spend just enough time in your comfort zone to recharge. But if you were experiencing just a little too much stress — too many straws on the camel's back — or you weren't quite getting as much recovery time as you needed, you were starting to hit the wall and become fatigued. At that point, your performance suffers. Beyond that, if life's slings and arrows seem to keep coming thick and fast and there's no respite. You become exhausted, burnt out. You break down and can't perform at all.

At the point where you're holding the glass effortlessly despite the demand you can feel from it, you're experiencing eustress, the optimal performance level. Not only are you able to cope, but the demand you are experiencing will strengthen your shoulder muscles, which will enable you to hold more water for longer in future. Once it really starts to hurt and consumes all of your focus, however, you're in what we'll call distress (from *dys*-stress, or bad stress). It's the kind of stress you feel when you're overwhelmed; when you can't cope.

It's interesting to note that in our everyday language we talk about stress as if it is inherently negative, whereas psychology conceptualises stress as anything that places a demand on you. If that demand is manageable in duration and intensity it is likely to be experienced as eustress, but once it becomes too intense or prolonged it slips into the distress domain.

And it's not just having too many stressors at once that can overload the camel. The same feeling can arise if any one challenge demands more of you than you can deliver — in other words, a crisis. And as we've seen — and will go on to explore — people's capacity to cope is highly individual. One person's crisis is just another day in the office for someone else.

Importantly, your capacity to cope is to some extent a function of whether or not you perceive yourself to be *choosing* to hold the glass. If you see yourself as *choosing to embrace the challenge voluntarily*, this activates a part of the brain associated with eustress which leads you to experience emotions such as determination and satisfaction. This part of the brain is also associated with learning and memory. But if you see the glass of water as thrust upon you with no voluntary component, this activates the distress part of the brain. You are more likely to crumble and be damaged by the stress associated with the experience.

Whatever situation you find yourself in, it will reduce your stress level if you choose to focus on your choices and what's in your control. I know this from the research, but I can also relate to it from practical experience. Of the 10 years, 10 months I spent in prison, I did nearly a year in solitary confinement. Being in solitary is a very stressful and challenging experience, but one of the strategies that helped me survive it and avoid mental breakdown was seeing it as a challenge to be embraced and overcome.

I (correctly) saw solitary as an attempt to break my spirit and change my more problematic behaviour through force. I resented this, and my bloody-minded response was to *embrace* whatever the system threw at me. Come at me! I've read about the same thing in books such as Ant Middleton's *First Man In*. In it, he speaks of how he initially reacted with anger to the gruelling selection process he was subjected to in the British Army Special Forces. By harnessing that anger, he was able to persevere, make it through the training and go on to perform in combat. In *Can't Hurt Me*, American David Goggins describes a similar thing: at the very point where he thought he would buckle under the physical and mental strain he was being subjected to by the instructors in his US Navy SEAL training programme, he experienced a surge of resentment and anger that made him determined, at all costs, not to give in.

In each of these examples, the key ingredient was *making a choice* to view the stress experienced as a challenge to be embraced rather than a threat to be avoided. This is consistent with Lisa Feldman Barrett's theory that our emotions are a part of us, not something separate from us. They also show how unpleasant emotions can be turned into useful fuel to overcome adversity.

Sick of it

It's not just your performance that suffers when you're under stress. There is a large and growing body of research suggesting that psychological stress — particularly chronic stress — negatively impacts your physical health. We saw, when we looked at the physiology of stress in Chapter 3, that one of the effects of cortisol on your bodily systems is suppression of your immune system. Needless to say, this opens the door for disease to take hold. How often do you get a cold as soon as you are through a period of stress and about to go on holiday?

For a very long time, it was believed that stress caused high stomach acidity, which in turn led to peptic ulcers. This was eventually discredited (stomach and intestinal ulcers are likely to be caused by a bacterium called *Helicobacter pylori*), but this did not altogether invalidate the link between stress and ulcers. It is now believed that while having *H. pylori* in your digestive system is a prerequisite for developing an ulcer, only around 10 per cent of people with *H. pylori* actually get one. Instead, a complex interplay between troughs in your immune response, poor dietary habits, smoking and alcohol abuse (some of the behaviours that we commonly display in times of stress), and the use of some medications are now thought to promote ulcer formation.

If you've ever contracted any of the herpes viruses — such as herpes simplex itself or chickenpox — you'll find that in times of stress the virus re-emerges, usually in the form of a cold sore or, worse, shingles. The virus lies latent along your nerve fibres, and at times when your immunity is compromised — such as when you're stressed — it stages a resurgence.

In cases like this, the connection between stress and physical health is reasonably direct and easy to understand. But stress has been associated with far less obvious negative impacts, too.

In the early 1990s, a pair of American psychologists, Bruce McEwen and Eliot Stellar, suggested that chronic stress imposed a kind of 'wear and tear' on the body's systems. They called this effect the 'allostatic load'. Allostasis is connected with the process of homeostasis that we met in Chapter 3: while homeostasis comes from Greek words meaning 'balancing in roughly the same place', 'allostasis' means more like 'returning to balance from a different place'. Allostatic change, as McEwen and Stellar conceived it, is the kind of adaptation that people (and animals) constantly make in response to changes in their environment, especially to stressors: in other words, it is the process we go through to restore homeostatic balance.

If we are forced to make those changes often enough — with those hormonal cascades and their physiological responses that we were looking at in Chapter 3 — this allostatic load takes its toll on our bodies. This makes us more susceptible to psychological disturbances such as sleep disorders and depression, and to physical illness as well. There's even evidence that our telomeres — structures on the ends of our chromosomes that determine the rate at which our cells age — are shortened by stress. That means that stress, quite literally, shortens our life!

Balm of hurt minds

After he killed his rival Duncan, the rightful king of Scotland, Macbeth had trouble sleeping. 'Sleep!' he mourned, 'that knits up the [un]ravelled sleeve of care! Balm of hurt minds ...' Like much of what the Bard wrote, this was an acute psychological observation. Anyone who has ever experienced episodes of severe or prolonged stress will know that it has a pronounced impact on sleep.

A decent night's sleep is vital to 'recharge our batteries'. Problems that seem insurmountable at day's end are far less formidable when you wake refreshed from a good night's sleep. The converse is also true. All of our problems seem greater, and the resources with which we are equipped to deal with them are reduced, when we are tired.

Lack of sleep is both an aggravating factor in stressful times (as in the cascade of events with which this chapter opened) and a stressor in its own right. Insomniacs know only too well how much anxiety you feel when the hours of darkness are ticking away and you can't get to sleep. And when you're stressed, it's not just the quantity, but also the quality of sleep that is negatively impacted.

In higher mammals (including humans), and even in other animals such as birds, sleep occurs in several phases. These can be divided into two broad categories: REM (rapid-eye-movement sleep) and NREM (non-rapid-eye-movement sleep). REM sleep corresponds with dreaming, which is thought to serve as a powerful restorative for the brain, much like 'defragging' a computer. NREM sleep tends to be 'deeper' sleep, but enough of both kinds is thought to be vital to refresh the body, and especially the brain.

Chronic stress alters the balance between these two types of sleep, although to what extent is not currently understood. It seems that elevated cortisol can reduce the duration of REM episodes. It also seems that lack of REM sleep can reduce the receptivity of those areas of the hypothalamus that detect and respond to those levels of cortisol. It would appear it's that same vicious cycle: stress, which promotes the release of cortisol, deprives us of the REM sleep we need to keep our waking brain functioning at its best. And this lack of REM sleep interferes with the mechanism that inhibits the release of cortisol. In simpler terms: stress messes with sleep; messed-up sleep causes stress.

We'll have a more detailed look at sleep and how to get more of the right kind of it in Chapter 6.

Down in the dumps

One of the complicating factors in determining the precise relationship between stress and sleep is that stress — and especially chronic stress — also has a complex relationship with depression. Depression also messes with sleep, and messed-up sleep contributes to depression. It's important to note that depression is different from simply feeling sad, which all of us do from time to time: as the poet Longfellow wrote, 'into each life some rain must fall'. Depression is characterised by a persistently low mood, often accompanied by a loss of interest in the things that once gave you pleasure, to the point where your ability to function on a day-to-day level is impaired. Those suffering severe depression will often experience very low energy levels and motivation.

Stress can cause depression, and depression can amplify our response to stressors. Depression has much in common with an effect named 'learned helplessness', where a person (or animal) becomes convinced by repeated failures to perform a task or control a situation that they have no power at all. They can't perform the task and will never be able to. They can't control the situation and never will be able to. Those experiencing depression often feel helpless in exactly this way, and powerless to do anything to improve their mood or their situation.

It's not hard to understand how a depressed person might regard a stressor which might be way down there at the 'petty annoyance' end of the scale for a normally functioning person as an insurmountable obstacle. That is, you may feel overwhelmed by something that wouldn't normally pose any kind of challenge at all. Similarly, if you are in a constant state of anxiety — you're stressed, and there is no end in sight — it's easy to see how you might become certain that nothing you can do will improve your situation. Stress thus contributes to depression.

The big C

You'll often hear people speculate that the stresses of modern life are the reason for what appears to be an increase in cancer cases.

And yes, many studies have associated stress with major illnesses such as heart disease, high blood pressure and certain types of cancer. However, there is little scientific basis for connecting stress directly with these ailments. There is no convincing evidence for a direct causal link between stress and cancer (although, as mentioned above, there is a straightforward *indirect* link in the form of some of the behaviours we might indulge in to cope with stress: notably, the consumption of alcohol and tobacco, both of which are known to increase the chances of developing cancer).

But thanks to advances in molecular biology, those studying the process of metastasis — the spread of cancer from its original site to other organs of the body — have detected what they believe to be a link between chronic stress and rates of metastatic cancer. A series of quite improbable things have to happen at a cellular level in order for cancer cells to successfully migrate from one part of the body to another: there is what you might think of as a set of locked doors between the original tumour and other tissues. But it turns out that the hormones associated with stress, especially cortisol and others related to chronic stress, can open the locks to those doors, allowing the cancer to waltz right on in.

How much is too much?

This is all a roundabout way of saying that too much stress is bad, right? You knew that already. But we were arguing only a few pages ago that a certain amount of stress is not only good for you, but also necessary for you to perform at your best. So how much stress is too much?

At the beginning of the chapter, I listed a few stressors, first in isolation, then in combination. They were loosely drawn from the Holmes and Rahe stress scale, which lists a bunch of common stressors and assigns them a number of 'points'. A major life stressor, such as the death of a spouse, comes at the top of the list, and counts for 100 points. More minor things, such as significant changes in eating habits or going on holiday, are assigned 12 points. Out of the list, you're asked to choose each stressor that you've experienced in the previous year. If your total score is 150 or less, you've got it relatively easy and you're probably pretty chilled. If it's between 150 and 300 points, you're up there in terms of stress levels: there's as much as a 50 per cent chance that you'll suffer a breakdown in the next two years. That risk rises to 80 per cent if your score is over 300.

Assuming there were no other factors unaccounted for, the list at the beginning of the chapter would earn you roughly 120 points. You're at the top of the green on the dial, where it's just beginning to shade into orange.

To work out where you're currently standing, look at this list of stressors and add up your total score for events experienced in the past year:

EVENT	POINTS
1 Death of spouse	100
2 Divorce	73
3 Marital separation	65
4 Jail term	63
5 Death of close family member	63
6 Personal injury or illness	53
7 Marriage	50
8 Fired from job	47
9 Marital reconciliation	45
10 Retirement	45
11 Change in health of family member	44

EVENT	POINTS
12 Pregnancy	40
13 Sex difficulties	39
14 Gain of new family member	39
15 Business readjustment	39
16 Change in financial state	38
17 Death of close friend	37
18 Change to a different line of work	36
19 Change in number of arguments with spouse	35
20 A large mortgage or loan	31
21 Foreclosure of mortgage or loan	30
22 Change in responsibilities at work	29
23 Son or daughter leaving home	29
24 Trouble with in-laws	29
25 Outstanding personal achievement	28
26 Spouse begins or stops work	26
27 Begin or end school/college	26
28 Change in living conditions	25
29 Revision of personal habits	24
30 Trouble with boss	23
31 Change in work hours or conditions	20
32 Change in residence	20
33 Change in school/college	20
34 Change in recreation	19
35 Change in church activities	19
36 Change in social activities	18
37 A moderate loan or mortgage	17
38 Change in sleeping habits	16
39 Change in number of family get-togethers	15
40 Change in eating habits	15

EVENT	POINTS
41 Vacation	13
42 Christmas	12
43 Minor violations of the law	11
TOTAL SCORE	

Score interpretation

SCORE	COMMENT
11–150	You have only a low to moderate chance of developing a stress-related illness in the near future.
150–299	You have a moderate to high chance of developing a stress-related illness in the near future.
300–600	You have a high or very high risk of developing a stress-related illness in the near future.

We've made the point that different people have different levels of susceptibility to stress. Some people are taller and don't have to jump as high to keep their head above the water when waves come. But the most important point is that *everyone is susceptible*. Even those who are accustomed to flourishing and to coping with whatever comes their way will find themselves overwhelmed from time to time. There's nothing wrong with occasionally feeling overwhelmed — it is often just a sign that we are taking on meaningful challenges and leading full lives — but we need to ensure it stays an occasional experience and something we can learn to get better at predicting and managing in our lives.

Monitoring your stress is the first step in managing it. If you know what the danger signs are, you can head off the danger itself. It's simple enough to tell when you're in trouble at a surf beach: you can't keep your head above water for long enough to get enough air. It's not always as easy to tell when you're mentally and emotionally swamped.

The rollercoaster ride

Stress is supposed to be a cycle, designed to raise our performance to the level necessary to meet a challenge, then to allow us to relax again and conserve our resources. Most of us experience this fluctuation within the range of a normal state of alertness and functioning. But some people work in jobs that routinely put them into a state of hypervigilance, wherein they are always ready for something big to happen, so they constantly have some adrenaline running through their systems.

Under normal conditions, our bodies can effectively deal with this type of peaking and recover to return to a mid-zone level of functioning and stress, but those working in high-stress environments can acquire a distorted sense of what is normal, because they don't often get the 18–24 hours' respite required for their nervous system to reset back to normal. You work an 18-hour, high-adrenaline shift — in law enforcement, perhaps, or as a paramedic — and you're above the line, in a state of high arousal, throughout. You go home, but instead of just settling back into the normal range, you slump further and drop below the line because your mind and body have an increased need to recover after the adrenal high. You feel tired, you're irritable, you just want everyone to leave you alone. If you go back to work again within 24 hours you won't have made it back between the lines. But when you are at work again you feel energised, alert and focused. And so the extreme up-and-down cycle carries on. Over time, this state of high stress and associated hypervigilance will start to wear on you physically, mentally and emotionally.

The danger for such people is that instead of recognising that the down they experience following the high of work is the natural cycle of their nervous system, they come to associate the depleted, depressed, tired feeling they have when they're below the line with their home and family life. Work, shimmering with adrenaline, seems more attractive. So they spend even more time at work and further reduce the likelihood they will have sufficient recovery time to make it back between the lines of normalcy. It's even more important for these people to take their recovery seriously, and to be realistic about how long it will take.

If this is you, make sure you establish very clear boundaries between work and time off. Make sure you protect your personal life. Make sure you engage in the things you love outside of work. Don't give up your hobbies. Spend time with your family and children. Get back into the real world.

Psychological crutches

One sign that you're experiencing excessive amounts of distress is that you rely on what are called 'psychological crutches'. These are behaviours that offer a little relief from distress, mostly by delivering easy gratification or pleasure.

Like most higher mammals, we tend to seek pleasure and avoid pain. Pleasure is best thought of as a reward that we physiologically deliver to ourselves when we perform an action that is conducive to our survival. But we are masters at co-opting this mechanism, and some of the behaviours in which we indulge give us pleasure but aren't necessarily (or at all) useful to us.

Drinking alcohol is one obvious example, so is taking drugs. Others are less obvious, such as using pornography, indulging in comfort eating, gambling or retail therapy, and even sometimes over exercising. They are behaviours that deliver a little dose of pleasure that masks the distress we're suffering as we become fatigued, but which also serves as a substitute for the sense of satisfaction we have when we're flourishing — albeit a poor substitute. We can start to use them as crutches, a means of soldiering on when we're actually beginning to feel the pinch. An increase in your dependence upon such crutches is an indicator that your stress levels are rising and you're becoming fatigued. And unfortunately, taking drugs and drinking alcohol can precipitate mental-health issues for those with a predisposition.

Take Tiger Woods, for example. There's no doubt that in his prime, he was one of the mentally toughest sportsmen around. He seemed to thrive on the extreme pressure of being out in front of the pack in major golf tournaments. But that was only half the story. The rest of his life was off course in more than one sense: rather than relaxing and recovering properly, he resorted to drugs and having affairs to cope with the pressures he faced the rest of the time. It wasn't sustainable, and led — inevitably, it seemed in hindsight — to a fall from grace and a dramatic decline in his performance. In many respects Tiger Woods serves as a great example of the need to approach our mental fitness holistically. His capacity to remain effective in the heat of the moment was legendary, be it making a match-winning shot under incredible pressure, continuing to perform through the extreme pain of an injury, or put aside his bereavement to remain focused when it counted in a match. Yet he wasn't flourishing in other areas of his life. Chapter 13 will teach you some of the techniques used by the Special Forces in order to cultivate a Tiger Woods level of mental toughness to perform under pressure, but it's Chapters 7 to 11 that will enable you to have the emotional experiences and connections with others that ensure you can flourish through the rest of your life.

The 'flourishing versus fatigued' continuum

You know when you're flourishing. You feel on top of your game. You get everything done, then look around for the next thing. Others might be expressing doubts and fears, but you find it easy to be positive. You're fizzing with energy, and even if all you can see looking forward is challenges, you think 'Bring it on!' You sleep well, wake energised and feel fit and capable. You're alert and onto it. You're proactive, anticipating problems and dealing with them before they escalate. You're not using psychological crutches to cope: you're standing, balanced and relaxed, on the balls of your own two emotional feet. You're crushing it! On the 'flourishing versus fatigued' continuum, you're a dead-set 9 or 10.

Perhaps that's not quite you, or that's what you felt like earlier in the day. Right now, you're achieving, which is to say you're getting through what you need to get done. You're motivated and, for the most part, you're enjoying what you do, and you don't wake to contemplate the future with dread. You're mostly positive and cheerful and mostly you feel well. You can accept new challenges without resentment or anxiety. But from time to time you forget things, or find yourself needing to take a bit of psychological time-out. Perhaps you have the odd sick day, where you welcome the chance to recharge your batteries a bit. Perhaps you're resorting to psychological crutches in a low-key kind of way. You'd be a 7 to 8 on the continuum.

Or maybe you're not achieving that consistently. Perhaps it feels more as though you're just hanging on. You're managing most things that are on your plate, and even when you drop the ball, you're not really letting other people down. But you find you're not so much proactive as reactive, which means you deal with things as and when they're absolutely necessary rather than applying a stitch in time. You procrastinate, and you're often tired and feel listless and unmotivated. You get sick, and anything that looks like it will require effort makes you grumpy. You're aware that things are fairly delicately poised, and this makes you anxious. You deal with the stress and anxiety by resorting to crutches more often than you know you should. That's you at 5 or 6 on the continuum.

This 'surviving' zone is where a lot of us spend a reasonable amount of time, simply due to living a busy and meaningful life. It's not a problem to be in this zone so long as we are proactive and disciplined about our recovery and self-care. What constitutes 'self-care' is different for different people, and to follow the mental fitness analogy, self-care is simply your 'recovery time', to allow your brain to recover from the challenges you have been experiencing (more on the ways to proactively do this in Chapters 6 to 11).

But what if you're not keeping up? You're behind on some tasks, and doing anything in your power to avoid taking on any more responsibility. You don't feel as though you've got much of a personal stake in what you're doing, and perhaps you're taking sick days all over the place. You're prone to overreacting, you're hyper-sensitive to criticism, you feel put-upon and you wish people would just leave you alone and let you get on with it. Your relationships — both professional and personal — are suffering, and you find you're leaning on those psychological crutches more and more often. It's fatigue: you can feel it. You're struggling — you're a 3 or 4 on the continuum.

Or perhaps the wheels really are falling off. You're failing to perform tasks that used to be routine, and you're increasingly forgetful and distracted. You can't see a way out of the mess you've got yourself into. Your problems are vast and insurmountable, and they're here to stay. You're ineffectual, useless, a waste of space. You can't see the point in trying anymore, because your best efforts don't get you anywhere. You avoid others, and you always seem to be on the edge of panic, so that the slightest setback leaves you feeling doomed and overwhelmed ... You take refuge in problematic behaviours, avoidant strategies and psychological crutches. You're worn out. You're fatigued. You're a 2 on the flourishing versus fatigued continuum, perhaps even a 1. You're in real trouble.

These are crude descriptions of what life is like at each point on the scale. But it's important to point out that your position on the scale is a moveable feast. You might start the day on top of your game, but by the time you get home after a hard day at work, you're right down there in the low numbers and ill-prepared to deal with the demands from your family. The secret to managing stress, as mentioned above, is monitoring your levels and then employing the strategies covered in subsequent chapters to ensure you recover effectively and continue to build your capacity to cope with future stress.

The Occupational Health Service at Oxford University has assembled a checklist of the things you feel when you're under too much strain:

- can't concentrate
- indecisive
- suffer memory lapses
- make stupid errors
- lose your temper quickly
- anxious

- insecure
- moody
- overly sensitive
- frequent headaches
- tense
- tired, but you can't relax.

You sound like a bit of a nightmare to be around, don't you? And in fact, quite often, when we're running on adrenaline and are just coping or beginning to fail to cope, it's not us who notices. It's those around us who do. Here's what people might notice about a fatigued friend, colleague or loved one. They:

- are performing tasks inconsistently
- are making uncharacteristic errors
- are indecisive
- are emotional and/or subject to sudden changes of moods
- seem unusually tired
- are touchy and irritable
- are often late, even absent
- avoid people or tasks, or lavish too much attention on them (overcompensating)
- demonstrate a loss of perspective — worrying excessively about trivial things, for example, or reacting inappropriately
- are forgetful or suffer from lapses in concentration
- are resistant, even hostile, to change
- have begun to smoke, drink or eat more (or less — skipping meals, for example).

These are all early warning signs that you or someone you are observing has reached the point on the performance curve where stress is ceasing to do them good and has the potential to do harm.

As I hinted earlier, different people will reach this point at different moments and in the face of different stressors or combinations of stressors. And it's important to recognise this fact. We're familiar with the instructions as to how to deal with people suffering from depression: it does no good — indeed, it does actual harm — to tell them to cheer up, that they don't know how hard they've got it, that they should harden up. It's the same with stress. It does no good whatsoever to take any given camel to task for buckling under what you might regard as a light load of straw. Because as we mentioned in the previous chapter, everyone is wired differently.

Flourishing versus fatigued continuum

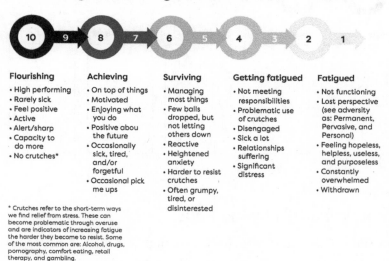

Flourishing	Achieving	Surviving	Getting fatigued	Fatigued
• High performing	• On top of things	• Managing most things	• Not meeting responsibilities	• Not functioning
• Rarely sick	• Motivated	• Few balls dropped, but not letting others down	• Problematic use of crutches	• Lost perspective (see adversity as: Permanent, Pervasive, and Personal)
• Feel positive	• Enjoying what you do			
• Active	• Positive abou the future	• Reactive	• Disengaged	
• Alert/sharp		• Heightened anxiety	• Sick a lot	• Feeling hopeless, helpless, useless, and purposeless
• Capacity to do more	• Occasionally sick, tired, and/or forgetful	• Harder to resist crutches	• Relationships suffering	
• No crutches*			• Significant distress	• Constantly overwhelmed
	• Occasional pick me ups	• Often grumpy, tired, or disinterested		• Withdrawn

* Crutches refer to the short-term ways we find relief from stress. These can become problematic through overuse and are indicators of increasing fatigue the harder they become to resist. Some of the most common are: Alcohol, drugs, pornography, comfort eating, retail therapy, and gambling.

The 'flourishing versus fatigued' continuum provides a gauge of the signs and indicators discussed regarding your current capacity for stress and the impact it is having on you. This continuum provides a way to monitor your level of emotional and mental fatigue so that you can more effectively manage the impact of stress.

The blank continuum below is for you to personalise, based on what you notice about yourself relative to the impact of stress you are experiencing. Have a go at recording below some of the crutches you find yourself drawn to, some of the behaviours you display (for me, procrastination is a biggie), and thoughts and emotions you experience at different points along the continuum. Use the continuum above and the Oxford checklist as references.

Flourishing versus fatigued continuum

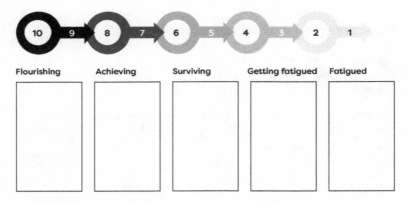

What do I do? What do I do?

Remember that glass you were holding? When it is getting too heavy to hold, what do you do? Simple! You put it down, until you've recovered sufficiently to pick it up again.

As with physical fitness, your need for psychological recovery is proportional to your level of fatigue, and the earlier you ease the pace, the faster and more fully you recover. Think of levels 5 through 10 on the flourishing versus fatigued continuum as the same as aerobic exercise. You recover as you go, and you can maintain that level of exercise for long periods without fatigue setting in. A physically fit person can jog for a long way without needing to stop to recover. Similarly, a mentally fit person, or a person whose resources match or exceed the demands placed upon them, can cope without needing to take a break. More than that, they can even step up and help those who are finding it tougher, because they have the extra capacity.

The lower levels, by contrast, are like anaerobic exercise. You can't get enough air in your lungs to sustain your level of activity, so you have to stop to catch your breath. This will happen to literally everyone at some point. An ultramarathon runner will keep going long after everyone else has hit the wall. But at some point, the ultramarathon runner, too, will hit the wall. We're not mental perpetual-motion machines, any more than physical.

At levels 5 and 6, your stress levels are sending you a warning. If you continue to place demands upon your resources, you will burn more fuel than you have at your disposal, and you will become overwhelmed and fatigued. For this reason, it's important that when you find yourself at this stage, you heed the warnings and treat your self-care as a necessity. You need to identify what it is you need to do to recover (we'll look at some of the steps you can take shortly) and do it as a matter of urgency. The longer you delay your effort to recover and get back on track when you're fatigued, the worse your situation will become and the harder your eventual road to recovery will be.

The urgency of the need to look after yourself can never be overstated. It's a discipline, not a luxury, because if you don't do it, you'll find yourself slipping further down the scale. Below level 5, where you're becoming fatigued, it's important that you stick your hand up and call for help.

If you're a type-A personality this might be hard to do. For very driven and goal-focused people, fatigue feels like weakness, feels like failure. It can be the same for those who may not be type-A personalities, but might have been brought up to believe that it's bad to feel vulnerable or weak. One of the great fallacies of our modern, individualistic society is that our fate is entirely in our own hands, and that courage is the ability to face stuff by yourself. Our culture has made it difficult to admit 'weakness', to admit to others and to yourself that you can't meet the demands upon you out of your own resources.

Admitting fatigue and prioritising self-care is also a challenge if you're a type-E personality. The E stands for Everything to Everyone. Type-E people more often feel fatigue as guilt, because they feel they are failing to deliver what others need from them and that they are supposed to always put the needs of others first. But think about the emergency card on an airliner. In the unlikely event of an emergency, what's the first thing it tells you to do if oxygen masks fall from the ceiling? *Put your own mask on first, before attending to others!* You're no use to your children if you pass out through lack of oxygen: likewise, you're no use to the people who matter to you if you can't cope yourself. If you are not squared away, you can't be who you need to be for yourself or for others.

The paradoxical thing is that it takes true courage to ask for help. The ability to recognise the moment when we need the tribe on the job is something to be admired, because it is actually drawing on one of the greatest strengths that you have as a human being. We're a social species, and are far more effective in a group than we are on our own. After all, 'no man is an island', as the poet John Donne once put it.

What's wrong with me?

It's important at this point to talk about depression and anxiety as a normal part of human experience. The states of mind to which we attach labels such as 'depressed', 'stressed', 'anxious', etc are simply points on a continuum of normal human responses. Just as no one who ever lived has been fortunate enough to avoid stress and aggravation altogether, it's unlikely there was ever a human being who did not find themselves at a very low point at some stage or another. We all experience highs and lows.

When you're low — especially when you're very low — it can feel as though what you're going through is due to some flaw or failing unique to you. We talked about 'learned helplessness' and how depressed people can form the idea that nothing they do will affect their situation for the better. In Chapter 7, we'll talk about the opposite: the value of 'learned optimism' as an essential part of mental fitness.

Perhaps the single most important thing to tell yourself when you're feeling fatigued — depressed, stressed out, exhausted, used up, wrung out, crushed, cornered, defeated — is that 'this too shall pass'. By prioritising your self-care and by reaching out to others who can help, you can begin to recover, impossible as this may seem when you're really down.

There is nothing wrong with you, and what you are experiencing is just a normal part of what it is to be human. Even scary-sounding labels like depression are just that: they're labels for parts of normal human experience. Don't be afraid to own this moment in your life's journey and to reach out for help if you need it.

Distress: the facts

We can become overwhelmed (distressed) by chronic or excessive stress.

Distress can be harmful to both our mental and physical health.

Different individuals have different vulnerabilities to stress.

There are a variety of common stressors that individually cause distress and in combination have a greater impact.

There are a number of warning signs that you (or another) are distressed: that is, experiencing intolerable levels of stress.

Monitoring the indicators of stress allows you to manage it more effectively.

Self-care is a discipline, not a luxury.

The Myth of Perpetual Happiness

Desire hath no rest, is infinite in itself, endless, and as one calls it, a perpetual rack, or horse-mill.

Robert Burton, *The Anatomy of Melancholy,* **1621**

The modern notion of emotional experience is that it occurs as a function of changes on a continuum of high/low arousal on the one hand, and pleasantness and unpleasantness on the other. There are no objectively good or bad emotions according to this conceptualisation: what we are feeling can be categorised only as helpful or unhelpful according to how we interpret the signals we are receiving, the situation we are in, how we respond and the outcomes we get.

The chief ingredients of emotions — high/low arousal and pleasant/unpleasant — are universal. However, as we have discussed, our perceptions of them, like our names for them, are not. These are culturally determined, and will vary from individual to individual even from the same culture. For example, Lisa Feldman Barrett's research shows that 'anger' is a cultural concept that we apply to hugely divergent patterns of change in the body. There's no single facial expression reliably associated with it, even in the same person. (Some cultures don't even have a concept that corresponds to 'anger', such as the Utku Inuit of Canada's Northwest Territories.)

The 'mood meter' below captures these continuums and replaces the more technical term of 'arousal' with 'energy'. Reflecting on how you feel right now, where on this meter would you be located? What label would you give this combination of high/low energy and unpleasantness/pleasantness? Is your interpretation of this mix the most helpful to you?

Energy/feeling matrix

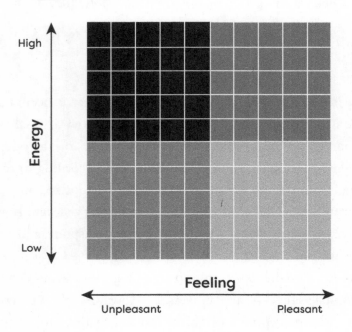

For example, you might be a mix of medium unpleasantness and energy because of something you should be doing other than reading this book. This could be interpreted as guilt or worry, but it could equally be interpreted as feeling motivated to put this book down and get back to whatever it is you are supposed to be doing right now!

Remember how I said I lacked the emotional self-awareness and literacy to know that I was feeling scared in maximum security? As mentioned, had you asked me at the time what I was feeling I would have interpreted the mix of unpleasantness and energy/arousal as feeling 'ready'. Although this deficiency of emotional range wouldn't serve me well in my life now, it was a beneficial interpretation in the situation I was in. The interpretation directed me towards actions likely to increase my survival, and focused attention on the threats to me rather than my experience of them.

What feelings do you regularly identify in your life that might be more helpful if you reinterpreted them? Perhaps you find yourself feeling attacked by your partner, when reinterpreting the signals your body is sending you as feeling challenged, disappointed or guilty would be more helpful? Or do you find yourself thinking you are feeling anxious, when switched on or excited might be a more useful interpretation?

Of all the emotions, the one that preoccupies people in the modern world most of the time is happiness. Philosophers, psychologists, theologians and greeting-card manufacturers have been struggling to complete the sentence 'Happiness is ...' for millennia. From time to time, you'll hear a news report that people living in some country or another have been declared 'the happiest', based on self-reported responses to a survey designed to measure some version of happiness or another.

Don't worry, be happy!

Pretty much all of us believe we know happiness when we feel it. We can all agree that happiness is a positive emotion. But how positive? Is it simply the absence of unpleasant emotion? Is it a sense of wellbeing and, if so, how do you define that? Is it contentment — satisfaction with our lot and our prospects — or does it have to be more intense than that, more like what you might call 'bliss' or 'ecstasy', to qualify as happiness, as we're encouraged to believe by sunlit television advertisements and picture-perfect posts by our social media 'friends'? And is it therefore simply sensual pleasure, or does there have to be an intellectual, even a moral component for it to qualify as 'proper' happiness?

In some respects, it's meaningless to talk about 'happiness' as a measure of pleasant emotion, as it seems to be the default human mode. In the 1970s, a team of researchers led by Philip Brickman and Donald T Campbell indicated that major life events, good or bad, had at most only a temporary impact upon our base level of happiness.

These findings have been replicated again and again. In 1978, a study of 22 people who had won a lottery and 29 people who had become paraplegic — in each case, around a year on from the event — showed that both groups reported themselves pretty much neither more nor less 'happy' or satisfied with their lives than they had been before their change in fortunes. This effect has been called 'hedonic adaptation' or 'the hedonic treadmill' — the notion that we cut the cloth of our expectations to fit our circumstances.

If we receive a sudden windfall, we change our expectations — we want a bigger car, a flasher house, more exotic holidays than we did before we were suddenly enriched, so that our wants stand in much the same relation to our means as they did when we could only afford a small car, a modest house, a simple holiday (an effect called 'abundance denial'). This is easy to understand. It's more surprising to learn that if we suffer a major adverse life event, we adapt in much the same way. People who had lost the use of their legs through accident or injury had more or less come to terms with their new circumstances a year on from the event. They still had hopes and dreams: just different hopes or dreams than the ones they'd had when fully able-bodied.

I lived the truth of this in prison. I experienced all kinds of emotions when I was first jailed, but after a while, I had adapted and was almost what you'd describe as 'happy' inside. We are programmed to find a comfort zone in whatever circumstances we find ourselves in. It's as though we, as a species, are capable of 'synthesising happiness', as Harvard psychology professor Dan Gilbert puts it.

It seems strange, then, that if happiness is something we naturally make for ourselves, it is treated as some kind of holy grail in the developed world. One of the most harmful myths in modern society is the idea that our principal goal is to be happy — experiencing pleasant emotions or even pleasure — most or even all of the time. Of course, there are entire industries that exist to foster and profit from this notion. Indeed, the founding principle of the advertising industry is that if we can be persuaded to believe that a product or service will make us happy (or happier), then we'll buy it. So, in the consumerist society in which we in the developed world live, we are constantly encouraged to believe not only that we could be happier, but also that we actually *should* be happier, and all it will take to make us happier is for us to open our wallets.

Glossy magazines are sold on our aspirations — to be as blessed and happy as the celebrities with which we are obsessed (somehow, in spite of all of the evidence to the contrary, we equate fame with happiness); to live in the houses and gardens that they show in such rich, full colour; to travel to those exotic places; to eat that delicious food ... Our friends, whether they know it or not, are complicit, when they post pictures and stories on social media that show all of the various ways in which their lives measure up to those unrealistic standards. Scrolling down our newsfeed, we can feel inadequate and deprived by comparison. Even the news media has traditionally been in the selling happiness game, in that they can tend to prey on our fears. Making us feel anxious — and therefore unhappy — is a way of capturing audiences and selling newspapers, because we like to believe that if we have the facts, we will be more in control of what worries us.

The false notion of happiness we're being directed towards sets us on a very different kind of hedonic treadmill. The happiness we're encouraged to pursue in modern, ultra-consumerist society is an illusion, dangled in front of us like a carrot before a hamster in a wheel.

There are big cultural differences in our understanding of 'happiness'. The American constitution even gives 'the pursuit of happiness' the status of a fundamental right, up there with freedom of religion, speech and the right to bear arms. It may mean different things to different individuals within a culture, and our own sense of what it is to be happy changes at different stages in our life.

But here's the thing. What the United States founding fathers understood by the term 'happiness' and what it has come to mean in our ultra-materialistic society are two very different things. Put simply, we expect too much of the wrong kind of happiness. And this has been shown — by the University of Colorado's June

Gruber, among others — to be counterproductive. Our excessive expectations actually make us worse off, because they make us feel as though we're failing. If we believe that our life's purpose is to find our comfort zone and stay there, avoiding all unpleasant emotions, then we'll regard any discomfort we experience as failure. This, in turn, will detract from our wellbeing.

In fact, as human beings, we are here to grow, and growing pains are all part of the deal. I believe we need either to recalibrate our sense of what it is to be happy, or even set the whole unhelpful notion of 'happiness' as a pleasant emotional experience aside and concentrate on what's *good* for us — what will help us flourish, to be effective and, as we strive towards our potential, to be *satisfied* with our lives and find meaning within them, regardless of what challenges may come our way. It's much like something Greek philosopher Epicurus said a couple of thousand years ago: 'Live according to nature and you will never be poor. Live according to opinion and you will never be rich.'

The modern misconception, carefully nurtured by the advertising industry and the media, is that our goal is to reach a certain level of happiness, at which point there's no further need for change or aspiration, and all unpleasant emotions will be a thing of the past. It's a natural human impulse to find our comfort zone and stay there, but it's an impulse that was designed to help us survive in a very different world — the world of a few hundred thousand years ago. To expect to be comfortable all the time wilfully ignores not only the nature of the universe, which has never simply fallen into line with human aspirations, but also what it is to be human.

To live according to nature is to accept that you will regularly experience unpleasant emotions because that's the way our brains are wired. There will be no point where you have reached a certain goal or age and your unpleasant emotions vanish. No matter how successful your life from the outside, or what inner spiritual journey you have embarked on, you will continue to carry around a Stone Age brain on the constant look out for something to worry about.

The prevailing twenty-first-century definition of happiness, at least in consumerist societies, is closer to the classical Greek concept of hedonism, which boils down to the pursuit of pleasure (the word derives from the Greek word for 'delight', *hedone*). Like all animals, we instinctively seek to avoid pain and discomfort. And, like all animals, our bodies produce feel-good chemicals when we perform certain functions that are conducive to our survival or that of our species — quenching our thirst, satisfying our hunger or our sexual desire, breastfeeding a baby, for example. These chemicals act on a receptive region of the brain, and the process of their reception is what we call pleasure. Hedonism is the notion that the sole object of human endeavour is to minimise discomfort and maximise pleasure.

But we are not born fully formed, with a clear destiny. We are born with *potential*. Life is therefore all about growth. Modern research has tended to suggest that true happiness (insofar as you can define it) has more to do with striving to reach our potential than any feeling of having got there and being left with nothing further to do. The goal in this scenario is not to feel happy *in* your life, all the time. Instead, it's to feel happy *with* your life. In this way, you'll be able to experience unpleasant emotions when they arise without feeling as though you're a failure or there's something wrong with your life.

This is closer to the definition of happiness that Thomas Jefferson had in mind when he enshrined 'the pursuit of happiness' in the US constitution. And this, in turn, is closer to a classical definition of happiness. While there was varied opinion in ancient Greece about what happiness actually was, one influential school of thought equated it with the concept of *eudaimonia*. This word literally means something like 'well in spirit' (from *eu* 'good' or 'well' and *daimonia* 'spirit'), but underlying it was the notion that like everything else in the universe, human beings have a purpose, and they are happiest when they are fulfilling that purpose. Aristotle, who was the best known proponent of this notion, identified the capacity for rational thought as the quality that was unique to humans. Therefore, he believed a human being was happiest when fully exercising their capacity for rational thought. If nothing else, this was a clear statement of how much he enjoyed his 'job' as a philosopher!

Implied in the concept of eudaimonia was the full realisation of other human potential, too. Our bodies are healthiest and happiest when we use them for the performance of physical work and the pursuit of athletic prowess. Aristotle even went so far as to suggest that some men — even whole races of men — were so much better suited to physical work than rational thought that they were designed by nature to be slaves. Similarly, women, whose bodies are designed for childbearing and rearing, drew nearest the state of eudaimonia as in their role as mothers.

Well, we can disagree with the detail but still accept the concept: happiness arises from the struggle to realise our potential. The eudaimonic definition of happiness has been pervasive throughout history. Victorian schoolmasters were fond of repeating the Roman formulation of it — *mens sana in corpore sano* ('a healthy mind in a healthy body') — to their pupils. Karl Marx, when describing a socialist utopia, wrote that unlike a society that forced us to become one thing only, the ideal society would make it 'possible for me to do one thing today and another tomorrow, to hunt in the morning, fish in the afternoon, rear cattle in the evening, criticise after dinner, just as I have a mind, without ever becoming hunter, fisherman, herdsman or critic.' Ironically, Thomas Jefferson, founding father of a nation that has virtually defined itself through its opposition to communism, would probably have wholeheartedly agreed with Marx's vision of what it is to pursue happiness.

Whatever it means personally to you to pursue your potential, there is research to suggest that asking yourself the following three questions on a regular basis will ensure you experience a life of greater meaning and satisfaction along the way.

- Am I present?
- Am I open?
- Am I doing what matters?

If you can answer 'yes' to these questions, you will have a life of greater meaning and satisfaction; when you can't, it will give you a nudge to get you back on the path.

The first of these questions refers to you being mentally present for the experience of life as it's happening, rather than mentally stuck in the past or prospecting into the future. The second question can be conceptualised in two ways: firstly, am I open to the world? To learning new things, being exposed to other ways of thinking and changing my mind? Secondly, am I open with the world about who I am, what I think and feel, and what really matters to me?

These first two questions are challenging, but the third question — am I doing what matters? — is the one most likely to result in an imitation of Edvard Munch's painting *The Scream*. In Chapter 10 we look at exploring our values to help ensure we are doing what matters, but there is a simpler question that we can ask on a moment-by-moment basis that comes from famous Notre Dame football coach Lou Holtz. It is captured by the acronym WIN, which stands for 'What's Important Now?'

Holtz instructed his players to ask themselves this question 35 times a day, and it's a question I powerfully employ in my own life. When I find myself in the surviving zone, I regularly procrastinate and spend time on things that don't reduce the pressure I am under (such as answering emails that aren't actually urgent). But when I ask myself 'What's Important Now?', it helps me cut through the noise and focus on what really matters in the moment.

The reason the preceding questions are so impactful is that they increase what is known as 'psychological flexibility'. Having psychological flexibility is being able to stay in contact with the present moment and based on the situation we find ourselves in, being able to act on longer term values and goals rather than short-term impulses, thoughts and feelings.

Pain and gain

There is a passive element to human growth. But there is also an active component. You don't build physical strength or stamina simply by sitting around doing nothing. You have to do the mahi — to expend the effort. And this entails accepting an amount of physical discomfort.

If you want to run a marathon, you have to get out there and pound the pavement. On the very first day you start training, you'll reach a point relatively quickly where your limbs feel heavy and your lungs are burning (I can speak with some authority on this, because I'm not a great runner but I've trained for and run a marathon). This is physical stress, and it's your body's way of telling you to stop doing what you're doing in order to conserve your resources. But you're well short of your goal of being fit enough to run 42.2 kilometres. If you listen to your body and stop as soon as it begins to hurt, or even soon after it begins to hurt, you'll never build your level of fitness. It's only by pushing yourself outside your comfort zone that you will improve: you have to exert some measure of self-control to endure physical discomfort in order to reap the benefits. You have to actively choose to embrace the challenge.

The whole premise of this book is that there is such a thing as mental fitness, too. We all know about mental stress (or we think we do). We've definitely all experienced it, and none of us like it. It's the same as physical stress, in that it is the mind's way of telling us that what we are attempting to do is challenging our resources (running a deficit, in Lisa Feldman Barrett's terms).

When we feel stress, we have a choice. We can heed the body's signal and stop — after all, we're meant to stay in our psychic comfort zone all the time, right? — or we can recognise that the discomfort we are feeling is simply nature's way of enabling us to rise to the occasion. It's a caveman reflex, and just as it enabled our remote ancestors to think quickly and coolly enough to perform whatever challenging task they happened to be confronted with — catching an animal, for example, or avoiding being caught by an animal — it's equipping us to deal with a situation that is demanding something extra of us.

In exactly the same way as the experience of physical stress increases our fitness and future capacity to cope with physiological challenge, the experience of psychological stress is how we get mentally tougher and more resilient. The worst thing you can do for your mental fitness is to avoid stress and pressure, for it is this experience of discomfort that builds our mental fitness.

Just as we have to work to gain physical fitness, and then to work to maintain it, mental fitness is the same deal. We have to step outside our psychic comfort zone to develop mental toughness, resilience and resourcefulness, and accept that there will never be a point at which we can string a banner over our heads with the words 'Mission Accomplished' printed on it. *Staying* mentally fit, just like becoming mentally fitter, is a lifelong struggle. But the joy is in the struggle. A mentally fit person is a flourishing person, one who will be able to show up as the best version of themselves time and again, and one who will cope when a crisis comes along.

When we start to look at what it is to flourish, we'll be using a model devised by one of my psychology heroes, Martin Seligman. For a very great deal of its history, the study of psychology was deficiency focused, because it tended to ask the question: how is it that people's thoughts and emotions become problematic? Take the discovery of the behaviour called 'learned helplessness' (discussed in Chapter 4). This came about (as many scientific advances do) as the unforeseen by-product of an experiment. The experiment was designed to explore 'conditioning' — where a stimulus is delivered in order to produce a response. The most famous example of this is Pavlov's dogs. Russian doctor Ivan Pavlov set up an experiment where he rang a gong each time he fed his test subjects, dogs. After the dogs had been given time to become accustomed to this regime, he began ringing the gong without offering food immediately afterwards. It made no difference to the dogs' conditioned physical response, which was to start drooling as though a nice, big bowl of dogroll had been set in front of them (actually, Pavlov used a type of flavour powder, but that doesn't conjure up as good an image!).

In the 1970s, Martin Seligman was a member of a team working on conditioned responses, again with dogs. They discovered a weird thing while conducting what would now be considered quite a questionable experiment. What they were doing was delivering an unpleasant stimulus to the dogs — they were kept in a cage that had a floor that could deliver an electric shock. The shock was preceded by a light and a noise. For most iterations of the experiment, the dog could escape the electrified floor by jumping a hurdle, and the dogs quickly learned that when the light came on, they needed to jump over the hurdle. But what the researchers weren't expecting was what happened when, for any reason, the dog found itself unable to escape the shock. All it took was a few repetitions of the dog finding itself to be helpless against the shock before it began to stop trying to escape by jumping the hurdle, even when escape was possible. The team called this 'learned helplessness' — the conditioned belief that you are powerless to avoid or improve an unpleasant situation.

The parallels with the thought processes of severely depressed people was immediately obvious. The psychologists suggested that depression involves a kind of learned helplessness: the hopelessness that a depressed person feels arising from the feeling that the forces ranged against them are out of their control. The component of learned helplessness in depression has now become widely accepted, even as it has also become accepted that the symptoms of depression occur on a continuum, and even those of us who are not depressed can still identify with and relate to the thoughts and associated feelings at times.

Soon after his team had been hailed for their description of one of the things that can go wrong with a person's thought processes, it occurred to Seligman that if a simple idea could exert this kind of negative influence over your thought processes and the actions you took, then surely other simple ideas could have a positive impact. Just as the feeling that you can't do anything might prevent you from trying to improve your situation, surely the feeling that you *can* take control of your life and circumstances could harness your mental energy to produce positive outcomes?

This idea was a turning point in Seligman's career and, in many ways, the course of twentieth century psychology more generally. For Seligman, his first book on the subject, *Learned Optimism: How to Change Your Mind and Your Life* (1991), was the beginning of a new career focusing not on what had gone wrong with people's thought processes, but on how you could use the power of your mind to improve your life.

The basic idea wasn't new. Indeed, it is very, very old: the whole notion of mastering the self with a set of worthy ideas to live a better life is fundamental to systems such as that of the Stoic philosophers of ancient Greece (whose writings helped me not only to survive but even to flourish through over a decade in some of New Zealand's toughest prisons). In 1902, the British poet and philosopher James Allen wrote a book named *As a Man Thinketh*, in which he declared that 'a man is literally what he thinks, his character being the complete sum of all his thoughts.' One of the most famous examples of what we now call a 'self-help' book was Dale Carnegie's *How to Win Friends and Influence People*, published in 1936, which explored the notion that material success often comes from self-belief. Similarly, Stephen Covey wrote in *The 7 Habits of Highly Effective People* (1989) that success in business is largely determined by your mindset.

Seligman's focus, however, was broader. In his work since the late 1980s, he has sought to show how our mental habits are crucial in creating wellbeing and what he (and we) have called 'flourishing'. In 2011 (in a book called *Flourish*), Seligman set out five elements that he considers pivotal to leading a fulfilled and meaningful life — any kind of life that is, as he puts it, 'north of zero', or characterised by something more positive than mere lassitude and indifference. He called this the PERMA model (more recently extended to PERMA-H or PERMA-V, where the last letter stands for Health or Vitality). PERMA is an acronym for:

- Positive emotion
- Engagement
- Relationships
- Meaning
- Accomplishment.

In this book, the PERMA-H model will be used to help you to identify how you can proactively ensure you have the fuel in your tank to move closer to the flourishing end of the flourishing versus fatigued continuum. We'll look at each of the elements in more detail in turn in the next few chapters, starting with the Health component, which forms the foundation upon which all other elements are built.

As you go through this chapter, ask yourself: if you had to score yourself on a 0–10 scale each of the Health areas (sleep, diet and exercise), what number would you give yourself, where 0 means you *never* meet the outlined standards and 10 is you *always* meet the standards? If you don't score yourself at least a 7 out of 10 in any of these areas, this is where your journey needs to begin. Nothing will have a bigger impact on your mental fitness than improvements in these three foundations.

At the end of each subsequent chapter for the PERMA-H domains, I will ask you to complete and score a simple questionnaire that you can use to figure out where in the remainder of the PERMA-H model your biggest mental fitness gains are to be had.

But while the PERMA-H model will help facilitate flourishing and enhance your mental fitness in general, in Chapters 12 and 13 we will focus on the mental toughness side of the mental fitness equation, through exploring a number of strategies used by the Special Forces, elite athletes and others to remain effective in the heat of the moment — when the pressure is at its greatest.

What we've learned about happiness

Trying to feel happy all the time is a fool's errand.

Pursuing your potential requires mental fitness and will lead to a more satisfying and meaningful life.

You can increase your mental fitness, just as you can increase your physical fitness.

In order to effectively increase and maintain your mental fitness, you need to embrace discomfort and work at it proactively.

When you are mentally fit, you can cope effectively for longer before you get fatigued or exhausted: it doesn't mean you don't feel the struggle.

Everyone gets fatigued: it's just a question of at what point fatigue sets in. You have to pay attention to the indicators of fatigue in order to marshal your resources.

The PERMA-H model can be used to ensure you holistically tap into those areas likely to facilitate flourishing and resilience.

6

Health — Fit for Life

Our species evolved to be hunter-gatherers. Our ancestors woke shortly before first light and were on the go — *literally on the go* — from that point onwards, hunting and gathering food and avoiding dangers along the way. Eating was done opportunistically, and we probably had a nap some time during the day. Nightfall usually found us in a sheltered, protected location, and we were asleep soon after the fall of darkness, only to wake up the following morning to do it all again. Every day will have brought a constant stream of new challenges, demanding full presence, focus and attention. There was no need for our ancestors to find ways to entertain themselves: every waking hour would have totally absorbed their attention in the deceptively simple-sounding business of staying alive.

Compare that with the lifestyle of the typical citizen of the developed world. By contrast, we lead sedentary lives. We wake, eat, commute (sitting down in a car or public transport) to our place of work and then spend most of the rest of the day indoors under artificial lighting, sitting down (or standing) in one place with our eyes focused on objects in our immediate vicinity, if not literally right in front of our nose. Along the way we have a meal and, in most cases, a snack or two as well — often high-energy, processed foods and drinks. In the evening, we eat yet another large meal, then typically sit around in artificially lit rooms, interacting with screens, then go to bed when we choose, often many hours after nightfall.

In most cases, our lifestyle is seriously at odds with our biology. And unless we make a conscious effort to align the way we live with the way we have evolved to live, it will be difficult for us to flourish. So the very first step in our pursuit of mental fitness is addressing our physiological needs — our health. Without doing so is like building on sand.

As previously mentioned, the Health component of the PERMA-H model is the last letter of the acronym, but I believe it is the most important part of setting ourselves up for a flourishing life. It focuses on getting three things right: sleep, exercise and nutrition.

Sleep

As part of my research for writing the mental toughness chapter of this book, I was fortunate enough to observe those who had made it through initial SAS selection now undertaking an element of SERE (Survive, Evade, Resist, Escape) training, in particular the resistance element aka 'conduct after capture' or CAC training. The first part of this training involves a non-stop escape and evasion exercise for approximately a week wherein the SAS candidates are chased by a 'hunter force' with dogs and helicopters. During this exercise they must cover approximately 130km of off-road terrain through an inhospitable Waiouru, primarily at night, on little to no sleep or food. They are then captured and spend the next several days subjected to further food and sleep deprivation, stress conditioning, and simulated interrogation. During this process they are closely monitored by the Defence Force oversight team, including CAC command, medical officers and psychologists, to ensure that the exercise conforms to its 'train not break' intention, and that the training is in accordance with international best practice. Participants are also aware that they can withdraw from the exercise at any time. Prior to this experience, participants had already been trained in the skills and tools they needed to cope with the training and ultimately survive captivity if they ever found themselves in that situation. Included in that is a model that will be covered later in this book, which is intended to assist their ability to cope and survive, and be deliberate in their responses. Yet another part of this prior training involved learning that one of the key methods an enemy will use to increase confusion and reduce the capacity to cope and resist is sleep deprivation.

*

Sleep is the primary foundation that the other fundamental pillars of diet and exercise are built upon. Like most things in life, sleep comes easily when you're young. But as you age, chances are you'll experience some level of sleep disturbance, perhaps for a period in your life, perhaps chronically. Sleep is something we have in common with many other species, and any behaviour that is favoured by evolution tends to be essential to survival. It serves to restore us, both physically and mentally. Getting enough quality sleep is crucial in maintaining both our physical and our mental health and wellbeing.

When we go to sleep, our body is replenished. It has a significant impact on our cardiovascular systems and metabolism. Our sleep also significantly impacts levels of hormones such as testosterone in our bodies. Men who sleep for only five to six hours a night tend to have testosterone levels similar to someone ten years their senior. This means a reduced quantity of sleep can result in significant ageing in an area critical to wellness, virility, muscle strength and sexual performance. As well as bodily and wellbeing benefits, sleep is directly linked to skill-learning and memory. Inadequate sleep, on the other hand, is linked to negative outcomes such as:

- cancer
- diabetes
- weight gain
- heart disease
- reduced fertility
- weakened immune system
- DNA damage.

Motor and cognitive learning and performance are heavily impacted by sleep, for it is when we are asleep that our minds scoop out episodes from the previous day's activities and commit them to memory. According to neuroscientist and sleep expert Professor Matthew Walker, sleep is the greatest performance-enhancing drug that most people are neglecting. His research shows that skilled performance is between 20 and 30 per cent better the following day for athletes who get at least seven hours' quality sleep following a training session, compared with those who don't. His research shows that an athlete who gets six hours or less sleep the night before an event will become physically exhausted 30 per cent sooner.

Besides performance, a lack of sleep depletes your reserves of mental fitness. You start the day pre-fatigued rather than recovered. When you're lacking sleep, small things will get to you sooner, minor hindrances will seem like insurmountable obstacles and you will feel emotional and lacking in self-control. It's no coincidence that it has become routine for interrogators to use sleep deprivation as a simple tool to break down resistance.

We need different amounts of sleep at different stages of our lives. Babies sleep most of the time — between 14 and 15 hours in a 24-hour period — waking up only to feed and engage in short periods of activity, which wipe them out completely. Children generally sleep anywhere from 10 to 14 hours a day. With the onset of puberty, teenagers find it more difficult to go to sleep in the early hours of the night, but tend to wake later, too, and sleep for roughly eight or nine hours a day. Adults need between seven and nine hours. People over the age of 60 sleep a little less than this — not because they need less sleep, but rather because the circadian rhythm responsible for the release of the sleep-related hormone melatonin is impaired with age.

Of course, not all of this sleep has to happen in one session, or all at night. In much of the developed world, we have grown accustomed to trying to get a single good night's kip (what's called monophasic sleep). Prior to industrialisation, it was much more common for a night-time sleep to be supplemented with a short sleep during daylight hours: some cultures, and many people, still enjoy a nap or a siesta, and this 'bimodal' sleep arrangement has been connected with some improved health aspects. But regardless of when you get your sleep, the quantity is important. Your body seems to keep a kind of ledger of sleep and wakefulness, and if you get too little sleep (you're in 'sleep deficit'), you will find it difficult to fully function.

The impact of not getting enough sleep is dramatic. Epidemiological studies across millions of people have shown that the shorter your sleep, the shorter your life. Insufficient sleep is a lifestyle factor associated with increased rates of cancer and Alzheimer's disease. The explanation for this is that during the day we experience a kind of low-level brain damage from the build-up of metabolic toxins associated with keeping our brains and bodies working. Just like driving a car with a combustion energy creates some pollutants, so does using your brain. It is during deep sleep at night that such toxins are purged from the brain.

Furthermore — and particularly relevant to the focus of this book — sleep is critical for emotional regulation, mood management and mental health. The prefrontal cortex, the logical and rational part of our brains, is the first thing to reduce in effectiveness when you're sleep deprived — its performance simply gets dialled down when you're tired. One of the functions of the prefrontal cortex is to control the deep emotional centres in the brain and keep them in check. At the same time, your amygdala — a part of your brain associated with strong, unpleasant emotional experiences and fight/flight/freeze response— is dialled up when you're fatigued. For this reason, when you're sleep deprived, you're all emotional gas pedal and too little regulatory brake!

For this reason, sleep deprivation doesn't just impact on your physical health: it also affects productivity, performance and your ability to be the best version of yourself when dealing with others. People who haven't had between seven and nine hours' sleep are less productive and efficient. The less sleep you've had, the more 'social loafing' you do — where you coast instead of pulling your weight in group and team activities. You also tend to focus on easier tasks at work, being less capable of and less likely to engage in deep and innovative work. It's also been shown that the less sleep a leader has had, the less charismatic their employees rate them as being, even when they know nothing about how much sleep their boss has had! Part of this is attributed to the impact sleep deprivation has on both performance and emotional regulation.

Yet according to international studies of industrialised nations, one out of two adults are not getting the recommended minimum of seven hours of sleep a night. And one out of three adults are trying to survive on six hours or less. The average nightly sleep for adults in industrialised nations has decreased from 7.9 hours in the 1940s to 6.3 hours now. Research clearly shows that no one operates effectively on six hours of sleep, and it also shows that people who are this sleep deprived can't accurately gauge the level of impairment they are experiencing. Furthermore, you can't make up for lost sleep. You'll sleep more on subsequent days, but it's never enough to make up the deficit.

If all of that isn't enough to convince you to invest in more bed-time, not getting enough sleep makes you fat! Two hormones control appetite and hunger, and insufficient sleep results in a suppression of the hormone that tells you you're full and have had enough to eat, and ramps up the hormone that tells you you're hungry! This causes us to eat more, but we're also more likely to eat the wrong kinds of foods when sleep deprived: carbohydrates, sugars and processed foods. Obesity has increased over the last 70 years as our sleep hours have reduced. Coincidence?

It's not just the quantity of the sleep that is important: it's also the quality. In any given night's sleep, we pass through several phases (broadly: deep and shallow), interspersed with periods where we actually wake up (although these are brief enough that we rarely remember them in the morning). The precise biological benefits of each phase aren't fully understood, but it's very well documented that too much of one kind or not enough of another means that the full restorative effect is compromised.

For example, alcohol will send you off to sleep just fine, and you may even stay fast asleep all night. But you won't wake as refreshed as you would have if you hadn't indulged, as alcohol tends to keep you longer in the deep phase of sleep rather than in the shallow phase. Similarly, anyone who has travelled a lot will know that hotels are rarely a place for getting replenishing sleep. The latest research suggests that this is because when we sleep in an unfamiliar setting, half of our brain stays in a lighter level of sleep. It is thought that this is an evolutionary adaption for ensuring we are better prepared to effectively detect and avoid or confront any potential threats in a novel environment. This half-brain sleeping is something shared with sea-based mammals such as the dolphin, which always sleep with only half of their brains at a time.

14 key tips for good sleep
1. STICK TO A SLEEP SCHEDULE

Aim to go to bed and wake up at the same time each day. Unfortunately, sleeping late on weekends doesn't make up for poor sleep during the week, and people generally have a hard time adjusting to changes in sleep patterns. If necessary, set an alarm for bedtime, and stick to it. Professor Matthew Walker's research suggests sticking to a sleep schedule should be the number-one priority.

2. DON'T EXERCISE TOO LATE IN THE DAY

Exercise is great, and we should try to exercise for at least 30 minutes on most days. Exercising during the day does help us sleep at night, but try to time it no later than two to three hours before bed. This is because the adrenaline released from exercising stimulates our nervous system and can stop us getting off to sleep.

3. AVOID CAFFEINE AND NICOTINE

Cola, coffee, non-herbal teas and chocolate all contain caffeine, which is a stimulant. Consuming these even in the afternoon can have an affect on your sleep. Nicotine is also a mild stimulant, and smokers will often wake up earlier than they would otherwise, due to nicotine withdrawal.

4. AVOID ALCOHOLIC DRINKS BEFORE BED

The presence of alcohol in the body can reduce your REM sleep and the general quality of your sleep.

5. DON'T GO TO BED TOO FULL OR TOO HUNGRY

A light snack before bed is OK, but a heavy meal closer than a couple of hours to sleep-time can cause digestive issues, which interfere with sleep. Drinking too much fluids can cause frequent awakenings, when you need to pee. Yet going to bed too long after eating can also reduce sleep quality, due to hunger. The perfect amount and time to eat before bed is different for different people, so you will have to experiment. While there is not yet a lot of research about diet and sleep, what is known is that diets heavy in sugars and stodgy carbohydrates and low in fibre result in less deep and more fragmented sleep.

6. AVOID MEDICINES THAT DELAY OR DISRUPT YOUR SLEEP (WHERE POSSIBLE)

Some commonly prescribed heart, blood pressure or asthma medications, as well as some over-the-counter and herbal medicines for coughs, colds or allergies, can disrupt sleep patterns. If you have trouble sleeping, it may be worth speaking to your doctor or pharmacist to see if any of the drugs you're taking may be contributing to this. It may be possible to take them earlier in the day.

7. DON'T NAP AFTER 3PM

Naps are great, but taking them too late in the day can make it hard to fall asleep at night.

8. MAKE SURE TO LEAVE TIME TO RELAX BEFORE BED

It's important to have time before bed to unwind. Try to schedule your days so that there is time to relax before bed.

9. KEEP COOL

Your brain and body need to drop in temperature before sleep, and for this reason it is always easier to fall asleep in a room that is too cold than too hot. Studies show that cooling the body results in getting to sleep quicker, and better-quality restorative sleep during the night. Those living in hunter-gatherer societies start to get drowsy as temperature drops in the evening, which signals to the brain that it is time to sleep. They go to sleep about two hours after dusk, then wake up about 30 minutes before dawn, due to the rise in temperature. This places temperature right up there with light when it comes to sleep regulation.

Sleeping semi-naked is one way to cool the body down. Another highly recommended approach is to have a hot bath before bed. This is because being submerged in hot water causes vasodilation — blood rushing to the surface of your skin — so once you get out of the bath you experience a massive thermal dump that causes your core temperature to plummet. Having a bath may also help you to slow down and relax before bed.

10. HAVE A DARK AND GADGET-FREE BEDROOM

Artificial light suppresses the production of melatonin, which is the hormone that tells your body it is time to sleep. People exposed to natural light only tend to go to sleep two hours earlier than what they think is their 'natural' time to go to sleep when artificial lighting is available. This is because their brain releases melatonin earlier. To encourage melatonin production, try dimming your lights or turn off half the lights in your house a couple of hours before you plan on going to bed.

Gadgets such as mobile phones and computers can be a distraction in the bedroom, and it is recommended that you stay away from them in the last hour before sleep. Additionally, the light they emit, especially the blue light, suppresses the secretion of melatonin. In fact, research has shown that one hour reading on an iPad, as opposed to reading a traditional book in dim light, delayed the release of melatonin by three hours and melatonin levels peaked at 50 per cent lower. Subjects didn't get as much REM sleep and didn't wake the next morning feeling as refreshed or restored by their sleep as those who read a traditional book.

You can use filters to reduce the amount of blue light you're exposed to at night. Some newer Apple phones and tablets have this built in (look for Night Shift), and there are also Android apps for this, such as Twilight. On computers, f.lux software can be used to adjust the colour of light from displays, and is a popular solution. Windows 10 also has a built-in 'Night Light' function that offers similar functionality. You can also adjust the amount of blue light being emitted by your home lighting system, by using products such as Philips Hue 'smart' lightbulbs, which connect wirelessly to your router and can be programmed to reduce blue light at certain times of day. For example, if your bedtime is 11 pm, you can set the bulbs to reduce blue light from 9 pm onwards, which will encourage your brain to produce melatonin, preparing you for sleep.

11. GET COMFY

A comfortable mattress and pillow can help set you up for a good sleep. Those with insomnia will often watch the clock, so turn it away from view so you don't have to worry about the time while trying to get to sleep.

12. GET THE RIGHT AMOUNT OF SUNLIGHT EXPOSURE

Being exposed to natural sunlight during the day helps to regulate sleeping patterns. Try to get outside in natural light for at least 30 minutes per day.

13. DON'T STAY IN BED IF YOU (REALLY) CAN'T SLEEP

If you find yourself still awake after about 20 minutes of trying to get to sleep, or you're starting to get anxious lying in bed, get up and do something else until you feel sleepy. Anxiety can make it harder to fall asleep.

14. USE EARPLUGS

Our hearing is our biological burglar alarm, designed to drag us out of a deep sleep the moment a potential threat announces itself through an unexpected noise. You know what it's like: on a windy night, creaks and groans and sudden roaring and whistling noises will keep you awake or, at best, allow you only a light and fretful sleep.

(For more on the research mentioned in this section, refer to Professor Matthew Walker's book *Why We Sleep*.)

*

After reading this section, you might find yourself worrying about not getting enough sleep or not being able to go to sleep. If you don't score yourself at least a 7 out of 10 for the general quality and quantity of your sleep, experiment with the above suggestions and focus on giving yourself eight hours' sleep *opportunity* each night. We can't always control our sleep, but we can control how much opportunity for sleep we provide ourselves. Let that be your focus.

Exercise

Psychologists often talk about 'movement' rather than exercise in the context of resilience, mental toughness and wellbeing. Some people have a mental barrier to exercise: they find it hard and don't like it because it's painful. Using the term 'movement' avoids triggering this negative association. Well, I'm not going to baby you like that. You already know that hard and painful things make you grow and develop. A better reason to refer to movement is that 'exercise' is a modern construct we have created due to our relatively sedentary lives. When I say 'modern', I don't mean the 2000s: I mean the last 10,000 years, since the first agricultural revolution when humans began moving away from a hunter-gatherer lifestyle. Your early ancestors weren't likely to have started the day with a quick set of burpees — they moved enough just doing what it took to stay alive, and it was their lifestyle that our bodies' needs are adapted to. Once the concept of 'exercise' was introduced, it was as a means of keeping warriors fit and practised for warfare.

In modern times, in the developed world, deliberate exercise can quite literally be the only way people get the opportunity to use their bodies as they were intended. The conventional way to increase the amount of movement you do is by building some sort of exercise regime into your life. So that's what we are going to focus on.

Although I've suggested you can handle me calling this section 'exercise', if the barrier for you isn't the pain or challenge, but rather conjured-up images of fake-tan-drenched buff men and sleek women pumping iron in front of wall-to-ceiling mirrors at the gym, or Lycra-clad people with their bums in the air and their noses to the aero bars of their road bikes, then maybe the word 'movement' is better for you, because it focuses attention upon our tendency to suffer from a lack of it. It's easier to resolve to walk instead of drive on some of your outings than it is to commit to 'doing exercise' at the gym.

Movement more accurately captures the benefits that can be gained from very small things that we wouldn't normally think of as exercise — for example, simply standing up and having a stretch, or making your hands into fists and holding them above your head as high as you can for five seconds. Go on: give one of those a try! Notice the benefit? Motion changes emotion, and it doesn't take much to put a little fuel in the tank.

Pretty much everyone knows that we need a certain level of physical activity in our lives. We were designed by nature to be physically active, and if we are not, our health, both physical and mental, tends to suffer. Study after study has shown that a certain level of movement has benefits for health and wellbeing regardless of age, gender or ethnicity. Some of the benefits are obvious. Some are quite surprising.

Among the obvious physical benefits is reaching and maintaining a healthy weight. Because such a mismatch exists between our modern lifestyles and our nutrition, obesity has reached epidemic proportions in the developed world. So, too, has dietary advice. We all want an easy path to a better, fitter, more attractive you, right? Simply giving some stuff up, or having more of some stuff and less of other stuff, seems much easier than making lifestyle changes, especially if those changes involve increasing the amount of time you're physically active. Exercise hurts, especially when you're unfit! But most diets fail, and not just because most people lack the willpower to stick to them.

Your body runs on pretty much the same principles as an internal combustion engine: it uses fuel at a rate that corresponds with the amount of work it's doing. But a mechanical engine has a means of balancing the amount of fuel consumed to the demands placed upon it. Our bodies are different, because when fuel is abundant, the human body is designed to lay up stores against times when it is scarce. And the way the body stores fuel is by converting the energy component of food to fat.

If you're seeking to lose weight, you need to alter the equation so that the amount of energy you're using is greater than the amount of energy readily available to your metabolism (your bodily furnace), so that your body begins to call upon its reserves. It does this by converting fat to other molecules that it can then burn.

Simply cutting down how much food, or how much of a certain kind of food, you eat won't cause you to lose weight, because your body's first response to this kind of deprivation is to slow your metabolism (like turning the heat down) so that it uses less energy and conserves its fat reserves. You need to dial up your metabolic rate (turn up the heat), and the way to do that is by increasing your amount of physical exertion. Mostly, people seek to do this by exercising.

The best kind of activity for this is aerobic, where your heart and breathing rate rise above their normal level. A good rule of thumb is that if you can only talk in short sentences because you're too puffed to talk normally, you've raised your metabolic rate and are in the aerobic zone. The best advice for adults currently is that 150 minutes of exercise at this level every week is beneficial. Activities that will get you in this zone include brisk walking, swimming, mowing the lawn, playing doubles tennis. Alternatively, if you get even more physical and engage in what they call 'vigorous aerobic exercise' — where you are too puffed to talk at all while you're doing it — 75 minutes will make a difference for the good. Stuff like cycling fast, running, swimming laps, playing singles tennis or doing a gym circuit or aerobics class will push you into this zone. Of course, any combination of activity levels will do the trick, and feel free to do more. And if you build resistance work — anything that makes your muscles strain to meet the demand, such as lifting weights or running up stairs — into your routine, you will achieve even more, because it will build muscle mass. Simply put, it's muscle that burns fat, and the more of it you have, the easier it will be to lose weight and to keep it off.

Older adults are advised to get 30 minutes of moderate physical activity on at least five days a week, and at least two sessions of activities that promote balance and flexibility. Children and teenagers should be moving practically all of the time, as there is plenty of research to suggest that our physique and physical capabilities are largely determined by what we do in our formative years. Encourage your kids to turn off that screen, put down that phone and get busy outside!

Doing 150 minutes of aerobic exercise a week at a minimum will help you reach and maintain a healthy body weight and composition (as in the ratio of muscle to fat). And this will, in turn, help to improve your health, by improving your cardiovascular system (your lungs, heart, and blood vessels) and your insulin sensitivity (we'll look at this in more detail when we discuss nutrition, below).

I just want to acknowledge here that for people who already do a lot of exercise, these recommendations will seem on the light side. I know that I like to get at least 360 minutes of relatively intense exercise a week. And that is nothing compared to an actual athlete. If you are someone who is doing more than the minimum recommendations you will have your own sense of what you require to feel like you are flourishing and effectively recovering from stress. Use this as your standard rather than the recommendations above.

This much is relatively obvious and well known. But research indicates that there are other, slightly counterintuitive physical benefits from getting enough exercise, too. Regular exercise improves not only your muscles, but also your bones. The fact that so-called 'high-impact' sports such as running seem better at promoting bone density than lower-impact activities such as swimming or cycling suggests that it's the stress to which you subject your bones that promotes their health, just as lifting weights promotes muscle growth — and just like psychological stress increases our mental fitness!

Not only that, but studies have shown that exercise improves your skin or, at least, seems to somewhat protect it against the effects of ageing. It's thought that this is because when you exercise, your body produces natural antioxidants, which mop up some of the by-products of our biochemistry that cause cell damage.

And even less obviously again, research seems to indicate that exercise can help arrest or at least slow ageing-related mental decline. Physical activity has been shown to produce the release of a cascade of growth factors which counteract the deterioration in memory and cognitive function that older people suffer if they simply sit and do nothing, and perhaps even recruit new brain cells and neural pathways (promoting what is known as 'neural plasticity').

That leads us nicely onto the other suite of unexpected benefits that accrue from getting a decent amount of exercise: the positive effect it has on your mental health. A link between physical activity and mental health has long been suspected (look at the Victorians with their *mens sana in corpore sano* — 'a healthy mind in a healthy body' — ideal), and research certainly seems to bear it out. A 2011 study followed 26 healthy men and women after they reduced the amount of exercise they did on a regular basis, and all were found to experience a negative change in their mood. Similarly, a 2016 study seeking the 'ideal' level of physical exercise to produce positive mental health outcomes looked at 24 women, all of whom had been diagnosed with major depressive disorder. In every case, exercise improved their mood, and it didn't seem to matter whether they engaged in light, moderate or hard physical activity. Other studies have shown that the improvement in the mood of depression sufferers produced by exercise is at least as great as that delivered by antidepressant medication.

On one level, the link is easy to understand. In most people's experience, exercise makes you feel physically better and promotes self-esteem. Various explanations have been advanced for this. Neurologists have shown that exercise actually alters your brain chemistry for the better. Researchers studying the neurological basis for learned helplessness (discussed in Chapter 4) have suggested that it comes about through the body's inability to produce enough serotonin and noradrenaline: we experience that deficit as a feeling of helplessness. Some antidepressants act by elevating levels of both of these chemicals, but exercise has been shown to do it at least as well as these drugs. Still more research suggests that a certain level of another brain chemical known as brain-derived neurotrophic factor (BDNF) is necessary for feeling good, and that any deficit results in feelings of stress and anxiety: exercise has been shown to increase levels of BDNF. And yet another school of thought has it that the release of endorphins (natural pain-killing chemicals produced by the body when under physical stress) has an effect on mood, resulting in experiences such as the 'runner's high' phenomenon.

Psychologists have got in on the act, too, as we'll see in more detail in the next couple of chapters. Getting up, getting out and moving your body delivers an 'experience of self-mastery', according to one researcher working in this field. Repeatedly experiencing self-mastery builds your conviction that you can master yourself in any situation, and promotes a state of mind called self-efficacy — the belief that when confronted with a threat or opportunity, you'll be able to cope with it or capitalise on it. And it's been shown that the positive impact on anxiety levels of regular exercise are roughly equivalent to those when a sufferer can be distracted from their anxiety and its sources, suggesting that perhaps the value of being physically active lies in its ability to engage and therefore distract us. Being physically active — especially outdoors: at the beach, in the bush — absorbs us and directs our attention to the present moment rather than to the future, where so many sources of our anxieties lie.

But the bottom line is this: whatever the mechanism or mechanisms at work, exercise is essential to both our physical and mental health, and enables us to flourish. We thrive on it — almost as though we were designed for physical activity and can't quite reach our potential unless we get enough of it.

If you don't score yourself at least a 7 out of 10 for your current exercise regime, use the tips below to get you moving in the right direction.

TIPS FOR GETTING ENOUGH MOVEMENT IN YOUR DAILY LIFE

If you're new to all this, start out slow. Concentrate on doing a little bit often rather than trying to get your quota over with in one, intense hit. The secret lies in building a habit, and as we will discuss further, this takes time. It's the habit that will stick. Try reinforcing the habit by, say, using a sticker chart.

Remind yourself why you're doing it: re-read this chapter whenever your resolve is flagging! Or ask yourself what kind of person you want to be, and what they would do in this situation.

Once you have established the habit of engaging in physical activity regularly, build up the amount and the intensity.

Experts recommend engaging in at least 150 minutes per week of moderate aerobic exercise (enough to get you moderately puffed while you're doing it), or 75 minutes of vigorous aerobic exercise (can't talk: too puffed), or some combination of the two.

Experts also recommend engaging in resistance-type activities at least twice a week. These build muscle mass, making weight-control easier. This could be weight training, push- or pull-ups, abdominal crunches and that sort of thing, which target a muscle group, or it could be as simple as running up the stairs.

Walk or exercise with a buddy so the social pressure of not letting someone down gets you out the door!

Take the stairs instead of using escalators.

If you plan on exercising in the morning, have all of your exercise gear laid out the night before so less effort is required to get out the door.

Nutrition

Reading the previous section, you might be forgiven for thinking that physical movement is the answer to all of your health and wellbeing problems. Sorry to be the bearer of bad news: it's not. It is, at best, about a third of the answer.

There's an old saying, 'you are what you eat'. If you look around you, you can see it's largely true. I use the term 'largely' advisedly: over the past 50 years or so, people in the developed world have been getting bigger and are therefore suffering from more and more associated health problems. As mentioned above, the root of all this evil is the serious mismatch between our biology and our diet. We evolved to be hunter-gatherers, eating (as the name suggests) whatever we could hunt or gather. Sometimes the foraging pickings were slim; sometimes the animals we hunted were too scarce, too scary or too cunning. We were accustomed to periods where food was short, and natural selection favoured those who could store energy to tide them over these times. What's more, most of the foods available to us were not only won with effort, they were also digested with effort. We became very efficient extractors of energy value from all of our food sources.

Technology changed all that. We became growers and farmers, and then we became bakers and brewers. We discovered, that is, how to reduce the amount of effort required to produce food in abundance. Soon enough, we discovered how to extract the energy value from raw and whole foods and make new foods that required much less energy to digest.

All of the ingredients for a dietary catastrophe were there, save one. This came along in the nineteenth century, when the idea that the whole point of human endeavour was to make money took root. There was an incentive to discover what it was that made people crave certain foods — and therefore buy them. We became confectioners. And that's basically what many food processors have been since the dawn of the twentieth century.

Because we're still hunter-gatherers at heart (and at stomach, if that's a valid expression), we crave the things that were hard to get by hunting and gathering: salt and (especially) sugar. Salt is essential to our survival, and we're naturally drawn to foods that contain it. And sweet, wild foods such as fruit and berries contain sugar, which is one short digestive step away from glucose, which is the fuel our bodies use. In the distant past, we mostly derived energy either from starchy foods, which require a lot of digestive effort to reduce to glucose, or from fats. Eating fruit or berries was a highly efficient way to get energy. But fruit and berries were, at best, seasonally scarce, and pretty much absent from some parts of the inhabited world. So our physiology evolved to reward us when we found and ate them.

Trouble is, our physiology *still* rewards us when we eat sugar, salt and fat. That's why we crave those kinds of foods. And that's why whole industries exist to supply them to us in exchange for money. When you put together the superabundance of sugar, salt and fat in processed foods and our natural, physiological expertise at storing excess energy, you can see why we in the developed world are suffering from epidemic levels of heart disease, hypertension (high blood pressure), type-2 diabetes, osteoporosis, many kinds of diet-related cancers, and more.

Dr Paul's Miracle Diet

So what do we do about it? If I could supply a simple answer to that question, I'd be a wealthy man! But here goes.

Diet is not rocket science, although a whole industry, more or less parasitical on the junk-food industry, exists to dazzle people with pseudo-scientific jargon and supply them with what sounds like an easy antidote to their problems with their weight. Think of all the fad diets you've heard of: low fat, high fat, low carbs, no carbs, apple cider vinegar, acai berries, paleo ... As I mentioned earlier, most (if not all of them) don't work, because they offer only a partial solution. Any real solution has to be holistic, and a good starting point is to remind ourselves what it is that nature designed us for. It designed us to be successful hunter-gatherers, active most of the time we're awake, sleeping well when we're not, and subsisting on an adequate diet derived from each of the main food groups. We need a balanced diet comprising fats and oils (from plant and animal sources), protein (principally from meat and vegetable-derived alternatives), carbohydrates (which can be simple — such as refined sugar — or complex, as in the case of starchy vegetables, wholegrains and seeds), and minerals and vitamins (which we get from fresh foods).

In some cases, we can improve our health and wellbeing simply by eating less. But in almost every case, we'll achieve even greater results by eating *better*.

If you don't give yourself a 7 out of 10 score for your current eating habits, use the tips below to get you moving in the right direction:

AVOID EXCESSIVE SUGAR INTAKE

This is far harder to do than you might suppose! You'll need to become adept at reading the consumer information labels on food packaging. Because we crave sugar, simply adding a bit of it improves the appeal of a food enormously. So that's what food processors do. Because sugar is a known dietary bad guy, they won't brag about it; instead, they'll engage in the kind of misdirection that food processors have raised to an art form. For example, on the box, big letters might proclaim a cereal to be 'high protein' or 'low fat', but if your kids love it, it's almost certainly full of sugar. Or food producers will list 'corn syrup' as an ingredient instead of sugar. And don't forget that 'natural' foods such as fruit and fruit juices are full of sugar, too. Just because it's naturally sourced doesn't mean it somehow doesn't count: a serving of dried fruit or a glass of fruit juice will contain the sugar equivalent of several pieces of whole fruit — and remember, sugary fruit and berries were rare in the diet of hunter-gatherers. In fact, drinking fruit juice is often no better for you (and frequently worse) than sugary soft-drinks. Even fruit has changed. For a long time, growers have been selectively breeding for a number of traits that have little to do with how good their produce is for you but for looks and taste: how red and shiny an apple or a tomato is and, just as important, how sweet it is.

Put simply, sugar is just about pure energy, and any energy we don't use immediately we store, so excessive sugar intake is likely to lead to obesity. What's more, our bodies are designed to deal with a fluctuating intake of energy from food, and to balance that unreliable supply with the demands of our metabolism. The mechanism the human body uses to regulate the consumption or conversion of glucose is the secretion of a hormone called insulin. When the level of glucose in our blood rises, our body produces insulin, which initiates the process of converting glucose to glycogen (from which body fat is produced). When insulin levels drop, the reverse process is initiated, with fat converted to glycogen and then to glucose. The integrity of this system relies upon the proper detection of insulin levels in our blood ('insulin sensitivity'). Some people are born with a congenital defect in insulin sensitivity, which is known as type-1 diabetes. Others, through swamping their bodies with a superabundance of glucose through long-term, excessive consumption of high-energy food, reduce their insulin sensitivity: this is known as type-2 diabetes. So there's another good reason to go easy on the sugar.

And one final thing: quite apart from the physical effects, a diet high in refined carbohydrates such as sugar has been shown to correlate with increased rates of anxiety and depression. Scientists believe that the brain's reward centre is activated by refined carbohydrates in a similar way as narcotics, which results in a come-down after the initial high.

EAT WHOLE FOODS

This includes eating a variety of fruit and vegetables. Their sugar content notwithstanding, fruit and vegetables are good for us. Weirdly, the colours of fruit and vegetables more or less correspond to the different vitamins and minerals they contain and which are necessary in our diet. And although to our hunter-gatherer ancestors the fruit and vegetables on supermarket shelves would be like a cartoonist's exaggerated depiction of their equivalent ancestral forms, the best way to ingest the nutrients in fruit and vegetables is the old-fashioned way: eating the fruits and veggies themselves.

The same advice applies to the grains we eat. Replace processed grain-based foods with wholegrain equivalents. Grain-based foods such as flour are amongst the oldest processed foods in humanity's pantry, but that doesn't mean we are biologically that well suited to eating them. Grains are the seeds of plants, and mostly comprise a hard husk and a starchy interior. Starch is digested to sucrose, which is then converted to glucose, but the effort required to extract its energy value — chewing the grain to crush the husk and mix the starch with saliva, the digestion of the starch and then the sucrose itself — somewhat offsets the raw energy value of the whole grain. Meanwhile, the husk provides fibre, which our bodies need too. Trouble is, we have developed methods of processing grains to make the energy more available (husking rice, for example, or milling and bleaching wheat to produce white flour) and the food less demanding on our digestion, sometimes dispensing with the fibrous content of the grain altogether. Breakfast cereals — as the name 'cereal' suggests — are made from grain, but they are so heavily refined that they provide little of the dietary benefit of the whole grains from which they were produced.

And nuts. Don't forget nuts! These were (and are) a staple of hunter-gatherer diets and, as such, they are good for us. They're high not just in protein (which is one of the most important of the essential nutrients in a diet), but also in fibre, a number of vitamins and minerals, and fat. While we should limit the amount of fat we eat, the kinds of fats available from nuts suit the human body and, in any case, much of the raw calorific value of nuts is offset by the energy used in digesting them.

WATCH YOUR FAT INTAKE

Fat is an essential component of the human diet: it is a source of energy, but it is also thought to be a trigger for the sensation of satisfaction or 'fullness'. And whereas there is lots of advice around that divides different types of fats into 'good' and 'bad' types, there is disagreement over which is which. These days, it is broadly agreed that fats from both animal and plant sources are beneficial: it is the so-called 'trans-fats' — a class of fats and oils synthesised by food processors, who learned that they trigger the body's reward mechanisms and therefore produce cravings — that are to be avoided. By contrast, some fats (such as those found in nuts) are good for us. Omega-3s, the type of fats you find in seafood and fish, are enormously beneficial to human health, especially brain function: hell, there is even a theory that it was the development of rudimentary fishing technology which provided access to Omega-3 fats that actually drove the evolution of the modern human brain!

REDUCE YOUR SODIUM INTAKE

We need sodium; its interplay with another mineral, potassium, in the body is essential to a whole range of biological processes. But as with most things, you can have too much of a good thing. Too much sodium is associated with all manner of health problems (and in surprisingly low doses, table salt — our principal dietary source of sodium — is toxic). But because it was hard to get back in the good old hunter-gatherer days, we crave it, and that's all encouragement the food processors need. It's everywhere and, as with sugar, the price of a healthy sodium intake is eternal vigilance — and the ability to read food analysis labels.

STAY HYDRATED

There is no hard or fast rule about how much water you should or should not drink: an easy way to gauge whether you are adequately hydrated is to take note of the colour of your pee. If it's pale, you're properly hydrated. If it is bright yellow or golden, you need to drink some water. If it's dark gold, you really, really need to drink some water.

*

There are lots of opinions about on when to eat, and which meal is the most important. A good-sized, healthy breakfast (delivering protein, fibre, complex carbohydrates and fat) sets you up for the day: eggs on wholegrain toast with avocado should do the trick. Processed breakfast cereals tend to be sugar-heavy and therefore give you lots of energy up front and a big slump in the middle of the afternoon. A large lunch can also play havoc with energy levels in the afternoon, and many people find a heavy evening meal affects their ability to sleep, all of which suggests that our traditional, three-big-meals-a-day approach is unhelpful. Better to start with a good breakfast and have a number of light meals throughout the rest of the day and evening. In some circles intermittent fasting is fashionable, and there is evidence that experiencing the pangs of hunger is both physiologically and mentally beneficial. But regardless of where you stand on any of these notions, the object is to balance our energy intake with the demands we face.

7

Positive Emotion

Not that long ago, I was due to speak at a conference. It was in a large venue, with attendees seated cabaret-style around tables. They were to have lunch just before I was introduced.

I arrived a bit early, and chose a seat towards the back of the space to wait for the programme to resume. As I was sitting there, a group of people came in and started chatting.

'Where d'you reckon we should sit?' asked one of them, scanning the room.

'Not too close to the front. This guy's a murderer.'

Well, that stung!

My story is pretty well known. I spend quite a lot of time telling it, because it's useful in showing people how it's possible to rise again from what looks like the ashes of your hopes and dreams.

As I told you at the beginning of this book, when I was 18, I killed the man from whom I used to buy drugs. It was almost the logical culmination of my life's story to that point — I hadn't exactly been a pro-social, contributing member of society — and now I was going to prison. I spent a little over a decade in there, and for close to half that time, I did very little — if anything — to change my direction.

But then I did change it. I enrolled in a university degree while inside prison, and whereas I had previously given little thought to the future (because I assumed I didn't have much of one, beyond drug use and prison), I began to sense that there were opportunities open to me after all. All I had to do is reach out and seize them.

Of course, it wasn't as straightforward as all that — it took a huge amount of effort — but I made that effort, I did the mahi and I took those opportunities. Nor did I stop there, because better never stops, right? Since my release, I have continued to work hard to achieve my potential and to be the best possible version of myself. And there's not a day that I wake up when I don't I reckon I can do better still.

Yet there I was with someone else's brutal impression of myself ringing in my ears. It hurt, but I had had years of practice in putting my story in perspective. So that's what I did, all over again.

The 'P' in the PERMA-H model mentioned in Chapter 5 stands for 'Positive Emotion', and a big part of what it takes to feel positive is, to view your past, present and future from a constructive perspective, and to remain optimistic. I have worked hard at becoming a positive person who regularly feels uplifted, can reduce the intensity and duration of my unpleasant emotions, and can take a positive view of my life and experiences. I have some insights to offer you about how you can do this, too. Sitting there, beset by unpleasant emotions, I found myself using the techniques I have learned to manage the unhelpful thoughts that were swirling in upon me. I'd like to share them with you now.

The power of positivity

Psychologist Martin Seligman, who I have mentioned above, has done lots of work in this area. Some of this earlier research indicated that positive people are more successful. They tend to be highly motivated and tenacious, more decisive and able to cope better in stressful situations.

Needless to say, this finding had interesting ramifications in the field of business psychology. In one of his paid gigs, Seligman was asked to analyse the performance of salespeople working for a struggling insurance company. He noted that the company screened its prospective employees using a questionnaire that determined whether they had the skills necessary to sell, but largely ignored other aspects of their character, such as whether they were optimistic or pessimistic. Based on his theory of how positivity affects performance, Seligman added a question that determined how optimistic a candidate was, and the company altered its policy so that it would hire less proficient salespeople if they possessed an optimistic outlook. By the time they came to review the effectiveness of the change, the company's fortunes had already turned around, and it was found that the optimists, even when the questionnaire indicated that they were less proficient at selling, had way outperformed the others.

And it's not just in selling life insurance policies that positive people excel. Other research has shown that cancer patients with a positive outlook cope better with the ravages of the treatment than those with a less positive outlook. What's more, positivity has been linked to better health generally, with people who describe themselves as optimists less likely to suffer stress-related illness such as cardiovascular disease.

Wouldn't it be nice to be an optimist? Well, here's the good news: you can be an optimist. And here is why.

Changing your mind

Most of us have seen stereotypical depictions of psychotherapists at work. They delve deep into a client's past, seeking to identify past life-events that cast a shadow over his or her present by conditioning their beliefs about themselves and their possibilities. This is a little out of date. Not long after Freud and his disciples introduced psychotherapy to the world, it occurred to some of those working in the field that it's not actually the *events* that give rise to the client's problematic beliefs that count: it's the beliefs themselves. This idea would lead the world into the age of cognitive therapy, which would shift the focus to what happened in one's childhood to present thoughts, emotions, and behaviours.

The pioneer of this approach was Albert Ellis, who called his own approach Rational-Emotive Behavioural Therapy (REBT). Ellis divided the beliefs that people hold into two categories: rational and irrational. To his way of seeing things, people who hold rational beliefs about themselves and the way the world works respond to adverse life events differently to people who hold irrational beliefs. He called the problematic, irrational beliefs 'cognitive distortions', and drew up a list of these. He encouraged his clients to examine the way they responded to adversity in order to identify the cognitive distortions to which they were prone, and which gave rise to negative behaviours.

Here's an example: Paul commits a crime, and is arrested and convicted. Paul believes that he's a criminal. Because he believes he's a criminal, he sees no point in trying to change who he is or what he does. So he spends his time in prison smoking drugs, fighting and planning his escape so that he can resume his criminal career.

Ellis usefully conceptualised this kind of chain of causation in terms of ABC. 'A' is the adverse situation or actuating event (in Paul's case, committing a crime and being convicted). 'B' is Paul's belief that he is a criminal, and that being a criminal is his destiny. 'C' is the consequence of this belief: his unwillingness, bordering on an inability, to seek to change his behaviour.

The way to disrupt this sequence, according to cognitive behavioural theorists such as Ellis, was to challenge the initial belief. They described the way you move from A to B — from experiencing an actuating event to your beliefs about it — as your 'explanatory style'. By changing your explanatory style, you could transform your response to adversity and begin to consider a whole new set of possible behaviours. (As an interesting aside, the latest research from Neuroscience Professor Andrew Huberman suggests that a more effective approach to changing your beliefs is to just change your behaviour. Beliefs will alter accordingly.)

It was possible, Ellis believed, to argue with your deeply held notions of yourself and the way the world worked, and to change them. In this book, I have already tried to challenge your beliefs in a number of ways likely to increase your mental fitness. I have tried to challenge the idea that you are not supposed to feel stress or unpleasant emotions. I have tried to shift your beliefs about stress, to see it as a positive catalyst for growth. I have tried to shift your belief that your unpleasant emotions are bad in some way, to seeing them as signals your body is sending you comparable to thirst and hunger. And I will be continuing to try to shift your beliefs about mental toughness and resilience as being fixed attributes to being readily developable traits consistent with physical fitness.

The explanatory style that helps people to flourish is what underpins an important component of mental fitness (the ability to weather and recover from adversity). We're going to call this explanatory style 'optimism'. Most people think of optimists as people who will look at a glass that contains half its capacity and describe it as half full. A pessimist will describe it as half empty. Both are right, but their descriptions are determined by their outlook, which selectively directs their attention to the feature of the glass that seems most relevant to them. To the pessimist, it's all that missing water. To the optimist, it's the water that remains.

Optimism is not the same as over-confidence, or sheer denial of what is actually going on in your life. For our purposes, optimists aren't people who hold a rose-tinted belief that things will work out, sometimes in the face of everything that indicates to the contrary. Optimists are people who find the most favourable explanation for challenges and adverse events. Optimists are people who face the reality of their challenges, but who see themselves as capable of taking the steps required to increase the likelihood they will overcome them.

Born that way?

A fascinating piece of research was published by American neurologist David Hecht in 2013, in which he and his team sought to determine whether there was a neural basis for optimism: that is, whether differences in our brains determine whether we are optimist or pessimists. Interestingly, it seems that they do.

The theory proposed by pioneering neurologist Roger Sperry in the 1960s is that people's personalities and aptitudes depend upon which half of their brain dominates. Our brains are divided down the middle into two hemispheres, usually called right and left. Curiously, information from our right eye is processed by the optic centre in the left hemisphere, and vice versa. Even more startling, Sperry and others had demonstrated that different kinds of thought processes are handled in one or other hemisphere, too.

Artistic creativity, lateral thinking and random ideas seem to originate in the right hemisphere. Sequential thinking, logic and scientific reasoning seem to originate in the left. Based on this, it was proposed that people's personalities are determined by which side of their brain is dominant.

That one side or the other was dominant to a greater or a lesser extent was borne out by an experiment that you can repeat at home. Take a sheet of blank paper and lie it on the table. Use a pencil to mark where you estimate the exact mid-point of top of the piece of paper to be. Now fold the page in half to work out where the mid-point really is.

Most people err on one side or the other, and this seems to correspond to a slight dominance of one cerebral hemisphere over the other. Because of the way in which our brain processes information, erring on the left side of the paper suggests a slight right dominance in your brain. Likewise, erring on the right side of the paper suggests a slight left-brain dominance.

It turns out, however, that Sperry's theory overstated the significance of this slight dominance. Research designed to sniff out right-brain or left-brain personalities has consistently failed to show that these exist. Unless afflicted by disease, injury or the results of surgery, the two hemispheres of our brain communicate and cooperate, so that for the most part, we are capable of both kinds of thought processes, and exhibit characteristics associated with both left- and right-brain personalities.

But here's the thing: it's been shown that positive thinking engages areas of the brain in the right hemisphere, as though the side of the brain responsible for art and creativity is also where our hopes and dreams come from. People thinking gloomy, negative thoughts do it with the left side of their brain, as though the logical, factual side of our personality is what helps us prepare for the worst. Perhaps we are born, as some suggest, predisposed to have a positive or a negative outlook.

But what we also know from a wealth of research into the brain's ability to remould and change itself is that, regardless of where we start, we can all learn to become more optimistic. (If you want to truly blow your mind when it comes to the extent to which our brain can be remoulded through practice, put this book down now and Google *blind people riding bicycles*.) That's why Martin Seligman describes it as 'learned optimism'.

Talking to yourself

Broadly speaking, many of the various thinking distortions that Ellis and other cognitive behavioural theorists identify boil down to beliefs about the world that place the control of outcomes ('locus of control' is the technical term for this) outside the individual — beliefs that make it unimaginable that you can do anything to change your own situation. You might think of yourself as unlovable, a born loser or useless: each of these is a self-administered assurance that there is nothing you can do about adverse events than accept them as your lot, as though your 'lot' was not of your own creation. Your relationship fails: it was bound to, because you think you are objectively unlovable. Why bother putting effort into forming a new relationship, or repairing or maintaining an existing one? You miss out on a job: the universe has always been against you. Why bother applying for any more jobs ever again? You failed at a task you attempted: I am hopeless, and there's no point in attempting to acquire new skills ...

The unhelpful ways in which we talk to ourselves like this are many and varied, but what they all have in common is that they serve to convince us that the troubles we have are due to forces outside our control. Seligman identified three key features of the negative self-talk that reduces positive emotional experiences and optimism, handily all described with a word beginning with P:

*

Personalisation. In the examples above, we personalise adversity when we decide that a relationship failed or we failed at a task because of a fault in ourselves (we're unlovable, we're useless). We personalise our failure to get a job by attributing it to our own, uniquely awful luck. Another way in which we personalise is by forgetting that such experiences happen to everyone — they are not things we alone are going through.

Permanence. We extrapolate from any given knock to a general, eternal principle: unlovable = never will be lovable; born loser = will never win; useless = failed this time and will always fail. Basically, things will never get better.

Pervasiveness. Similarly, we generalise setbacks beyond any shortcoming that may have contributed to it, to a more profound and wide-reaching belief: the fact that I failed in a relationship, that task, in getting that job = the story of my life. The negative parts of our life are like a drop of ink in a glass of water — they discolour everything else for us. We lose sight of the things that are actually OK or good. Maybe my relationship ends, but my work and health are OK. Or maybe I'm made redundant, but I lose sight of the fact my health and relationship are good.

*

People who are more optimistic are better at not considering their challenges and misfortunes to be personal, permanent and pervasive. An optimist views the same events through a different lens. Confronted with the failure of their relationship, an optimist will find reasons for that particular failure, as well as reasons why future relationships need not fail. 'I wasn't ready for the level of commitment he was asking of me,' you might say to yourself: this implies the problem was transient rather than permanent, and you will be ready in future to be successful. 'The timing was wrong,' you might say — absolving both parties of fault, and treating the problem as isolated and temporary rather than pervasive and enduring, and suggesting that in the future, the timing will be right. 'I couldn't find a way to be emotionally available in the way that she needed me to be,' you might say — it's brutally honest, but in saying it, you retain the ability to take control over your future behaviour and the outcomes you want. You can change. You can work on your emotional availability. You might also depersonalise the failure of your relationship by reminding yourself that many people's relationships fail.

You'll sometimes hear people — especially people like me — talk about growth mindsets and fixed mindsets. At their most basic, the difference between a growth and fixed mindset relates to your assumptions around the potential for change and growth. People with a fixed mindset see our abilities as being like our eye colour — fixed and unchangeable. People with a growth mindset, on the other hand, view our abilities and attributes as more like our muscles — we are not all created equally, or starting at the same place, but we are all capable of developing and getting closer to an as-yet-unreached potential, through practise and opportunity.

These two mindsets come into play here, too. People with a fixed mindset will be prone to respond to events using the three Ps — especially personalisation and permanence. Their mindset is fixed precisely because they have unilaterally declared the locus of control to be in someone else's hands — or at any rate, out of theirs. Someone with a growth mindset, by contrast, will analyse events in search of things that they can change in order to produce better outcomes — precisely because they start from the premise that they retain control over the actions that can improve their situation.

Decades of research into the previously mentioned field of neuroplasticity supports the accuracy of the growth mindset. If you are someone who tends towards a fixed mindset, you will benefit from reminding yourself that life is about progress not perfection; that the goal is getting better, not being good all the time; and that failures are how we learn and grow and improve. This will increase your volume of positive emotional experiences by reducing the amount of time you spend dwelling on and beating yourself up for your misfortunes and mistakes.

Mindset self-assessment

Respond to these questions honestly, giving a score from 1 (strongly disagree) to 6 (strongly agree), then add up your total score.

You have a certain amount of intelligence, and you can't change it.
   Strongly disagree   1   2   3   4   5   6   Strongly agree

Your confidence is something about you that you can't change very much.
   Strongly disagree   1   2   3   4   5   6   Strongly agree

To be honest, you can't really change whether you are a high or low performer.
   Strongly disagree   1   2   3   4   5   6   Strongly agree

You can learn new things, but you can't really change your basic level of intelligence.

Strongly disagree 1 2 3 4 5 6 Strongly agree

No matter who you are, you can't significantly change your level of talent.

Strongly disagree 1 2 3 4 5 6 Strongly agree

Scores of 10 or less suggest tendencies towards a growth mindset. Scores above 20 suggest a fixed mindset tendency. To foster a more consistent growth mindset:

1. Learn to hear/observe your 'fixed mindset' inner voice.
2. Recognise that you have a choice about how you think.
3. Talk back to it with a 'growth mindset' voice.

*

To increase your optimism and encourage more positive emotional experiences, you don't have to believe that you're all-powerful and responsible for everything that happens: only that we can change things about the way we think and act. The art of optimism lies in recognising those things.

Perhaps the simplest way to achieve this is to ask yourself what is in your 'circle of control' in whatever situation you find yourself in. The 'circle of control' idea was popularised by Stephen Covey in his book *The 7 Habits of Highly Effective People*, first published in 1989. The only thing you can ever hope to control in life is yourself and your attitude and responses to the situations you find yourself in. Your circle of control refers to exactly that: what can I *choose* to think or do in this situation.

While this concept was popularised by Covey, its true origins lie with the Stoic philosophers of antiquity, who believed that the only thing of any real value was focusing on how you choose to perceive and respond to your circumstances. Its psychological origins, however, are more associated with Viktor Frankl, an Austrian Holocaust survivor and the author of one of the bestselling books on psychotherapy of all time: *Man's Search for Meaning.*

Frankl was already a practising psychotherapist when he was interned in several Nazi concentration camps in the early 1940s. After the war, when Tuerkheim, a sub-camp of Dachau, was liberated and he returned to his life and practice, he wrote of his experiences and sought to answer the question: how was it possible to survive in circumstances such as those faced by the inmates of the death camps? Frankl's answer was that the freedom of choice we always retain, no matter how constrained our choices or brutalised we are, gives our lives meaning, and it is this meaning that makes life worth living. A Viktor Frankl mentality insists on our freedom to choose, never surrendering our sense of control over our thoughts and actions. Whatever our situation might be, we always have choices that can make our future better.

The value of focusing on your circle of control to get through challenging circumstances reminds me of a story a friend of mine told me about when he was on deployment in Afghanistan with the SAS. They were engaged in strategic reconnaissance in two six-man teams, deep behind enemy lines. After completing their observations of enemy vehicle movements, they moved to high ground for helicopter extraction. However, once they got to high ground it started snowing and the helicopters were unable to come and get them. They couldn't afford to be seen by anyone, as they weren't a fighting force, and no one else would come to their rescue this far behind enemy lines. They each had a 24-hour emergency ration pack, but they couldn't predict how long it would be before the weather cleared and they could be picked up.

My friend didn't focus on the weather, which wasn't within his control. He instead focused on what was within his circle of control. He believed the helicopters would come, but knew he had to be a realistic optimist and not assume that it would be soon. So he rationed out his 24-hour food supply into four days' worth of small meals.

It was indeed four days of freezing conditions, staying hidden on a mountainside, before the helicopters could make it back in to pick them up. During that time he regularly changed his socks and did what was in his control to keep his feet warm and dry. He kept focusing on his circle of control. He also didn't let his mind focus on their eventual rescue, but instead concentrated on the next thing he needed to do or could look forward to on that mountain. His next piece of muesli bar. The next time he would be on watch. I will talk more about the benefit of focusing on such mini-goals in Chapter 13 on the Big Four skills for mental toughness.

On another tour of Afghanistan, this same friend was tasked with capturing 'high-value targets' through night raids on enemy compounds. When I asked him how he managed his emotions in anticipation of such a high-stress activity, he said he again came back to his circle of control. In particular, he would clean and diligently check and prepare all of his equipment, including always ensuring he had new batteries in his night-vision goggles and other pieces of electronic equipment. Circle of control, every time.

Turn that frown upside down

So if we're born with a tendency towards pessimism and its associated negative emotions, are we stuck with that style? No, we aren't! With a little effort, we can change. We have already discussed some of the ways you can enhance your optimism. There are also several simple things you can do to keep the negative at bay and experience more positive emotions — but remember, like most aspects of mental fitness, they require you to put continuous, consistent effort into them, so that they become an engrained, automatic habit. Here are four things you can try:

1. COMPARING DOWN

No matter how bad you've got it, as they say, worse things happen at sea. For example, because I was far from a model prisoner in the early part of my term, I spent quite a lot of time in solitary confinement. Believe me, you go to some pretty dark places when you're in there, with nothing but four concrete walls to look at. What got me through times like that was comparing my situation to that of people who were worse off than me. Because there is pretty much always someone in a worse situation. Later in my term, after I had discovered the transformative power of reading books, I found comparing down easier, because I was able to read the stories of people who had it far, far worse than me. Even in my darkest moments, I was able to thank my lucky stars that in all likelihood I would be released from prison within 15 years — unlike Nelson Mandela, say, who had every reason to believe that he would die on Robben Island. And no matter how hard I was doing it, at least I wasn't being tortured, like Vice-Admiral James Stockdale, a US Navy pilot who was shot down and imprisoned by the Viet Cong during the Vietnam war.

2. TREATING ADVERSITY AS A CHALLENGE TO BE EMBRACED RATHER THAN A CURSE TO BE ENDURED

This is something else I did in solitary, what US Navy SEAL David Goggins (whom I mentioned earlier) did when he realised his trainers were doing everything in their power to see him fail, and what Stockdale did when he realised he was facing a long stint in captivity. There is, as Shakespeare put it, neither good nor bad, but thinking makes it so. This applies to every event, no matter how shitty. If you change your perception of adversity — thinking, this is a challenge that I embrace, rather than a desperately unfair affliction — you can meet fire with mental fire.

3. KEEP A GRATITUDE DIARY

This may seem like a childish idea, but it works! Get in the habit of writing down three good things that have happened each day, trying to ensure that you find three generally small but different things each day. Even on your shittiest day ever, you'll find three (and likely far more). Write them down. It may seem tedious, but so does going to the gym, until you remind yourself that this is an investment in your future. It's repetitions that count. A lot of people who try gratitude diaries give up pretty quickly because recounting their three things doesn't make them feel uplifted immediately. Yet Harvard research suggests that if people carry on the practice for 21 days, they will notice the benefit through an increased sense of wellbeing and positivity. This exercise trains you to look for and recognise the good things — to look for the water in the half-full glass rather than the emptiness. If you stick at it for those 21 days, you will find yourself noticing all the candidates in your day to be those three things, and getting additional fuel in your emotional tank as a result. As we noted above, one of the things that differentiates optimists from pessimists is the focus of their attention. You can teach yourself to pay attention to the good things, which serves to reduce the amount of attention you direct at the bad and the crippling sense that those challenging things are pervasive. In deliberately directing our attention to positive things, we're basically re-wiring our brains. We're disposed by nature to look for threats — it's estimated that we have three times as many neural pathways devoted to expecting the worst than to identifying potential benefits. But the neurons that fire together wire together and we can wire new pathways by deliberately directing our attention to the positive things we experience in our days.

4. NOTICE AND LABEL THE PLEASANT FEELINGS YOU HAVE

Often we don't savour our positive emotional experiences, so their impact on us is not maximised. If you get into the habit of noticing and labelling the pleasant emotions you experience, you will prolong the release of the neurotransmitters that give you that sense of pleasantness, putting more fuel in your emotional tank as a result. Here's the meme, folks: say it to savour it! To get the most from this approach, you will benefit from developing your emotional vocabulary enough to correctly recognise the pleasant emotions you are experiencing. More on this in Chapter 12.

Positive emotion self-assessment

This self-assessment will give you an indication of the extent to which the positive emotion domain is a priority work-on for you, or an area in which more deliberate focus will move you closer to your mental fitness potential. Answer these questions according to what is most true and accurate for you. Don't overthink them — go with the first answer that comes to mind.

Question	Very slightly or not at all (1)	A little (2)	Moderately (3)	Quite a bit (4)	Extremely (5)
To what extent do you feel enthusiastic at the present moment or within the past week?					
To what extent do you feel pleasant or calm at the present moment or within the past week?					
To what extent do you feel determined at the present moment or within the past week?					
To what extent do you feel excited at the present moment or within the past week?					
To what extent do you feel carefree, confident or relaxed at the present moment or within the past week?					

Total score: _____

You should get a number between 5 and 25. A higher score indicates greater levels of positive emotion.

The power of positivity — a summary

Positive thinking helps us to cope, but is not about denying the reality of our circumstances or challenges.

Whether we feel capable of improving our situation depends upon our tendencies towards optimism and pessimism, which in turn is determined by where we habitually think the control of our future lies — with ourselves and the choices we can make, or with the whims of the fates.

Learned optimism involves reminding ourselves that adverse events are temporary, transient and isolated.

Cultivating a growth mindset will increase our optimism and experience of positive emotions.

Building our emotional vocabulary to recognise and label the pleasant emotions we experience helps us to savour those experiences and puts more fuel in our emotional tank, as does cultivating gratitude and reminding ourselves that things could be worse.

8

Engagement

Engagement is a bit of a buzzword in the workplace these days. It's one of the things that management likes to see in their employees, and for good reason: research suggests 30 per cent of an organisation's bottom line can be attributed to employee engagement. If you work for a large organisation, at some stage you've probably been asked to fill out an 'engagement' survey. This type of engagement is about how much emotional buy-in employees have to their work and organisation. It is generally demonstrated in whether people perform according to their capability, are willing to take on discretionary tasks and persevere when times are challenging, try to get better at what they do, and talk positively about their organisation in informal settings (remembered as Perform, Preserve, Perfect and Praise).

This kind of engagement isn't necessarily what we're talking about here. The 'E' for Engagement in Seligman's PERMA-H model (discussed in Chapter 5) equates with entering what is called a 'flow state' wherein you are fully deploying your skills, strengths and attention on a challenging task. This is not the only way in which we can be engaged, but flow is the aspect of engagement we will focus on in this chapter. It is the aspect of engagement that's best for your mental fitness — reflected in the feeling you get when you are fully present in the moment, often because you're learning something new, or doing something you're passionate about or intensely interested in.

Peak flow

You've been there. It's almost like you lose yourself, you are so immersed and engrossed in what you're doing. You're all focus. Your decisions and actions are spontaneous and effective. There's no distinction between past, present or future. Time flies by. You're not thinking, not even really feeling, although you might be dimly aware of a sense of deep satisfaction, like the vibration you get through an axe handle when you cleanly split a round of wood: you're simply doing.

In the late 1980s, American psychologist Mihaly Csikszentmihalyi (his surname is pronounced 'Chick-Zent-My-High') set out to determine what mental characteristics were shared by top performers in a number of fields of endeavour. Time and again, he struck high-flying people who gave slightly baffled descriptions of the state they were in when they found themselves capable of effortless, optimal performance — composers watching their hand marking musical notes on a score as though it was being dictated by someone else, writers typing sentences without having to pause to grope for words, scientists making the kind of intuitive leaps that lead to breakthroughs, businesspeople conducting negotiations as though their reluctant partners to the transaction had already been persuaded ... Csikszentmihalyi called it a 'flow state'. All his subjects reported entering a flow state when their skills and abilities were being tested yet proved equal to the demands imposed by the challenges they faced.

You remember the optimal performance curve from Chapter 3, right? Well, when you're operating right at the peak of that curve, you're likely to be in a flow state. This means that what we're talking about here is another way of describing a situation where you're experiencing eustress, rising to a challenge and meeting it from your own (or, if you're in a group, your shared) resources. Each such experience, as we've noted, puts fuel in the tank of your mental fitness. Your belief in your ability to positively influence outcomes is raised, and your self-esteem along with it. Your outlook becomes more optimistic.

The ability to enter a flow state isn't just one of the secrets to greater success and productivity: it makes a positive contribution to our mental fitness and wellbeing and (as is so often the way) produces a virtuous circle, where the experience of entering a flow state equips us to seek out and enter the flow state more often and easily. In this chapter, we'll look at what a flow state is and how you can maximise your chances of entering it.

One of the leading theorists of the flow state is American psychologist Steven Kotler, author of *The Rise of Superman: Decoding the Science of Ultimate Human Performance*, who experienced at first-hand its extraordinary power. Kotler had contracted Lyme disease, a bacterial infection spread to human beings by the bite of a tick that hangs around in foliage in North American woodland looking for deer (its natural host) to infest. The early stages of the disease are characterised by the typical symptoms of an infection: fever, headache, a rash. But if left untreated, it can progress to an awful auto-immune syndrome, causing arthritis, muscle spasms and nerve disorders, breathing difficulties, heart dysrhythmia, meningitis and even death. Although he had been successfully treated with antibiotics for the original infection, Kotler was struggling with the auto-immune effects, to the point where he couldn't care for himself and could barely walk across a room. Because there is no known effective treatment for the secondary stage of Lyme disease, he was in despair, and had actually resolved to kill himself.

It was at this low moment that a friend visited and made the ridiculous suggestion that Kotler go surfing with him. Quite apart from his advanced debilitation, Kotler had given up surfing years before, after a big-wave accident. He scoffed at the proposal. But his friend was insistent and, after a while, Kotler shrugged.

'What have I got to lose?' he asked himself. 'I can always kill myself tomorrow.'

They went to Sunset Beach in southern Los Angeles, where there was hardly a swell. Kotler was given a huge board, making it more buoyant and stable and easier to paddle.

Out on the ocean, he lay miserably on his stomach for many minutes. But then a wave came along. Something like muscle memory kicked in. Without really thinking about it, Kotler spun his board towards the shore and started paddling. The board locked in the wave and Kotler got to his feet, just like that. It was as though, he said, he had stood up and found himself in an altered state of consciousness — as though the wreck that he was had been disassembled and put together again as something that worked. Whereas he had, only hours before, seen no future for himself, he felt again 'the thrum of possibility'.

Afterwards, he was at a complete loss to explain what had happened. He feared that he had entered the last stages of Lyme disease, and that his sudden feeling of wellbeing was actually the prelude to rapid mental degradation and death.

He didn't die, and nor did he kill himself. While he was doubtful that he would ever recover, he decided he would use the time left to him to try to find out what it was about surfing that had brought about the change he felt. He knew about Csikszentmihalyi's 'flow state' and wondered if this had something to do with it.

He went surfing again, and again. Each time, he felt it work its magic, and in six months, he went from what he estimated was the 10 per cent of his physical and mental functionality that the disease had left him to 80 per cent. His immune system, which had been reacting out of control, was recalibrated and settled down.

Once sufficiently recovered to resume work, Kotler devoted his career to researching exponents of high-adrenaline sports — climbers, mountaineers, extreme skiers and snowboarders, base jumpers and big-wave surfers — whom he considered to be masters of flow: people who were better at accessing the state (or 'hacking' it, as he puts it). He later widened the scope of his research to include Special Forces operatives and Silicon Valley pioneers. Like Csikszentmihalyi before him, he began to see patterns in the self-reported experiences of these 'supermen'. And it so happened that the new tools available to neuroscience made it possible to study what was actually going on in the brain when such people were 'in the zone'.

TUNE IN, TURN OFF

Scientists now know that the changes in brain processes that occur when we enter a flow state are quite pronounced. The wave forms that occur when we're concentrating hard (beta waves) resolve into alpha waves, which are associated with relaxation, and theta waves, which occur when we're experiencing the kind of deep relaxation we enter when meditating. At the same time (and either because of these changes in activity, or as their cause), several neurotransmitters are secreted at elevated levels. These include the biggies, dopamine and noradrenaline, both associated with states of heightened arousal. Dopamine, in particular, is responsible for feelings of enjoyment and anticipatory excitement, and upon its release, we are capable of heightened attention and reduced distraction. These neurotransmitters aren't just significant when we are 'in the zone': they are also markers of important events, and signal to our neural system to commit the experience to memory.

Contrary to what you might imagine, it turns out that the secret to entering a flow state is actually shutting down a large part of our brain, namely the prefrontal cortex, which is responsible for a whole bunch of higher brain functions, known as 'executive function' — the ability to judge good and bad, better and best, same and different, to predict outcomes (including the consequences of actions) and to determine whether actions will be socially acceptable. In this state (the technical term is 'transient hypofrontality'), we don't overthink stuff: we just do it. And one of the overthinking functions that gets switched off is our self-doubt. Kotler puts it beautifully: 'Flow is such a hyper-concentrated state that your ghosts can't follow you into it ... your inner critic is silenced.'

When you are confronted by a challenge that you can meet only by performing at the peak of your abilities, that little voice that tells you that you won't be able to do it is gone from your mind, so preoccupied are you with the task. Your awareness of time is diminished, if not altogether banished, which is not surprising, as perception of time is another of the functions of the prefrontal cortex.

Going with the flow

You won't be surprised to learn that the flow state has become something of a holy grail for sports and workplace psychologists. After all, if you can find a way of getting people into this state when they're at work or competing in a sport or fighting in a war, then you'll get the very best out of them.

Researchers consider flow to be a spectrum of experience, on a continuum between micro and macro versions of the state. A state of micro-flow, or a lighter version of the state, is experienced in situations like when you fall into a great conversation at work and one great idea leads to the another, and you're having so much fun you lose track of time. Or you can experience a much more intense state of macro-flow, when the experience itself takes on non-ordinary qualities — for example, time seems to slow to a crawl and you feel one with the universe.

Macro/micro flow

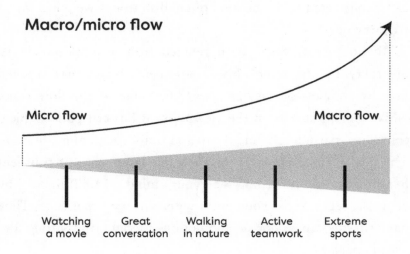

Micro flow   Macro flow

Watching a movie   Great conversation   Walking in nature   Active teamwork   Extreme sports

So how do you enter a flow state, and how do you get to spend more time there? There are three steps:

1. HAVE A LOOK AT YOUR LIFE AND THE THINGS YOU DO, AND SEEK TO IDENTIFY THOSE MOMENTS WHERE YOU ARE IN A FLOW STATE

It might not be at work: it might be at play. You might find yourself in the zone when you're exercising, or playing sport, or playing music (or even just listening to it), or engaging in a favourite hobby. My most common experiences of flow state occur when I am fighting in judo or navigating downhill on a mountain bike or speaking at a conference.

A survey conducted a while back found that 15 per cent of people couldn't identify a time or activity when they were in a flow state. This is probably an accurate reflection of how totally our lives have been dominated by a rigid set of expectations about what it is that we ought to do as adults. Flow states are a natural part of childhood, as 'play' is such an important part of childhood. Unfortunately, pursuits that feel like playing have come to be considered to be the kind of childish things we put away as we grow up.

To an extent, we've been rescued from this old-fashioned mentality by the mindfulness movement, which has reached broadly similar conclusions about the value of the flow state, while coming at it from the viewpoint of Eastern philosophical traditions, particularly Buddhism and transcendental meditation. The goal of meditation is to reach the same state of transient hypofrontalism by emptying your mind. Mindfulness, by contrast, seeks to fill your mind with sensory experience. Time has little relevance: nor do the notions of right and wrong and social approval.

Rather than getting caught up in buzzwords like mindfulness, a more useful way to conceptualise this might be 'attentional control' or 'focus control', which are the terms for mindfulness sometimes used in psychology and the defence forces respectively. It doesn't matter how we get into this state: it is enough that we spend time there — that we spend time focused on life as it is happening without the distraction of thoughts of the past or future. The great value of this 'living in the moment' is that it gives permission to grown-ups to do the kind of things that so absorbed us as children, so that we can experience the benefits of entering the same state of child-like absorption. That's why you'll see colouring-in books for adults in bookshops these days: imagine what our grandparents would have thought of that! But other activities can achieve the same thing: surfing, playing a sport, participating in martial arts … each will drag you fully into the present and keep your attention there. It's both restorative and therapeutic, serving to lower cortisol levels and put fuel in your emotional tank. Focus control is also a powerful tool for managing strong emotional experiences. More on this in Chapter 13.

2. CULTIVATE YOUR PASSIONS

Once you've found the areas in which you experience a flow state, spend time there! Because as we've seen, the benefits of spending time in the zone aren't limited to your performance in that activity. So whether it's physical activity (sports or exercise), music or practising another skill, do your best to devise ways of producing the flow state. The experience of pushing yourself to the limit of your skill and coping builds your capacity to do it again and again, and the habit is transferable from one field of activity to another (in psychology, this is called self-efficacy).

3. BE AWARE OF, AND SEEK OUT WHEREVER POSSIBLE, THE FACTORS THAT TRIGGER FLOW STATE ACTIVITY

Different researchers have produced different lists of these, but they can all be sheeted back to the requirement that you step out of your comfort zone. The flow state, Kotler argues, is a product of evolution: it's a state of consciousness we were designed by nature to achieve, so that we could perform tasks that demanded our undivided attention. Accordingly, anything that 'drives our attention into the now' will trigger a flow state.

Flow profiles

Steve Kotler and his team have created four flow profiles to assist people figure out which types of activities are most likely to get them into a flow state. Have a look and consider which of the four profiles below most resonates with you. What does this suggest about how you can be increasing your time in flow?

Read through the descriptions and 'flow hacks' and then rank the four profiles from 1 to 4, where 1 is most like you and 4 is least like you.

Profile	Description	Likely flow hacks	Rank (1 to 4)
Crowd pleaser	You thrive on the energy and inspiration of interacting with others. You lose yourself in the company of friends and like-minded others. Likely to be extroverted. For you, intensity is likely to come from the power of shared experience.	Social/political causes, festivals, conferences, social media, sports teams (playing and watching), nightlife and work teams.	

Profile	Description	Likely flow hacks	Rank (1 to 4)
Flow goer	Your life, attitude, activities and maybe even clothing show commitment to flow as a lifestyle. Likely to have done some soul searching. You may believe in synchronicity, serendipity and that everything happens for a reason.	Yoga, meditation, personal growth retreats, non-contact martial arts, eco-tourism, new circus, ecstatic dance.	
Hard charger	Easily bored go-getter who craves intensity and challenge. Flow is likely to offer an escape from your relentless drive to succeed and a strong inner critic who is always pushing you to raise the bar.	Adventure sports, mountain biking, skiing, snowboarding, surfing, rock climbing, paintball, contact martial arts, skydiving.	
Deep thinker	Introspective and more likely to achieve flow through solitary activities. Flow is likely to occur in relaxing, creative and sometimes soothingly repetitive activities.	Likely flow hacks: painting, music, poetry, gaming, coding, gardening, hiking and working with animals.	

Although there are some individual differences in which activities people sometimes prefer to experience flow states, there are also some general ingredients that make flow more likely. So what are some of the more general aspects of experiences that may trigger a flow state?

Risk. When the stakes are high, we focus. This is obviously true of adventure sports. If you're free climbing, for example, any lapse in your attention to the here and now, to this handhold, to that foothold, could spell curtains for you. But it needn't be life and limb that you're risking. Social risk is just as liable to capture your attention. After all, when we were members of a tribe and depended upon the tribe for our survival, banishment was little short of a death sentence. So taking a social risk was basically the same as performing a double somersault on a BMX bike: mess up, you'll probably die. That's why some of us find it almost unbearably difficult to take social risks (initiating conversation with an attractive stranger, for example). We have evolved to rate social risk almost as highly as death and serious injury. (We'll talk about this more in the next chapter.) By the way, an additional benefit of choosing to take any risk that makes you feel vulnerable is that it also exercises your 'courage muscle', which makes it easier to show courage on subsequent occasions. And who doesn't want a greater capacity to do what's right and true in their lives, even if it's a bit scary, rather than what's emotionally easier and more convenient in the moment?

Rich environments. When we're in a situation that is highly stimulating, our attention tends to be concentrated in the here and now. That's because our caveman ancestors — like maximum-security prisoners — were adept at analysing complex situations for threats. We can choose to seek out this kind of environment: activities in the natural world present us with an abundance of sensory stimulation, even if it's something no more threatening than a stroll in the bush or visiting a new art gallery or exhibition. Rich environments are also often found by going to new places and seeking out new experiences.

Deep embodiment. This term refers to the engagement of multiple sensory streams at once. This one will be very familiar to the mindful and the meditative. These activities encourage us to pay attention to our senses, and any situation that delivers stimuli to us through many senses at once will draw us into the present (almost as though it's creating a rich environment in our minds). Physical activity such as yoga, martial arts and many sports are good for this. So, too, is anything that takes you out into the natural world. We were never intended to spend all our time sitting at a desk in an air-conditioned, windowless room, under artificial lights, staring at a screen. There is a whole, growing movement in psychology called ecotherapy, which holds that time spent in nature — at the beach, in the bush, up in the hills, out in the fields — is vital to recalibrating our mental systems, and that deprivation of these things is a major cause of dys-stress. We'll come back to this (and call it 'environmental scanning') when we come to talk about the skills required to cope in a crisis in Chapter 13.

Tasks with clear goals. We focus best when we know we can achieve the task at hand. Think of mountaineering: quite apart from the risk involved, it engages those who do it because the goal is simple and clear. You're there to stay alive while attempting to reach the summit. And even if the overarching goal of summitting might seem monumentally difficult, setting clear, realisable intermediate goals serves the same purpose. For the mountaineer, it's putting one foot in front of another, concentrating on each rope pitch and each difficulty en route to the summit. For me, when running a marathon, I'm not focusing on the 42.2 kilometres I need to complete. I set myself much smaller, achievable goals that will serve to progress me towards the larger goal. Remember the Special Forces operative in Afghanistan and his next bit of muesli bar? Once again, we'll return to goals and their importance for mental toughness in Chapter 13.

Tasks that we truly want to accomplish. The technical term for this is 'intrinsic motivation' — where the desire to get something done comes from us, not from the boss, or some

159

societal expectation (extrinsic motivation). You'll sometimes hear this called a 'pull' factor, as distinct from a 'push' factor. Pull factors, where we are drawn towards a desirable goal, have been shown to be far more effective motivators than 'push' factors.

Tasks that provide immediate feedback. If we get instant, measurable results from our actions, it tends to focus us on the now, as we can make small adjustments to what we're doing without having to stop and re-think (which would re-engage our prefrontal cortex).

Tasks where the challenge slightly exceeds our skill set. If we tackle something that is too far beyond us, we become overwhelmed. Excessively difficult challenges are stressful and demotivating. But similarly, taking on something that is too easy is boring, and boredom is as unattractive to us as a sense of futility (and as unconducive to fully occupying our minds). We learn from experiences that stretch and fully engage us.

Tasks that demand deep concentration. Commonly, when we are required to perform at the peak of our ability, we focus intently on the 'right here, right now'. All else is shut out.

Control. When we are fully in control of what we're doing, it sometimes seems as though we are being controlled by some higher force or power that is directing us to best effect. (Kotler calls it the 'paradox of control', because you are in control without consciously controlling.)

Creativity. We are equipped by evolution to sniff out novelty. When we are on the trail of something new — whether it's something we're creating, something we're discovering, a trick/move we are trying to land, or a new skill we are trying to learn — we're likely to be in a flow state, intensely focused and in the now.

Those who conduct research in this area describe flow not only as something achieved by individuals, but also as a state into which a group can enter, where you lose your sense of self and feel 'at one' with the others engaged in the joint enterprise. It turns out there is even a neurobiological reason for this. Measurement of brain activity has found that people who are experiencing that sense of transcendent unity with the others in their group show less activity in their right parietal lobe, the part of the brain that is typically responsible for forming a sense of our own identity as distinct from others.

Of course, if you could discover the secret to producing group flow, you'd be set for life! Some reckon they've come close. American psychologist Keith Sawyer has created a list of ten 'triggers' for group flow:

Shared goals. If everyone is bought into line on what it is the group is to achieve, each person 'owns' the goal (remember the difference between extrinsic and intrinsic motivation mentioned above?). It's a different thing to desire to achieve the group's goals than merely to obey an instruction.

Close listening. This is both a sign and a trigger of the group-flow state: where members of a group pay close, focused attention to what other members have to say.

'Yes, and ...' Also known as the 'accept, don't argue' principle.) The approach of every member is affirmative and constructive rather than negative and critical. It's as though each member has the potential to function as a prefrontal cortex, the group's inner critic, but suspends judgement in favour of adding to rather than detracting from the group's direction.

Complete concentration. This is broadly similar to point 2, close listening. It is both a signifier and a trigger of the flow state: everyone is focused on the here and now.

Sense of control. This can only occur where each member of the group identifies with the group and its goals, rather than feeling taken along for the ride, especially unwillingly.

Blending egos. There's no 'I' in 'team', right? A consequence of wholly identifying with the group and its goals is that you don't see the need to achieve anything different from the group.

Equal participation. Typically, for group flow to be achieved, all members must be capable of making a contribution, whether because their skills are similar or complementary. Anyone who feels they are 'carrying' the group will find it difficult to treat it as a joint enterprise; anyone who feels like a passenger will find it hard to fully identify with its endeavours.

Familiarity. The most effective teams in most joint enterprises know one another backwards — their strengths, weaknesses, foibles, blind spots and super powers.

Constant communication. This is the group version of immediate feedback. While everyone might start off on the same page, without keeping track of where each member is — and this can only be done by communication — the danger is that people will find themselves at odds with the collective goal or drop out of synch with it.

Shared group risk. If everyone at the table (or on the field, or the battlefield) has 'skin in the game', they will be more likely to be motivated to identify with the group's goals. If the outcome of the group's endeavours has no consequences for a member, it is highly unlikely they will be intrinsically motivated.

*

Obviously, the way the world works, it is impossible for everyone to find a job that will both meet their material needs and keep them operating at a level of optimal performance. But there is nothing stopping us, as individuals or groups, seeking to maximise the opportunity to spend time in a flow state. Ideally, given how much of our waking time we spend working, this would be in the workplace. But failing that, we should strive to find areas of our lives where we can go with the flow.

And ... rest

While we've been talking up the benefits and attractions of time spent in a flow state, it's important to note that we can't be there all the time. We're fully engaged when we're being stretched, and this is good only up to a point: too much stretching and we'll become fatigued and break. So we need to rest after periods of intense, flow state, concentrated effort. This restores us and ensures we have maximum resources available to us next time we're called upon to perform at our optimum. And an important part of resting is reflecting. Reflection is essential in consolidating the learning and the benefits from the flow state itself.

As previously mentioned, for me, judo is an activity in which I most commonly experience flow. After every judo training session I reflect and make notes on what worked well for me in that session, and what could be done differently going forward. This is a very simple reflective practice that can be used to enhance your life and mental fitness more generally. Once a day, every day, reflect on what has worked well for you and what you might do differently going forward.

ENGAGEMENT SELF-ASSESSMENT

This self-assessment will give you an indication of the extent to which the engagement domain is a priority work-on for you, or an area in which more deliberate focus will move you closer to your mental fitness potential. Answer these questions according to what is most true and accurate for you. Don't overthink them — go with the first answer that comes to mind.

Question	Very slightly or not at all (1)	A little (2)	Moderately (3)	Quite a bit (4)	Extremely (5)
To what extent have you found yourself completely absorbed in a task today or within the past week?					
To what extent have you avoided procrastinating today or within the past week?					
To what extent have you lost track of time during a task or activity today or within the past week?					
To what extent have you found yourself working on satisfying and/or fun tasks today or within the past week?					
To what extent have you found yourself interested or entertained while trying to complete tasks today or within the past week?					

Total score: _____

You should get a number between 5 and 25. A higher score indicates greater levels of engagement.

Congratulations on your engagement

When we're operating at our peak, we are just outside our comfort zone; the challenge we are facing slightly exceeds our skill set. When we rise to such a challenge, we commonly enter a flow state.

In a flow state, we lose our self-consciousness and our sense of time. We are fully present in the here and now.

The flow state not only enables us to perform at our peak, it offers genuine and lasting neurobiological benefits.

We can maximise our chances of entering a flow state by identifying those areas of our lives where we experience it. Choose one of the flow hacks mentioned in your top flow profile to try or practise more consistently and deliberately.

Cultivate your passions (which, by definition, are those pursuits that we find most engaging) and fill your life with as many 'flow-state triggers' as you can.

It's possible for groups of people to enter a 'group flow-state'.

It's vital to rest and reflect after intense, concentrated activity.

9

Relationships

'No man is an island, entire of itself.'

John Donne, 1624

In 1864, an Australian sealing vessel named the *Grafton* dragged her anchors in Carnley Harbour in the Auckland Islands (480 kilometres south of New Zealand) and was wrecked. All five crew aboard survived, but they were immediately confronted with the challenge of staying alive until they were rescued. They had some elements of good luck (compared with other castaways): they had access to the wreck of their vessel, they had a shotgun and ammunition, and they were in a relatively hospitable part of the grim, bleak Auckland group. But the rest was up to them.

All five men were pretty capable, but one was more capable than most: Frenchman François Raynal was a former goldminer, and a resourceful, determined, DIY sort of guy. Among his many achievements on the island were that he had devised methods of tanning seal hides for shoes and clothing, manufacturing soap and cement, and making tools and fasteners from scrap iron in a forge that he also made. But perhaps his greatest achievement of all was in keeping the group together.

The *Grafton*'s captain, Thomas Musgrave, assumed that he would lead the men, but he was moody and ineffective. In a stroke of genius, Raynal proposed that as they were now a group of castaways rather than a ship's company, they should elect a new leader. He cast his own vote for Musgrave. The rest followed his example, and Musgrave took renewed heart at the endorsement. Raynal also found a way of brewing alcohol, and made playing cards, but when both threatened group harmony — drunken arguments broke out, and Musgrave proved to be a sore loser at cards — the Frenchman stopped brewing and quietly disappeared the cards. Instead, as they were a crew of mixed nationalities, he established language classes and instigated Bible readings. In short, Raynal tended the little team's morale as assiduously as they all tended the fire: both were essential to keeping them alive.

We can be sure of this, because it so happens that a few months after the *Grafton* was wrecked on the southern end of Auckland Island, another vessel, the *Invercauld*, was wrecked at the northern end. Of the 25 men aboard, only 19 made it ashore, and they were entirely without supplies.

In order to survive, it was essential that they crossed from the little beach where they were huddled at the foot of the formidable cliffs that form the west coast of Auckland Island to the slightly more hospitable east coast. The march was accomplished in an 'every man for himself' manner, and by the time they had regrouped at Port Ross on the east coast, only five men were left alive, the rest having given up or perhaps even been killed and cannibalised by their shipmates.

Nor were their problems over. The captain, George Dalgarno, insisted on maintaining the shipboard hierarchy, including the strict division between officers and men. Four of the survivors were officers (including Dalgarno himself): the only able seaman left alive was young Robert Holding, who turned out to be the only one among them with much of a work ethic or a sense of how they might eke out a living in the desperate conditions in which they found themselves. The group was profoundly dysfunctional, and as a consequence, when they were finally rescued, there were only three men left (Holding, Dalgarno and the first mate).

It's a terrific story, and it's really well told in a book named *Island of the Lost* by maritime historian Joan Druett. It was as though history had set out to provide humanity with a real-life example of one of those 'compare and contrast' questions that university examiners love so much. The *Grafton*'s five men all survived: only three of the *Invercauld*'s nineteen made it. The stark difference was in the *Grafton*'s crew's resolute determination to maintain their *esprit de corps*.

Being a social animal

Unlike many mammals, we are born helpless, and depend wholly upon others for our survival years afterwards. In our hunter-gatherer past, a pregnant and breastfeeding mother depended upon others for her survival, too. So in order to reproduce the species, we formed social groups — tribes — that worked for the collective good. Human beings evolved to be social animals. A group of human beings working together is more than the sum of its parts.

Despite the technological advances of the last few thousand years, nothing about that has changed. We remain social animals, equipped with a suite of adaptations that drive us to seek and foster relationships with others. We dread loneliness. Indeed, enforced loneliness has been used as a punishment throughout human history. As I've said earlier, for a hunter-gatherer, being turfed out of the tribe would have amounted to a death sentence. For the ancient Greeks and Romans, ostracism — exile from society — was considered second only to death as a punishment. Some religious groups use a form of exclusion to punish wrongdoers — the Amish temporarily 'shun' straying members of the flock, the Pope has the power to excommunicate naughty Catholics — and in our own penal system, prisoners who won't toe the institutional line are deprived of social contact by being assigned spells of solitary confinement. And those who don't toe the line of inmate culture are treated by other inmates as if they are invisible, if more grizzly fates do not await.

Social deprivation hurts. And you don't need to have been in solitary yourself to know it: everyone knows what it feels like to have been excluded from a group that we wanted to be part of — being given the cold shoulder by a clique when you were at school, discovering you've been unfriended by someone on Facebook ... It hurts all right, and it's not just imaginary pain. Neurologists have shown that the parts of the brain that process the pain of social exclusion are the same ones that process the pain arising from physical injury. And research has shown that the negative health impacts of chronic loneliness are similar to those of smoking!

There are measurable benefits to our health and wellbeing when we enjoy functional relationships:

- We suffer less from dys-stress (as indicated by lower cortisol levels).
- We are less likely to suffer anxiety and depression.
- We have higher self-esteem.

- We are healthier (perhaps as a consequence of lower cortisol levels, or perhaps because the relationships that are best for us are ones in which we reinforce healthy behaviours for one another).
- We bounce back better from illness and injury.
- We are happier (due to the happiness-enhancing effect of doing things for others, and the psychological boost we receive from feeling part of something larger than ourselves: more on both in the next chapter).
- As a consequence of many of the factors above operating as a virtuous cycle, we are better at making and maintaining new relationships.

We thrive when we are properly connected with others. A study involving a large number of American undergraduate students sought to rank them from the most to the least satisfied with their lives, and then compared the factors at play in the lives of the top 10 per cent with the bottom 10 per cent. The difference in almost every case lay in their satisfaction with their relationships.

You might be sceptical about this finding, given it was based on the preoccupations of a distinctly image-conscious, popularity-seeking and downright horny cohort (Americans of both sexes just on either side of 20), and you wouldn't be alone. But many of those who have repeated the experiment found that much the same held true for other age groups, nationalities and gender mixes. How well we perceive ourselves to be connected to others really does seem to be a major determinant of life satisfaction.

So what is a 'functional' relationship?

We have various levels of social connection to others. All are important, and it's likely that we need connections at each level to truly thrive. Psychologists often divide the kinds of relationships we have into three categories:

Intimate connections. These can be with our spouse or partner, with our wider family, or with our friends. The distinguishing feature of a functional intimate relationship is that we feel accepted within it — unafraid to be ourselves, to show our weaknesses, vulnerabilities and character flaws. There are degrees of intimacy, of course: we might not be afraid to cry, or swear, to be seen naked or to fart in front of our spouse or partner. We might be a little more reserved with our children, more reserved again with our parents, and then more reserved again around our friends.

Relational connections. These are the kinds of connections we have with people with whom we share an enterprise but who are outside our intimate relationships —workmates, say, or members of clubs. These relationships are usually a little more formal and constrained than intimate relationships.

Collective connections. These are more the kinds of affiliations we have to 'tribes' — shared political views, religion, nationality, etc. We share a world view, and we're united by the story we tell ourselves about how the world works and where we belong in it. These kinds of relationships are important because they give us a sense of belonging to something larger than ourselves, which in turn bestows a sense of meaning and purpose. We'll return to this in the next chapter.

*

Needless to say, measuring how much benefit we are deriving from our social connections is a difficult task. We can start by taking a piece of paper, heading it up with the three categories above (intimate, relational and collective) and listing the various connections we have with others in each column. This can provide us with an objective, quantitative measurement of our social connections.

But it's not just the *quantity* of relationships that counts. The *quality* is important, too; indeed, it's perhaps the most important factor of all.

In order to assess how 'good' any given relationship is, try asking yourself the following questions:

- Do I and the other person always treat one another with respect?
- Do we both equally protect and value the relationship?
- Do we listen to one another, and do we give ground when we recognise the other's point of view has more merit than our own?
- Are we both functional within the relationship? That is, does it feel like a free and equal arrangement, where we are both independently responsible for our own needs and for maintaining the relationship?
- Do I feel I can speak openly and share my point of view, my thoughts and my feelings within the relationship?
- Can we both set boundaries for the relationship (that is, make the rules and determine what we can and can't ask of the other)?
- Do we resolve disagreements without resorting to threats or actual physical, emotional or psychological abuse?
- Are there any physically, emotionally or psychologically abusive aspects to the relationship?

Of course, if there are aspects of a relationship that leave a bit to be desired, it doesn't mean the relationship is doomed or has nothing to offer. Few relationships are perfect! Finding yours is less than perfect often means you are in the completely normal situation of needing to put some work into it!

The things that *do* predict real dysfunction and ultimate collapse in relationships have been identified through the extensive research by American psychologist John Gottman, who calls them 'the Four Horsemen of the Apocalypse', after the biblical harbingers of doom. They are criticism, defensiveness, contempt and stonewalling.

A lot of people who are used to managing high stress in their work or have had difficult childhoods can find themselves prone to stonewalling when they are working through challenges and upsets in their relationships. Part of the reason for this is that they may have learned very effective strategies for dealing with high-stress situations that involve shutting down or 'parking' their emotional responses. On the plus side, these strategies serve us very well when we are required to perform under pressure, and are used in the defence forces and among elite athletes. These will be outlined in the mental toughness section of this book (Chapter 12).

Unfortunately, our ways of coping with stress and effectively moving through discomfort to better times are 'domain-specific'. That is a technical term which means that what works well for you in one situation may not work as well for you in another. Lieutenant Colonel Steve Kearney, chief mental health officer for the New Zealand Defence Force, uses the analogy of being fit and conditioned for running not helping you a whole heap when thrown in the pool! When someone uses techniques such as shutting down and focusing on immediate sensory experiences, which work so well in high-stress and high-pressure environments, their significant other is likely to perceive them as cold and distant, which aggravates rather than helps the situation! Instead, they need to shift tack and employ some of the tips below, particularly those relating to listening and being listened to.

TOP TIPS FOR IMPROVING RELATIONSHIPS

Be grateful. Research suggests that gratitude is the single most important relationship-strengthening emotion, because it requires us to see how we have been affirmed and supported by other people.

Give time. If something is worth doing (and forming and maintaining relationships is one of the most worthwhile things we do), then it's worth doing properly. The very least a relationship asks of you is the time to make it work.

Be present. It's not just the amount of time that you put in, it's the quality of that time, too. It's getting harder and harder in the modern world to give other people their due. How often do you try to have a conversation with someone and they're glancing at their phone, or gazing beyond you at a television screen? Focus on being there and giving the other party or parties to a relationship your full attention — it's the most effective way to make people feel seen and valued.

Listen. Listening is one of the most important social skills there is. Try practising 'active' listening (where you give feedback to the person speaking by, for example, repeating or rephrasing each important part of what they're telling you. For example, if your partner tells you she thinks you're spending too much time at the office, say: 'So you think I should try to get home from the office a bit earlier ...'). This not only reassures the person speaking that their words are being received and understood, but also helps to focus your attention on what they're saying. But keep your tone neutral! Part of listening is being non-judgemental: it's all about receiving and understanding another's point of view, which is a necessary step before you start passing judgement. A useful tip to improve your listening skills is to listen as though you might be tested on what the other person is sharing. This way, you're likely to clarify ambiguities and ask better questions.

Be listened to. This is perhaps the hardest and scariest part of any relationship. Communication is a two-way thing, and it is hard for another person to feel you're committed to making the relationship work if you're not forthcoming or honest about how you're feeling and your point of view. More on the benefits of such communication and how to increase your capacity to do this in the section on emotional literacy in Chapter 12.

Recognise that relationships can be bad for one, both or all parties. This can be because they're substitutes for the kinds of relationships that we really need (junk relationships), or because they're actually harmful (toxic relationships) — see below for more on both.

Junk relationships

In the modern world, it's pretty easy to form relationships that seem to serve a purpose, but in fact act only as a poor substitute for a functional, fulfilling connection. Look no further than social media, the junk food of the relationship world. On one level, such apps as Facebook might seem to be a useful tool in building and maintaining relationships: you can keep in touch with a far wider circle of people than ever before, regardless of the tyranny of distance. You can see what they're up to (or what they choose to let you see), and you can interact with them any time you want. But a social-media connection is a poor substitute for a real relationship, just as a packet of potato chips is a poor substitute for real, nutritious food.

As we grow and develop, we learn to 'read' other people. Every interaction we have with another person adds to our store of knowledge of the blizzard of cues we receive from them through our senses — visual cues (such as facial expression, body language), aural cues (such as speech intonation) and even olfactory cues (such as pheromones, primal and little understood as they are). Collectively, this store of knowledge is known as 'social intelligence'. There's plenty of evidence to suggest that the rise of social media has coincided with a decline in social intelligence, and little wonder: the communication we engage in over social media is limited to one or two channels, compared with the multi-channel communication we have in real life. That's why misunderstandings arising from texts and emails happen so often: sarcasm and humour, stock-in-trade when we're conversing with someone in person, often don't survive electronic transmission.

The reason social media has become so addictive is because it provides the same kind of instant gratification to our need for social interaction as junk food does to our physiology. You post on Facebook and lean forward expectantly, waiting for the reactions to roll in. You feel a little burst of pleasure each time someone likes your post. You feel rejected, isolated and irrelevant if no one does. And you lay yourself open to be 'hated on', because there's nothing quite like sitting down at a computer with your anonymity assured or without having to deal with the consequences of your actions to bring out the malevolent troll in people. It's very hard to detach your sense of self-worth from the fickle reactions of your social-media contacts.

Conducting relationships in public is a bad idea, but that's what social media encourages. When you're going through tough times, there can be a temptation to seek the support of your Facebook friends and Twitter followers and overshare in the process. This can come back to bite you in the bum. While some platforms offer the facility to delete ill-considered and regretted posts, sometimes the damage has already been done.

Our craving for approval — a desire instilled in us by all the evolutionary pressure that turned us into creatures anxious to be valued members of the tribe — places enormous pressure on us to conform. We create social-media personas calculated to attract approval, admiration, even envy. And of course, we see the glittering social personas of others, and can't help but compare ourselves unfavourably.

Furthermore, our drive to compulsively cultivate a perfect virtual version of our 'story' often threatens to crowd out the interaction we have with real people, in the real world. Top tip for improving your real relationships? Put your bloody phone down and engage!

Toxic relationships

We all know people in relationships that seem all wrong for them. Sometimes we find ourselves in relationships that are wrong for us. It's not always (perhaps not even often) that it's a matter of having entered a relationship with the wrong person — although, of course, this happens. People and what they want out of life change, and it is often the case that previously compatible friends, life partners, etc find themselves at loggerheads because one of the other person's life direction has changed.

Sometimes a relationship can change to accommodate the new demands placed upon it. Sometimes it can't, and no longer serves the needs of one, both or all parties. Too often, people will remain in a relationship for all the wrong reasons — fear of loneliness, a sense of obligation arising out of concern for the other person or because there is 'history' between them ... but if a relationship is no longer serving your needs and the only one prepared to make any effort to improve it is you, it's time to call it off. Flogging a dead horse will get you nowhere but tired.

The following are signs that a relationship is toxic:

There is emotional, psychological or physical abuse. *This is a deal-breaker.* Abuse is always unhealthy and cannot be tolerated. If it can't be stopped, the relationship has to end.

You or your partner feels scared when you argue. One step back from actual abuse is the threat of it — anything that inhibits open communication and prevents those within a relationship from airing their thoughts, feelings and needs. The threat doesn't need to be of physical violence. A bad emotional reaction, such as anger, tears or such passive-aggressive behaviour as playing the martyr, are also unhelpful.

One person makes the rules and the other feels they have to toe the line. A functional relationship caters to the needs of everyone in it, and doesn't just serve as a means of control by one party.

One or more person in the relationship is co-dependent (that is, they wouldn't get far outside the relationship).

You feel you're wasting your breath when you express your point of view, or you tend not to listen when the other person/ people speak their mind. It's a problem if one party takes a 'my way or the highway' approach on every issue.

One person does all the work maintaining the relationship or one party behaves in ways that threaten the relationship.

If you have good reason to believe one of your relationships is toxic most of the time, it's time to consider walking away. It might be a hard and painful decision, but I've said it before in this book and I'll say it again: discomfort is often a sign that we're growing.

The SCARF model

Relationships are important to us because we each have a set of social needs, and just like our physical needs, if they're not met, we'll fail to thrive. So what are these social needs?

Based on 30 interviews with the world's leading neuroscientists, Dr David Rock captured our most universal social needs in what he calls the SCARF model. As usual, SCARF is an acronym, with each letter standing for a social need: Status/Significance, Certainty, Autonomy, Relatedness and Fairness. The SCARF model sits within a field called social neuroscience, which is the area of research that explores how the brain works as a function of our social interactions. As mentioned above, our brain treats these interactions as incredibly important.

At its most basic, our brain is constantly scanning the environment to identify potential threats and rewards. If something is perceived to be a potential reward, the 'approach' system in our brain fires up and neurotransmitters that make us feel good, bond with others, learn and perform effectively kick in. If we experience a high level of activation in this approach system, we will go into what is called in psychology 'broaden and build', a state of functioning wherein our perspectives are broadened and our capacity to try new things, risk failure and get out of our comfort zones is built or increased. Broaden and build is the polar opposite of the previously discussed state of fight/ flight/freeze, which is what we kick into when the 'avoid' system is strongly activated. When something is perceived as a potential physical, psychological or social threat, neurotransmitters are released that cause us to feel unpleasant emotions and to prepare to react automatically in the interests of survival. Instead of bonding with others we become guarded, defensive, closed-down and wary.

A key idea behind the SCARF model is that if we increase a person's sense of status/significance, certainty, autonomy, relatedness or fairness when we interact with them, they find us rewarding to deal with. But if we in any way diminish or reduce their sense of these things, they find us aversive or unpleasant. After a few interactions, people can become a trigger for pleasant or unpleasant emotions.

It didn't take Pavlov's dogs long to associate the ringing of the bell with the arrival of food. In the same way, there are some people who we need to just catch sight of to start feeling uneasy. In fact, I'm sure there are some people who feel that way at the prospect of dealing with me!

Yet understanding the SCARF model isn't just about being able to be more rewarding to deal with and therefore successful in any interaction and relationship: it's also about being able to depersonalise the things that other people do that cause us annoyance and distress. You will remember from Chapter 7 (about positive emotion) that taking things personally is the enemy of both optimism and wellbeing. When you better understand how someone else's attempt to meet their social needs might negatively impact on you, you can accept it is truly about them and can move on more quickly from the sting. You can also adapt your behaviour to be more effective in the relationship, if it is one you value.

Another reason to focus on being rewarding to deal with is that it is one of the three key factors found to predict career advancement and success, in one of the largest studies into the predictors of job success (the other two ingredients were the ability to learn what is required of you to be successful, and the willingness to do the work required to be successful).

The SCARF model is a useful tool not only for understanding the social needs we all have in our relationships, but also where our needs may be greater or lesser than others we interact with. This model will help you determine why you find some people easier to connect with than others, and what you can do to more effectively meet the social needs of those you need or want to connect with.

S IS FOR STATUS/SIGNIFICANCE

S is for Status in David Rock's original model; however, I think that Significance more effectively captures the universal nature of this need for most people. On this basis, I refer to the S as standing for Status/Significance.

We all have the need to feel seen, heard and valued. In fact, this is the primary driver of teenage behaviour! From an evolutionary perspective, you could say that as teenagers we are no longer able to simply exist in the tribe by virtue of our parents. We need to start making our own contribution. Our biological drive also means we need to establish how we can be seen as a viable mate. Either way, we need to be seen and valued. The most important influence for teenagers is the 'prestige economy' of their peers. What are the things that get you respected and valued amongst the other teens? This is why I always tell parents of teens to focus on the 'prestige economy' of their children's peers, as knowing what their friends value can tell you whether you need to worry about possible associated problems or can feel reassured.

However, we all have the need to feel seen and valued; to feel that we are respected and our contributions are appreciated.

Our sense of social significance is increased and we feel pleasant emotions if we perceive that we are appreciated, listened to, acknowledged, praised and successful. On the other hand, feeling embarrassed, judged, dismissed, condescended to, talked over or belittled leads us to experience unpleasant emotions.

Some people are more sensitive to these triggers than others. For people who have a greater need for Status/Significance than others, their social needs will be more focused on their relative importance compared to others (i.e. status); for example, thinking not only 'Am I perceived as smart and capable enough, but am I perceived as smarter and more capable than others here?' A useful way to conceptualise such people is as a Capital S.

In evolutionary psychology, we talk about the ways people meet their need for status as falling into two broad categories of behaviour: prestige and dominance. Prestige is what we get when others place value on our skills and knowledge, and the route to it is the pursuit of excellence and mastery in areas of value. The other path is dominance, which is about the assertion of social status, often through being domineering, dismissive, focused on power, prone to one-upmanship and hyper-competitive. The pursuit of prestige and making others feel seen and valued is just about always the path to more rewarding relationships.

I'm a Capital S, which isn't really consistent with New Zealand's 'the kumara doesn't talk about its own sweetness' ethos. Yet the strength of your social needs reflect unchosen preferences rather than aspirations, and if we know ourselves, we can better manage our relationships with others. Knowing I am a Capital S helps me focus on the pursuit of excellence and prestige while not taking it personally if someone doesn't show me the respect my emotional self feels I am due. It also means I can ensure that I focus on making others feel seen and valued through listening and asking rather than always sharing and opining. Yet on my worst days when I am slipping towards the fatigued end of the flourishing versus fatigued continuum, I can still be a hater and slip into the envious and domineering path of dominance. Progress, not perfection, is the goal!

C IS FOR CERTAINTY

Certainty is about predictability, and predictability is about safety. If we know what's going on and what's coming up, we feel safer.

To give you an idea of how much our species likes certainty, in 2018 a study was conducted in which participants were given two options. The first option was a low-intensity electric shock at random. The second option was a significantly stronger electric shock right now! You know what they chose? That's right: most people would rather have a stronger electric shock that is certain and predictable than deal with the emotional distress of not knowing when something is coming.

We all have the need for certainty when we interact with others. We need to feel that we know what is expected of us, how to achieve desired outcomes and what the future is going to look like. If you are a Capital C, this need for certainty will be even greater.

Capital Cs are often people who get stuck into the weeds and seek and provide too much detail when interacting with others. Have you ever worked with or lived with someone who does this, who likes a lot more predictability and information than others? In managerial positions this greater need for certainty often results in micromanagement. This is often mistaken for a lack of trust in the person being micromanaged, whereas it is actually just about a high need for certainty on the part of the manager.

If you know this, you can learn to take micromanagement less personally and 'manage up' more effectively to meet your superior's need for certainty.

When it comes to our relationships, certainty is more about knowing where we stand and that others are reliable. We like to be able to trust people.

If you have a Capital C in your life, make sure you follow through on what you say you will do. If you find them double-checking that things are as they would like them, remember that this is about their desire for certainty, not about a lack of trust in you.

A IS FOR AUTONOMY

We value control over our own lives and destinies. Few people cope well with the feeling of helplessness. As I mentioned earlier, in my preparation for writing this book, I observed the work that the defence force does with Special Forces troops on what they call 'conduct after capture' or CAC training. You can imagine what SAS soldiers are like: they're men of action, highly trained to become adept at making swift, effective decisions. None of this is much use when you're captured and your fate is no longer in your hands, hence the need for an entire training module on how to cope under circumstances where you can no longer control anything much.

Capital A people place greater value than most on autonomy and independence. If you are someone who likes to be left alone to get on with your work rather than working collaboratively on tasks, if you are someone who bristles when asked for additional information or updates on what you are doing, you may be a Capital A. If so you are the Capital C's nightmare as an employee! Learning to provide more certainty and information than you consider reasonable is the way to managing your relationships with Capital Cs. While it is a little annoying to have to do it rather than just getting on with things, it is less annoying than being micromanaged!

If you are dealing with a Capital A, make sure you are always giving them options and involve them in the decision-making around their work and schedule.

R IS FOR RELATEDNESS

We need to feel connected to others and to make common cause with other people, and to do this we need to feel safe with those we choose. Relatedness is our most fundamental friend-or-foe consideration for members of a tribal species. Are we part of the same tribe and therefore on the same side against enemies as we work towards our common interests?

In evolutionary psychology, we say there are two primary approaches to meeting your need for relatednesss — common enemy or common humanity. Suppose you have a problem with a co-worker. There are two ways for you to deal with it. Common humanity is the hard way, which is to not dismiss that difficult-to-deal-with colleague by trying to give them the benefit of the doubt, assume the best intentions from their side, put yourself into their shoes and understand what might be going on for them, or maybe even sit down with that person and address the issue with direct communication. Hard work, right? It makes you feel drained just thinking about doing it. A much easier (and thus more common, but unfortunately far less constructive) way of dealing with it is via 'common enemy'. This is where you seek out someone who you anticipate will be receptive and then moan about your co-worker to them. You form 'in' and 'out' groups to meet your need for relatedness. This is exactly how 'silos' in organisations often form, where people in a team get on well and like each other, but have the feeling they are separate and different from other teams within the organisation.

If you are a Capital R, you are likely to be very sensitive to perceptions of inclusion or exclusion. You are likely to be someone who places value on the harmony of relationships and avoids conflict where possible. This is likely to make you a lovely person to be around and work with, but it will also make you less likely to be good at getting your own needs met, standing up for yourself, and sharing your views and opinions, due to concern about losing popularity with others. Sometimes if you do appropriately assert yourself by saying no or honestly sharing your opinions, you might momentarily lose popularity, but you will trade popularity for respect. People hold others in higher esteem when they feel they will hear an honest view and opinion from them rather than simply hearing what they think someone else wants to hear.

Asking people about themselves and their lives is a good way to meet their need for relatedness — showing that you are genuinely interested in and care about the wellbeing of others.

F IS FOR FAIRNESS

We instinctively look for reciprocity in social exchanges. Some cultures even enshrine this human impulse into moral and ethical codes: think of the Maori concept of utu, the Melanesian principle of reciprocity or the biblical tenet of 'an eye for an eye, a tooth for a tooth'. These are far from isolated examples. Of course, you can take an insistence on fairness too far: you probably know one of those wearying people who are always affronted because they feel they're being short-changed in their dealings with others. A classic way in which fairness is negatively triggered in the workplace is where there's a perception of bias or favouritism.

An interesting difference between fairness and the other social needs outlined here is that if people feel unfairly treated, they experience far stronger, more visceral emotions such as disgust. I think the evolutionary origin of this probably relates to the crucial need for highly interdependent tribe members to be intolerant of people who don't pull their weight or who exploit others.

If someone is a Capital F, you will often hear it in their language, with them regularly talking about things being fair or unfair. To effectively meet this need in others, you need to focus on establishing win-win outcomes and making sure you always take ownership of your role in any issues or problems.

Knowing your triggers

To maximise the value you get from the SCARF model, it is important to know what your weaker and stronger triggers are. While all aspects of this model apply to each of us, most of us will have some that are stronger social needs.

Go through the descriptions below and then rank the SCARF domains from 1 to 5, where 1 represents the most impactful for you, and 5 equals the least impactful for you.

Need	Causes of negative emotions	Causes of positive emotions	Rank order 1–5
Status/ Significance	Suggestions from someone that you didn't do something very well.	Someone stating mutual needs and acknowledging the importance of the relationship.	
	Someone diminishing your thoughts or ideas.	People seeking to understand your point of view and reflecting that understanding.	
	People 'going over the top of you' to get things they need or want.	Others drawing on your thoughts and ideas.	

Need	Causes of negative emotions	Causes of positive emotions	Rank order 1–5
Certainty	People not telling the truth or acting incongruously. People who don't keep promises, miss deadlines or fail to do what they said they would. Unknown expectations, responsibilities, or a lack of feedback on the quality of work.	People being consistent in what they say and do. People clearly defining expectations, responsibilities, milestones for actions. People continually communicating on progress and keeping promises.	
Autonomy	Being micromanaged and given little choice in how to complete your work. Not being consulted on decisions that affect your work. Inflexible work practices (e.g. not being able to set up your own desk, take leave when you need to or organise your workflow).	People exploring with you different courses of action that could be taken to resolve conflict. Generally being consultative. People being flexible and open to your ideas.	
Relatedness	Being a different type of employee (e.g. contractor – permanent). Working in a silo culture and mentality. Colleagues who are guarded about their thoughts and feelings.	People being authentic. People establishing shared needs or goals. Others who build rapport and find common ground with you.	

Need	Causes of negative emotions	Causes of positive emotions	Rank order 1–5
Fairness	Different sets of rules seemingly applying for different people.	People establishing win-win outcomes with you.	
	Different people doing very similar work yet being paid different amounts.	People taking appropriate ownership and responsibility for issues.	
	Inequalities such as a higher percentage of men being promoted to senior positions.	When it is ensured that both parties are happy with negotiated outcomes.	

Awareness of the SCARF model is so important, because what people tend to do is just unconsciously interact with others according to their personal preference for what would meet their own needs. This will only get you so far, as people are different, according to which of these needs is strongest and most prioritised.

To make the most of this model for boosting your relationship skills, I suggest you complete the below relationship map. In this map you place yourself in the middle circle, and use the previous SCARF self-assessment exercise to list your strongest needs. In the other circles you then add people with whom you most need to effectively interact, and name what you think their strongest needs are. Include a mix of personal and professional relationships.

While all aspects of the SCARF model apply to all of us, most people will have two or three relatively stronger needs. Some people are consistent across needs, but most of us have some capital letters. If you are unsure of what capitals might apply to those in your relationship map, start observing your interactions through this lens. Once you have a better idea of the needs of the people around you, you can more effectively adapt your behaviour to improve your interactions, by meeting those needs.

Relationship map

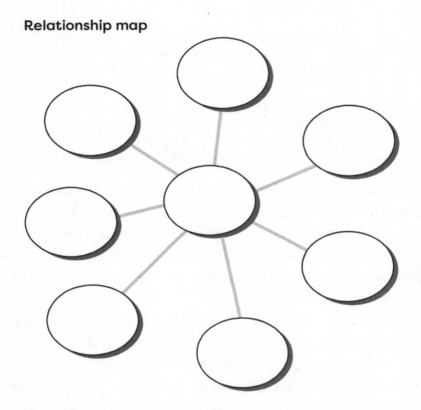

The unexpected benefits of connecting

Remember the hedonic treadmill, the tendency for us to settle back to more or less the same level of satisfaction regardless of good or bad life events? Most of the good feelings we experience — joy, bliss, ecstasy, pleasure — are temporary. They will raise us out of our default state of mind for a time, but we'll soon adapt and revert.

But here's something interesting that researchers have noticed:

we derive a significant and lasting surge of positive emotion from performing acts of kindness. One study followed people who were either undergoing major medical interventions or who were supporting a family member through a procedure. Some were asked to mentor and support other people who were to undergo the same treatment, and it was found that the mental health benefits to those who performed such volunteer work was greater than the benefits to those whom they were supporting. Another, similar study followed a group of sufferers of multiple sclerosis who provided peer support to other MS patients: the volunteers all reported improved levels of confidence and self-esteem and were less likely to suffer from depression.

It's also been shown that performing acts of kindness can lower your stress levels. When you're fatigued and verging on being overwhelmed, it might seem as though the last thing you need is to put yourself out for someone else. But strangely, the opposite seems to be true. The kind of positive emotion you generate by being kind puts fuel in your tank.

Why? Well, as I have said many times, we are social animals, and we are hardwired to feel good about doing things that are conducive to the wellbeing of the group. Most of us admire altruism — the performing of acts of kindness, without expecting anything in return. Most of us would like to be viewed as kind. If we value kindness, then being kind amounts to living up to one of our values, which gives us a sense of validation and purpose.

There are other benefits, too. The whole Buddhist notion of 'karma' is that what goes around comes around, so that if you are kind and generous, your kindness and generosity will be rewarded by the universe. Of course, the Buddhist doctrine of reincarnation suggests you needn't hold your breath while you wait for all that good karma to come your way in this life. For non-Buddhists, for whom this life is all there is, it's pretty plain that the karmic rewards system isn't infallible. But if you acquire a reputation for kindness and generosity, you will find people are more willing to be kind and generous to you, and to offer support when you need it. Kindness strengthens the bonds of unity.

We noted in Chapter 7 that one way to refocus your attention on the positive aspects of your life was to compare down. The willingness to be kind places you in a great position to do this. Helping others with their problems can give you an entirely different and refreshing perspective on your own circumstances.

What about my freedom?

All of this talk about community, kindness and altruism may seem deeply unfashionable. There's a very good reason for this: over the last 50 or so years, most Western societies have converted wholeheartedly to a set of political ideas based on radical individualism.

Individualism itself is a comparatively new philosophical idea. It arose during the Renaissance, when Protestant Reformers argued that individual believers ought to be able to find out what God wanted of and for them all by themselves. So long as you had access to the Bible, there was no need to bow to the authority of the church. The cry for religious freedom soon widened to an argument for political freedom — the novel idea that the state was there to serve the needs of its people, not the other way round. The democratic revolutions of the seventeenth and eighteenth centuries were fought on this principle.

What really sealed the deal was the identification of individual freedom with the personal right to make and keep as much money as possible, an idea that gained currency (so to speak) in the 1950s in the US (of course). An Austrian-born philosopher at the University of Chicago, F.A. Hayek, began to preach the idea that the free market could do a better job of organising society than any central planner — and it really caught on, especially among those who stood to gain from greater freedom from regulation and taxation. It's no surprise that it has become the ruling orthodoxy throughout the West that more 'freedom' is always better.

To practically anyone who lived at any point in human history prior to 1950, the idea that individuals should have unfettered personal freedom would have seemed not only ludicrous, but also downright dangerous, and in speaking up against it, they would have had a point. As I am writing this, the world is struggling to get to grips with a global pandemic. Nations that have adopted a strategy based on collective action have done notably better than nations where extreme interpretations of personal liberty have been swallowed hook, line and sinker. In America, birthplace of free-market economics, people insisting on their rights and freedoms refuse to follow the advice of medical experts: as of early 2021, America leads the world in rates of Covid-19 infection and per capita mortality. Great Britain, whose one-time prime minister Margaret Thatcher (an admirer of Hayek) once said: 'Society? There's no such thing. There's only individuals and families', is doing little better.

We are naturally suited to live in groups, and we can achieve more as a group than we can as individuals focused solely upon our own self-interest. Adam Smith, the eighteenth-century Scottish philosopher whose work inspired (and is quoted with admiration by) Hayek and other neo-liberal philosophers, recognised that altruism comes naturally to us. 'How selfish soever man may be supposed,' Smith wrote, 'there are evidently some principles in his nature, which interest him in the fortune of others, and render their happiness necessary to him though he derives nothing from it, except the pleasure of seeing it ... The greatest ruffian, the most hardened violator of the laws of society, is not altogether without it.'

Subsequent philosophers who insist upon identifying rationality with the pursuit of self-interest have found themselves obliged to explain altruism away in terms of such stilted concepts as 'psychic income' — the pleasure we get when we do something for others, which is worth almost as much to us as money. While I don't agree with this notion, there is value in seeing your relationships as investments. Every time you have a positive interaction with someone else it is like putting money in the bank. Every time you have a more difficult interaction it is like making a withdrawal. You don't have to be a Nobel Prize-winning economist to understand that if you are making only withdrawals, it doesn't take long to find yourself in trouble.

Human beings cannot flourish standing only on their own two feet. Among the most harmful myths that have arisen out of the wholesale worship of individual freedom is the idea that we must stand or fall on our own merits and drawing upon our own resources. You've heard the saying 'it takes a village to raise a child.' It's true, because we are born helpless. And the village's job isn't over when we reach adulthood. It takes families, neighbourhoods, villages, societies, to keep us all safe, happy and whole.

Relationships self-assessment

This self-assessment will give you an indication of the extent to which the relationships domain is a priority work-on for you, or an area in which more deliberate focus will move you closer to your mental fitness potential. Answer these questions according to what is most true and accurate for you. Don't overthink them — go with the first answer that comes to mind.

Question	Very slightly or not at all (1)	A little (2)	Moderately (3)	Quite a bit (4)	Extremely (5)
To what extent have you felt heard and understood by someone else today or within the past week?					
To what extent have you offered support or help to others today or within the past week?					
To what extent have you found yourself not avoiding interacting with another person today or within the past week?					
To what extent do you receive help and support from others when you need it?					
How satisfied are you with your personal relationships?					

You should get a number between 5 and 25. A higher score indicates greater levels of relationship strength.

Good relationships in summary

Human beings are social animals, and the quality of our relationships is a key ingredient in thriving.

Relationships can be improved — just as they can do us harm.

The coping strategies we use effectively in some situations may be problematic when used in our relationships.

A key to improving relationships is understanding what we need from them, and what others need from us (which we can do using the SCARF model).

Doing things for others is a proven way to increase your own mental fitness.

10

Meaning

'He who has a why to live for can bear almost any how.'

Friedrich Nietzsche

Human beings are best placed to flourish when they feel their lives have a purpose, and that they are connected to something that is greater than themselves. This is probably just another of the suite of adaptations that we have carried forward from the Stone Age, when identifying the survival of the tribe as your primary objective helped everyone work effectively together.

One of the most graphic illustrations of the importance to your health and wellbeing of feeling you're part of something larger than yourself is seeing how people fare when they're deprived of it. Look at the indigenous peoples around the world whose way of life was disrupted by colonisation: in practically every case, the social outcomes of their descendants are significantly worse than those of the descendants of the colonisers, and even of more recent migrants and refugees. You'll occasionally hear people from advantaged backgrounds complaining that Maori, for example, or Aboriginal Australians, or African or First Nations Americans have the same opportunities to get ahead as everyone else in society, and that their failure to grasp those opportunities is indicative of some character flaw, perhaps even racial inferiority. But this completely ignores the immensely demoralising effect of the destruction of the entire belief system from which these people formerly drew meaning and purpose, with nothing to take its place — not to mention historical inequalities in legislation, education and entitlements.

Societies have traditionally found meaning in belief systems such as religions, or a sense of nationalism. Both are of greatly diminished importance in our increasingly secular, globalised world. Where do you look for that kind of guiding light today?

If this were a clickbait ad on the internet, I'd be inviting you to find out what matters most to you using this one weird trick:

Suppose you were to attend your own funeral — what would you most hope to hear when people stood up to deliver your eulogy? Would you admire the person they're describing? Would the things they single out as significant about you and the type of person you were be the things you would want to be remembered for? What would you rather they said instead?

Of course, by the time everyone is hearing about who you were and what you did at your funeral, it's a bit late for you to do much about it. But you can start now. Identifying your values — the things that are important to you — provides you with your personal signposts to meaning and a sense of purpose. Knowing and living your values more consistently and deliberately will guide your choices, helping you to shape your future, as well as get the most out of now. It will:

- set your life's priorities
- give you a rule of thumb by which to make plans and decisions
- give you an incentive to keep going when the going gets tough
- help you to identify what's important if your circumstances change
- boost your mental fitness, self-confidence and general wellbeing
- clarify your short-term goals
- clarify your long-term goals.

By identifying your values and striving to live by them, you can derive a deeper satisfaction from your life than you will achieve by focusing upon transient 'happiness' and pleasures. Living a values-driven life is the pursuit of eudaimonic happiness (discussed in Chapter 5) — it's your ticket off the hedonic treadmill.

Human beings are best placed to flourish when they feel connected to something larger than themselves. Our caveman ancestors, when they were thriving, will have felt part of the tribe, working towards the common goal of the tribe's wellbeing. Down through the ages, people have found meaning in making common cause with others, such as where they have shared a political or religious purpose.

As we saw in the previous chapter, much of our wellbeing arises from the connections we have with other people. Partly, this is because we derive our sense of purpose from the ways in which we contribute to the groups of which we are a part. An easy win when you're looking for significance and merit in your actions is to perform acts of kindness. Similarly, if we share a sense of common purpose with others — if society becomes a joint project — we can derive meaning from performing pro-social acts. Research out of Harvard's happiness laboratory also suggests that journalling in as much detail as possible about something meaningful that happened to you or that you did for another is also an effective way to put more fuel in your emotional tank. And those of us lucky enough to be working in a job where we feel as though we're making a difference derive from it a reason to get out of bed in the morning and get stuck in.

You don't have to imagine your own funeral to get a sense of what it is that matters to you in life. All you have to do is think deeply and honestly about what it is that you love doing, what your passions are (to use a much-overused word). Imagine you had a 'bonus' day, a single day all to yourself, when you would wake refreshed, full of energy and with no demands or obligations: what would you spend the day doing? What is it that you wish you were doing apart from what you're obliged to do right now?

What it all means

Numerous studies have shown that a sense of meaning improves the quality — and perhaps even the quantity — of people's lives, especially in older people. A lack of this sense of meaning is also strongly associated with substance abuse, depression and suicide.

What we're talking about here is not 'the meaning of life' (which has been the subject of enquiry for every major religion and philosophy in the history of the world). It's rather a sense of meaning *in* life. We need a meaning because we are hardwired to look for one.

It's in the nature of our intelligence that we seek patterns and significance in everything, and our own lives are not exempt from this interrogation. We derive meaning in our lives from our sense of purpose — what our actions are *for*, what makes them seem significant and worthwhile. A sense of purpose can be 'an anchor we throw into the future', as the founder and director of the Center for Meaning and Purpose at Colorado State University, Professor Michael Steger, so beautifully puts it. Like an anchor, it provides focus and direction. If we're experiencing momentary turmoil and confusion in the present, it provides something fixed and steady that we can pull towards.

Having a purpose can also contribute to having a sense of a coherent self — a sense that our past, present and future actions make sense together. When we're young, when we're inhabiting our 'experiencing self', we're often too busy being in the thick of it to search for meaning. But as we age, and especially when we reach an advanced age, we more and more inhabit the 'remembering self', and it is a great comfort if the actions that we reflect upon seem meaningful and significant.

What drives you?

In the previous chapter, we touched on the difference between extrinsic and intrinsic motivation. We saw that people are more motivated when their reason for doing what they do comes from within themselves (a pull factor), rather than merely being imposed by others (a push factor — like your boss setting you a deadline, or social expectations). If you find what you're doing personally rewarding, you'll be far more motivated to start, you'll persist even when the task is difficult, and you'll work harder at it. And you are far more likely to find what you're doing personally rewarding if the task you're tackling aligns with your life goals and values.

Of course, doing what's important to you is not always the same thing as doing what's easy or pleasurable. Living according to your values can put you in some uncomfortable positions. But that's what eudaimonic happiness is all about: it's the ability to keep your eyes on the prize despite the discomfort. In psychology, we talk about 'decision points' as the daily forks in the road we encounter where it is possible to decide to take the path that leads you closer to being the person you want your reputation to reflect and be in the world, or to take the path that leads you further away from being that person.

Too few of us spend enough time figuring out our values. The things that matter to us aren't always obvious until we're forced to choose, or when we lose them. We take much of what we value for granted. Take your health, for example. When we're young, we feel bulletproof, and are unlikely to rank health high on a list of values, as it just doesn't occur to us that it's something we might have to work to preserve. For most of us, that comes later, unless we suffer some kind of life event where we're left with little else but our health: you crash your beloved car, for example, but you escape unscathed. You lose your life's savings, but you're still fit and healthy.

A quick look at your values

Values are your heart's deepest desires about how you want to behave as a human being. Values are not about what you want to get or achieve — they are about how you want to behave or act. Values are the things you aspire to live and demonstrate; they are not necessarily the things that come easiest to us. For example, I place value on compassion, but based on my natural tendencies towards striving for achievement and a relatively hard first 30 years of life, my default setting is to be quite a judgemental person, with limited empathy. This means I have to deliberately work to cultivate compassion. So, while some values will be easier

202

to demonstrate than others, don't confuse your values with your personality or what comes easiest to you.

There are hundreds of different values, but below you'll find a list of the most common ones adapted from the work of Australian psychologist Dr Russ Harris. Not all of them will be relevant to you. Keep in mind there are no such things as 'right' or 'wrong' values in an objective sense. While our values are influenced by culture and upbringing, they are fundamentally subjective. As Dr Harris says, it's a bit like our taste in pizza. If you prefer Hawaiian but I can't stand pineapple and love olives, that doesn't mean that my taste in pizza is right and yours is wrong. It just means we have different tastes. Similarly, we may have different values.

With this in mind, read through the list below and write a letter next to each value: V = Very important, Q = Quite important, and N = Not so important. Make sure to score at least 10 factors as Very important.

1. Acceptance: to be open to and accepting of myself, others, life, etc
2. Adventure: to be adventurous; to actively seek, create or explore novel or stimulating experiences
3. Assertiveness: to respectfully stand up for my rights and request what I want
4. Authenticity: to be authentic, genuine, real; to be true to myself
5. Beauty: to appreciate, create, nurture or cultivate beauty in myself, others, the environment, etc
6. Caring: to be caring towards myself, others, the environment, etc
7. Challenge: to keep challenging myself to grow, learn, improve

8. Compassion: to act with kindness towards those who are suffering

9. Connection: to engage fully in whatever I am doing, and be fully present with others

10. Contribution: to contribute, help, assist or make a positive difference to myself or others

11. Conformity: to be respectful and obedient of rules and obligations

12. Cooperation: to be cooperative and collaborative with others

13. Courage: to be courageous or brave; to persist in the face of fear, threat or difficulty

14. Creativity: to be creative or innovative

15. Curiosity: to be curious, open-minded and interested; to explore and discover

16. Encouragement: to encourage and reward behaviour that I value in myself or other

17. Equality: to treat others as equal to myself, and vice versa

18. Excitement: to seek, create and engage in activities that are exciting, stimulating or thrilling

19. Fairness: to be fair to myself or others

20. Fitness: to maintain or improve my fitness; to look after my physical and mental health and wellbeing

21. Flexibility: to adjust and adapt readily to changing circumstances

22. Freedom: to live freely; to choose how I live and behave, or help others do likewise

23. Friendliness: to be friendly, companionable or agreeable towards others

24. Forgiveness: to be forgiving towards myself or others

25. Fun: to be fun-loving; to seek, create and engage in fun-filled activities

26. Generosity: to be generous, sharing and giving, to myself or other

27. Gratitude: to be grateful for and appreciative of the positive aspects of myself, others and life

28. Honesty: to be honest, truthful and sincere with myself and others

29. Humour: to see and appreciate the humorous side of life

30. Humility: to be humble or modest; to let my achievements speak for themselves

31. Industry: to be industrious, hard-working and dedicated

32. Independence: to be self-supportive, and choose my own way of doing things

33. Intimacy: to open up, reveal and share myself in my close personal relationships

34. Justice: to uphold justice and fairness

35. Kindness: to be kind, compassionate, considerate, nurturing or caring towards myself or others

36. Love: to act lovingly or affectionately towards myself or other

37. Mindfulness: to be conscious of, open to and curious about my here-and-now experience

38. Order: to be orderly and organised

39. Open-mindedness: to consider ideas, see things from other's perspectives and weigh evidence fairly

40. Patience: to wait calmly for what I want

41. Persistence: to continue resolutely, despite problems or difficulties

42. Pleasure: to create and give pleasure to myself or others

43. Power: to strongly influence or wield authority over others (e.g. taking charge, leading and organising)

44. Reciprocity: to build relationships in which there is a fair balance of giving and taking
45. Respect: to be respectful towards myself or others; to be polite, considerate and show positive regard
46. Responsibility: to be responsible and accountable for my action
47. Romance: to be romantic; to display and express love or strong affection
48. Safety: to secure, protect or ensure safety of myself or others
49. Self-awareness: to know myself and be aware of my own thoughts, feelings and actions
50. Self-care: to look after my health and wellbeing, and get my needs met
51. Self-development: to keep growing, advancing or improving in knowledge, skills, character or life experience
52. Self-control: to act in accordance with my own ideals without giving in to whim
53. Sensuality: to create, explore and enjoy experiences that stimulate the five senses
54. Sexuality: to explore or express my sexuality
55. Spirituality: to connect with things bigger than myself
56. Skilfulness: to continually practise and improve my skills, and apply myself fully when using them
57. Supportiveness: to be supportive, helpful, encouraging and available to myself or others.
58. Trust: to be trustworthy; to be loyal, faithful, sincere and reliable.
59. Insert your own unlisted value here: _____

_____

60. Insert your own unlisted value here: _____

_____

Once you've marked each value as V, Q, N (Very, Quite or Not so important), go through all the Vs and select the top six that are *most* important to you. Write down those six values below, to remind yourself this is what you want to stand for as a human being.

Now score each of the below values according to how consistently/frequently you are demonstrating them. A ten equals a fully lived value that is demonstrated at every opportunity. A zero designates a value that you aspire to, but have not yet demonstrated.

1. _____

2. _____

3. _____

4. _____

5. _____

6. _____

Once you have scored your values, consider the daily opportunities you have to more deliberately live your lower-scored values and further play to those you already embody. Where, when, and with whom might you have the chance to demonstrate these values?

Scripting your life

As previously mentioned, our values are often aspirational. Even while we're falling short in a number of ways, we can have a pretty clear idea of who and what we want to be. The story we're living need not be the story we live in the future, even in the near future. To change our lives, often all that's necessary is to change the script. We can become authors of our own destiny, by writing ourselves a character and then striving to play that role. Here's an example:

I can certainly be a knob, as illustrated by the following exchange I had a few years back, when going through domestic airport security:

Aviation Security Officer: Do you have a laptop in your bag, sir?

Me: No, only a Surface Pro.

Aviation Security Officer: You'll have to take that out, sir.

Me: But it's a tablet. One of the reasons I purchased this was so that I wouldn't have to take it out of my bag when going through airport security. This is the only airport in the country that asks me to take it out of my bag.

Aviation Security Officer: I'm sorry, sir, but this is an airport committed to security and I need you to take it out of your bag.

Me [as I grudgingly take it out of my bag for the scan]: Are you suggesting other airports aren't concerned about security?

*

Almost immediately after this exchange, I felt embarrassed about my behaviour. The security person was simply trying to follow the procedure for scanning electronics. I had responded as though removing a tablet from my bag was a major hardship and affront to my dignity!

I've noticed that I often behave as a less desirable version of myself when travelling. I've come to think of this character as

Special Paul. Special Paul gets unhelpfully annoyed and frustrated at the slightest provocation and then proceeds to act entitled, special, judgemental and petty.

Special Paul is just one of the many versions of the person I am and can be. In fact, we are often different versions of ourselves at different times of day, in different situations, and with different people. There are certainly many ways in which I'm different when at the airport, at work and at home.

These different versions of ourselves generally develop when learning to navigate the terrain of our childhood and adolescence. The behaviours that define these various characters become habits because they have assisted us in some way in the past. Yet many no longer serve us as well as they once did.

Before I emerged from prison I had to start recalibrating my aggression to be appropriate in the everyday social situations I would encounter once released. I had grown up in an environment where the way to impress my mates was to be tough, uncompromising and aggressive. The Staunch Paul character who developed in this environment actually suited prison pretty well, where the only way to avoid being preyed upon and victimised was to convince potential predators that I would meet fire with even greater fire. But Staunch Paul would struggle when he was released and had to deal with ordinary people for whom physical and even verbal aggression was a social no-no. Staunch Paul wasn't going to get me far on the outside.

Fortunately, we can choose to rewrite the script for these characters and present as better versions of ourselves. This is quite a liberating idea: that we can choose to be someone other than who we feel we are or who we become at our worst. My friend and colleague Dr Paul Englert's research into 'Future

Selves' development suggests that a prerequisite to becoming someone better is the ability to imagine future versions of yourself. If you can't imagine who you might grow into, your personal development will be delayed or derailed.

Staunch Paul was written out of the script and replaced by Stoic Paul long before I left prison. Staunch Paul was focused on other people's opinions of him, while Stoic Paul was focused on controlling himself and his responses to challenging situations. It was Stoic Paul who got parole.

While we're all different in our own way, psychology recognises several common default characters that often emerge when people are at a low emotional ebb or have been triggered in some way. A first useful step in being a better version of ourselves is to identify our less desirable default. I first came across some of the most common of these defaults in the work of Dr Ben Palmer. These are listed in the table below, on the left-hand side, with potential aspirating alternatives on the right.

Attacker ⟷	Coach
Avoider ⟷	Engager
Sniper ⟷	Supporter
Saboteur ⟷	Problem solver
Fortune teller ⟷	Fortune seeker
Child ⟷	Adult
Victim ⟷	Strategist
Hero ⟷	Collaborator
Judge ⟷	Acceptor
Pollyanna ⟷	Pragmatist
Super-agreeable ⟷	Authentic
Gloomy Gus ⟷	Harmonious

Once you have identified your default character or characters (and yes, there can be more than one, as they are often situational or appear in combinations), the next step is to choose to present as a more aspirational alternative. As can be seen in the table above, the Attacker can become the Coach, the Avoider the Engager, the Judge the Acceptor, and the Super-agreeable the Authentic.

Instead of Special Paul, I now choose to show up as Cool Paul when travelling. Unlike Special Paul, Cool Paul is completely chill when faced with minor inconveniences, and even anticipates and avoids potential frustrations. Hell, Cool Paul takes his Surface Pro out of his bag before he's even asked to do it!

Because I know Special Paul often appears when I am travelling, I can pre-emptively choose to assume the character of Cool Paul instead. At the outset, this requires conscious consideration, but over time this will just become my new habitual way of behaving when travelling.

To identify your default character, think back to a situation that really didn't go as well as it could have, in part because of your behaviour. Anything that prompts an unpleasant emotional experience to think about should work. Write about this situation in a short , narrative/story, in the third person (i.e. rather than 'I was thinking …', write: 'Paul was thinking …'), which will help to create emotional distance and increase objectivity. Although one short story might do, the gold standard is to write about three different situations with less-than-optimal outcomes, to better understand the patterns of your behaviour. (This is also a great technique to help you move on and stop dwelling about a negative experience, too.)

Read back through your narratives to identify common character themes, such as losing your temper when tired, overreacting when hungry, or being sarcastic with co-workers when you feel they are not pulling their weight. Also look for clues regarding the types of situations in which certain characters appear. For example, the judge appears when at home in the evening or the sniper at work during meetings. The common elements of these situations could be reflected in who, what and/ or where triggers the response. This insight will allow you to predict when you need to pre-emptively start playing the part of your aspirational character.

You might find it helpful to label both your default and aspirational characters (like Special Paul and Cool Paul). These labels should reflect the essence of who we are being when we are at our worst and best respectively. If these character labels allow you to laugh a little at yourself, even better.

Showing up as a better version of yourself is a journey of progress not perfection. There will be times when your default character appears despite your best intentions, but over time you can more effectively rewrite the script and behave as a better version of yourself. I choose to be Cool Paul, and every time he is present I get more fuel in my emotional tank.

Game designer and author Professor Jane McGonigal, in line with her 'gameful' approach to creating personal change and enhancing wellbeing, conceptualises this approach as 'adopting a secret identity'. Her research suggests that those who do so report feeling stronger and braver, being better understood by their friends and family, and being happier even when tackling the toughest challenges of their lives. Ask yourself: who is it you'd rather be?

BECOMING A BETTER VERSION OF YOURSELF

You can choose to become a better version of yourself, through identifying your emotional defaults and choosing an aspirational alternative.

Once you can recognise your defaults and have an aspirational alternative to aim for, identify the situations in which your default appears and pre-emptively play the part of your aspirational character instead.

Becoming a better version of yourself is a journey of progress, not perfection. You won't get it right every time, and your goal should be getting better, not being good.

Back to nature

One connection to something greater than ourselves that our Stone Age ancestors enjoyed, but that we have all but severed in our busy modern lives, is our connection with the natural world. We spend a great deal of our time inside vehicles, or buildings with artificial lighting. We can go for days on end without encountering the natural world. There's plenty of evidence to suggest that this is not a healthy state of affairs. Indeed, research suggests that reconnecting with nature can promote mental fitness, reduce anxiety and help us to recover from trauma more quickly and completely. There are even organisations and individuals that offer 'ecotherapy' as a formal treatment for psychological disorders.

Being in nature — on a beach, in the bush, even in your own backyard — provides a rich sensory experience, and serves to draw the focus of your attention to the present moment. There's no single effective way of reconnecting with the natural world, but try to find ways of including interaction with nature into your working day, and make time for longer, more sustained experiences (over a long weekend, say) as often as you can. It's a matter of experimenting to find an activity that works for you. Here are some ideas:

- Gardening, especially community gardening, where you have the added benefit of connecting with others.
- Bush walking and/or 'forest bathing', as it is called: simply being in a wooded area where the sights, sounds, smells and textures absorb your attention.
- Exercising outdoors (instead of inside, at the gym). You can build in an element of altruism by 'plogging' (combining jogging with picking up rubbish). Take a bag with you and pick up litter as you walk or run.
- Animal experiences. Interacting with animals has proven benefits for the elderly and isolated, children on the autism spectrum or with behavioural difficulties, and people suffering from major mental illness such as schizophrenia and bipolar disorder. The beneficial effects have become accepted to the point where 'animal-assisted therapy' has become a thing.
- Adventure activities, such as tramping, surfing, mountain biking, skiing or ocean swimming. Activities that introduce an element of risk help to recalibrate our stress-response mechanisms by engaging all of our systems in the way they have evolved to operate.
- Night experiences. We city-based humans routinely avoid being outside in the dark, but going for a walk at night or simply standing outside and stargazing can be both stimulating and soothing.
- Looking out a window for 30 seconds. Go on: try this one right now!

Meaning self-assessment

This self-assessment will give you an indication of the extent to which the meaning domain is a priority work-on for you, or an area in which more deliberate focus will move you closer to your mental fitness potential. Answer these questions according to what is most true and accurate for you. Don't overthink them — go with the first answer that comes to mind.

Question	Very slightly or not at all (1)	A little (2)	Moderately (3)	Quite a bit (4)	Extremely (5)
To what extent have you felt a sense of purpose today or within the past week?					
To what extent have you confronted a challenging situation and done what you knew to be the right thing today or within the past week?					
To what extent have you made a meaningful contribution today or within the past week?					
To what extent have you chosen not to behave today or within the past week in a way that is inconsistent with who you want to be in the world?					
To what extent do you generally feel you have a sense of direction in your life?					

Total score: _____

You should get a number between 5 and 25. A higher score indicates greater levels of meaning.

Finding your meaning

Human beings are best placed to flourish when they feel they are part of something greater than themselves.

A key to finding a sense of meaning is identifying your values.

You can 'script your life', creating a role for yourself in stressful situations where you live up to your values and be the best version of yourself.

Often people can find a sense of meaning through finding a common cause with others.

The natural world is somewhere a sense of connection to something bigger than yourself is readily available.

11

Accomplishment

One of the ways in which we build mental fitness is by accomplishing things. This doesn't mean overcoming seemingly insurmountable obstacles — or, at least, not entirely. An accomplishment is any situation in which you successfully exercise willpower to achieve an objective.

Willpower is like a muscle: it gets stronger the more you use it, and it's repetition rather than the scale of any given accomplishment that builds endurance. Everywhere you look, there are opportunities to exercise your willpower. You walk past a sink full of dirty dishes on your way to sit down in your favourite armchair. Well, do the damn dishes, *then* sit down in your favourite armchair! You don't want to, and you experience a slight feeling of irritation at the thought of doing dishes when all you want to do is sit down, but once you've made yourself do it, you will feel a sense of satisfaction and have strengthened your willpower muscle.

Make things harder for yourself. Take the stairs instead of the lift. Walk to work instead of driving. Take the lid off a jar with your left hand instead of your right (or the other way around if you're left-handed). There's no shortage of small tasks that you can accomplish, each of which will be a little victory, another demonstration of your self-efficacy.

In the dishwashing example I've just given, you were faced with a choice. There was instant gratification available to you (sinking into your favourite armchair *right now*!), or there was delayed, and greater, satisfaction available to you (doing the dishes, *then* sinking into your favourite armchair, without the need to do the dishes hanging over you). The capacity that you exercised when you decided to do the dishes was what we call 'willpower'. Willpower is different from self-control. I'd define willpower as the internal energy you harness to act. Self-control, on the other hand, is the ability to resist an impulse.

Like most useful human capacities, willpower and self-control have been a popular subject for study by psychologists for a very long time. In 1972, a team of researchers led by Walter Mischel of Stanford University conducted the classic experiment into delayed gratification that has become known as 'the marshmallow test'. In this, preschool-aged children were offered a marshmallow (or a pretzel, if the child preferred: the fact that the test is known as 'the marshmallow test' is an indicator of your average child's opinion of the relative desirability of marshmallows and pretzels). Each child was told that the researcher was going to leave the room for a while. The child had a choice: they could either ring a bell, whereupon the researcher would return and the child would be allowed to eat the marshmallow immediately, or they could wait patiently until the researcher returned, whereupon they would receive two marshmallows.

Some rang the bell and settled for a single marshmallow. Others exercised self-control and waited (for roughly 15 minutes) and were rewarded with two marshmallows. And the fascinating thing was that when the study group was followed up a decade later, those who had successfully delayed gratification proved to be more competent teenagers (as reported by their parents). A few years later again, the same group was found to be higher achievers at academic tasks.

Although this experiment has been questioned in more recent times (other researchers have had difficulties replicating its results), we can take comfort from the fact that similar findings arose from a study conducted as part of New Zealand's own Dunedin longitudinal study, which has followed a group of 1000 individuals from birth. Those who considered themselves to have good self-control as children (and whose self-assessments were corroborated by teachers and parents) proved to be higher achievers as teenagers and adults. Self-control seemed to correlate with better self-esteem, better academic performance, lower incidence of obesity and drug and alcohol problems, and better relationship skills.

Walter 'Marshmallow' Mischel proposed an explanation for the presence or absence of willpower in terms of 'hot' and 'cool' reactive systems. The 'hot' system, he postulated, was impulsive and emotional. The 'cool' system was cognitive and deliberate. Some people, he suggested, tended to be better at engaging the 'cool' system than others, who responded 'hotly'.

Well, by now this should sound highly familiar. In this book, we have conceptualised human beings as comprising both systems — both the emotional and the coolly rational. If you read the work of Dr Ceri Evans, the All Blacks' psych-skills consultant, you'll see the same idea but with different labels. To Evans, we possess two sets of responses: the fast, emotional and impulsive (which he calls the 'red' brain), and the slower, more deliberate and considered (which he calls the 'blue' brain). Intriguingly, the two styles of response seem to correlate with the activity of the left and the right brain, with the right brain (predominantly associated with pessimism and threat detection) managing the 'red' brain functions and the left brain managing 'blue' brain functions.

We are capable of using either response system, or both in balanced combination. This is reflected in the practice of some sports psychologists of broadening this red/blue brain metaphor to include the green brain. Green is for go. The green brain reflects when we are sitting at the top of the stress performance curve with the perfect balance of emotional engagement and intellectual effectiveness. I find this way of thinking more consistent with the modern idea that we are our emotions rather than that they are something to be resisted and repressed. The centaur, rather than the rider and the horse remember?

We are all susceptible to being overtaken or overwhelmed by our emotions and impulses at times, but there are effective strategies for shifting from the red to the green brain in situations of high emotional intensity. These are covered in Chapter 13, which looks at the Big Four mental skills taught to Special Forces operatives to help them manage stressors like the intensity of gun battles. Fortunately, in situations of relatively low emotional intensity, we can exercise our willpower.

The cookie jar

I've already mentioned David Goggins in this book. He's such an exemplar of mental toughness that 'Goggins' has become a verb meaning pushing oneself to the extreme. If you haven't heard of him, he's a bestselling author who is absolutely legendary for using a mind-over-matter approach to realising our potential.

To me, he's an outlier example of what it's possible to achieve through sheer willpower. As a young man, he was determined to become a pararescue operative in the US military. He hadn't been any great shakes at school, and it took him three attempts to pass the aptitude test necessary to enter the pararescue training course.

Then, one week into the training course itself, he suffered a collapse and was diagnosed with sickle cell trait, a blood abnormality that compromises its ability to shift oxygen around the body, particularly when you're under physical stress. Once recovered, he returned to the course but was told he'd have to start all over again.

Bugger that, he decided, and instead did a five-year stint in the Air Force's Special Forces wing. He left the Air Force in 1999, having decided he would prefer to train as a Sea, Air and Land operative of the US Navy (the famous Navy SEALs). Trouble was, he was way overweight: he tipped the scales at nearly 150 kilograms, where the preferred weight of SEAL trainee intakes was half that. In less than three months, he managed to shed over 50 kilograms, and was accepted into the course.

The SEAL course is one of the most demanding in the world. In one phase — the so-called Basic Underwater Demolition, culminating in the evocatively named 'Hell Week' — recruits are made to undergo an almost unbelievably physically demanding programme interspersed with assaults on their mental and emotional fortitude by their instructors. During Hell Week, SEAL candidates participate in five and a half days of continuous training. Each candidate runs more than 320 kilometres, sleeps at most four hours during the entire week, and does physical training for more than 20 hours per day. Goggins didn't complete his first two attempts due to injuries, but passed on his third.

Having graduated as a SEAL, he served in Iraq. In 2004, some of his former special forces buddies were killed in a helicopter crash in Afghanistan. Goggins resolved to raise money to support their families, and hit upon ultra-distance running as the way to do it. He applied to enter the Badwater Ultramarathon, a 217-kilometre nightmare of a race that passes through Death Valley in Arizona and climbs high up the flanks of Mount Whitney, the highest mountain in the US outside Alaska. The Badwater is an invitation-only race: in order to be considered, the organisers told Goggins, he'd have to complete another couple of ultramarathons first.

So he did, completing 100 miles (161 kilometres) at San Diego in 19 hours, and placing ninth out of the 23 who finished the HURT100 in Hawai'i, managing to squeeze in a conventional marathon as well. In 2006, he was duly invited to take part in the Badwater, and placed fifth in a field comprising people who had trained all their lives to compete in events such as this.

Since then, he has raced and placed highly in many more ultra-distance events, including ultra-triathlons and cycle races — despite being diagnosed along the way with a congenital heart defect that should have prevented him reaching more than 75 per cent of his physical potential.

It probably makes you feel tired just reading a potted summary of his achievements; if you want to feel inspired by what is possible with willpower and mental and physical toughness, read his book, *Can't Hurt Me*.

One of my favourite ideas from *Can't Hurt Me* is the cookie jar. Goggins remembered that, as a child, his mother always managed to stock the cookie jar, no matter how hard times were. As a reward, he was able to choose one or two cookies. He writes that it was like 'a mini treasure hunt', and how each time he felt intensely thankful for what might be seen as a very simple gift.

When it came to developing his own mental skills programme, he remembered the jar, and how it had made him feel. He writes:

> I used that concept to stuff a new kind of Cookie Jar. Inside it were all my past victories ... We all have a cookie jar inside us, because life, being what it is, has always tested us. Even if you're feeling low and beat down by life right now, I guarantee you can think of a time or two when you overcame odds and tasted success. It doesn't have to be a big victory either. It can be something small.

That's the important point here. Your victories don't have to be things like the time you ran an ultramarathon even though your shins were fractured, or getting through Hell Week on the third attempt despite having a blood defect that put you at a significant disadvantage. Your victories can be small things. In the Navy SEALs, according to Admiral William H. McRaven in his book *Make Your Bed*, they tell you that the very first thing you should do when you get up in the morning is to make your bed tidily. That way, no matter what happens for the rest of the day, you've had your first success. No matter how bad things turn, you've accomplished one thing. It's a small victory, but it ensures that the cookie jar isn't empty.

When I was in prison, I saw the simple truth of this all around me. Prisoners are often obsessively tidy in how they keep their cells. When you consider how little control they have over their own lives — prison is designed to keep you as close to helpless as adult humans can be — this impulse makes sense. It's a way of controlling your environment, of asserting yourself, of reminding yourself that you can positively effect change and influence your life.

Think of Viktor Frankl in the concentration camp. He managed to keep hope alive because no matter what was done to him, he was determined to hold onto his sense of self-efficacy. Think, too, of the morale-boosting activities that François Raynal, the castaway we mentioned in Chapter 9, encouraged his companions to engage in: learning languages, making and building things to improve their standard of living. Each little accomplishment was a reminder that they could effect positive change in their own lives, even when their situation seemed hopeless. It was a victory, a cookie. It put fuel in the tank.

Making a list

We can divide the kinds of objectives that you have into two kinds: *identity* goals and *outcome* goals. Identity goals are the types of things that move you towards becoming the person you want to be (such as living to your values, as we discussed in the previous chapter, or building your strengths and capabilities). They are the kinds of things that give your life meaning. And let's face it: if you aren't living to your values or not working towards those identity goals, pretty much anything else you accomplish in life will be hollow.

The other kind of goals, outcome goals, is the stuff that populates your five-year plans and day-to-day task list. You don't have a list of your day's tasks? Well, start now! Take a piece of paper and write down what you want to get done before the end of the day. If the day is over, write down what you want to get done tomorrow. And when you get up in the morning, make your bed, pick up your list and start work on crossing things off straight away.

Some people dislike to-do lists because they see them as a self-deceiving means of avoiding what most needs to be done by justifying the distraction of less important tasks. I personally love them and avoid this concern by making sure not all items on my to-do list are given equal priority. These days, I make lists of stuff that I am going to make myself do, and I complete these tasks in order of priority, according to their urgency and importance. Those that are both urgent and important get top priority. Each item that I cross off gives me a little bit of pleasure — a little more fuel in the tank. I love the feeling you get when you're crossing off priority item after priority item on your list and you just know you're crushing it. As Navy SEAL legend, retired Lieutenant-Commander John 'Jocko' Willink, would say, prioritise and execute.

Better never stops

Another important component of Seligman's Accomplishment domain is 'mastery', which concerns the focused process of getting better at a skill or gaining knowledge in an area through persistent effort. When you think of top-level athletes, you'd imagine that they're 100 per cent focused on being the best all the time, wouldn't you? Take the All Blacks, for example. You'd expect all the talk in their dressing room and in their training camps to be about being the best in the world.

Wrong!

A little while back, I had the privilege of working with a rugby franchise, and former All Blacks coach Graham Henry was involved. I heard him addressing the players one day, and he used a phrase that has stayed with me. 'Better,' he said, 'never stops.'

I could see the genius of that straight away. From my perspective it does two things. First, it makes the pursuit of excellence and mastery a process rather than a goal. And second, it makes your own improvement the measure of success. When this is the measure, the things that most matter are under your control, such as your own training, learning and effort. And the things that we often focus on that we can't control, such as other people and how good they are, don't matter as much.

If you are focused on being the best at something, then there's a point at which you might actually achieve that goal. When the All Blacks win the Webb Ellis Cup, they're world champions, the best. What's left? To stay there? To become statistically the best All Black team of all time? Suppose they accomplish that, too. What then? There's sort of nowhere to go.

But if you're focused on getting *better*, that's a never-ending journey. You might win the Webb Ellis Cup, but you can still get better, because better never stops. You can be measurably the best of all time, but you don't stop trying to improve, because better never stops.

You don't have to be an elite athlete, or an athlete at all, to apply this to yourself and your own attempts to get better at what you do. No matter how much improvement you show, you can still improve, because better never stops.

And more importantly still, if you are solely focused on your own personal improvement — getting better — then your performance relative to others becomes less important to you. Your only benchmark is where you were yesterday in comparison to where you are today, and where you will be tomorrow. And as long as tomorrow's version of you is just a little bit better than yesterday's, that's what it means to progress, that's what it means to be on the path. Win, lose or draw, you can take satisfaction out of any improvement you've made because that's your mission: to get better.

You can probably see at once how liberating this mentality is: you don't have to be the best at anything — all that counts is where you are on your personal continuum of getting better. You might line up for a marathon and come last by some distance. If you were focused on being the best, this would come as quite a blow to you. But if you've clocked up a *personal* best, your placing will be irrelevant. You'll probably be more satisfied than the winner of the marathon, who is five minutes slower than last time they raced.

Better never stops.

Dreams into goals

Most of us have dreams. Some of them can seem nearly unattainable from our immediate vantage point. Looking at the summit of a mountain you're about to climb, it seems so high, so far away.

When I first decided that I would like to be someone who had run a marathon, it was a struggle to run 2.2 kilometres. 42.2 kilometres certainly didn't look any closer after my very first training run! But not even David Goggins always expects to realise all his dreams and ambitions as soon as he comes up with them. Like all achievers, he's adept at mapping the path to his goal and breaking it down into practical stages.

When working with clients I often talk about 'ultimate' and 'proximate' goals. Ultimate goals are the big things you finally want to achieve. Proximate goals are the smaller steps that close the gap from where you are to the ultimate goal. When goals seem too big or far away, focus on the proximate goals that will get you there.

You climb mountains through a series of proximate goals that involve putting one foot in front of another, and with each step you take, the summit comes closer. Every step is an achievement, a cookie in the jar. It is by repetitively tackling small, realisable proximate goals that our lofty ultimate goals come within our grasp. As the full quote goes, Rome wasn't built in a day, but bricks were laid every hour.

That's SMART

A popular way of setting goals has been to analyse them according to the so-called SMART template. SMART is — you guessed it — an acronym for:

Specific: What exactly do you hope to achieve? What is the specific goal?

Measurable: How will you be able to gauge your progress towards your ultimate goal, and your eventual success? What will be the milestones and proximate goals along the way?

Achievable: Is your goal something that you have the personal skills, time, energy and resources to accomplish? If not, can you acquire those skills, deprioritise other commitments or get the resources required to make your goal achievable?

Relevant: Does achieving this goal advance you towards your larger, longer-term aims (living up to a value, advancing your career, growing into the type of person you want to be, etc)?

Time-bound: When do you hope to have achieved this goal? What are the timelines for the proximate goals that will take you there?

*

As an example, let's look at how this applied to my own goal of getting a black belt in judo:

Specific: I want to get a black belt in judo.

Measurable: This will involve progressing through all the belts and associated requirements leading up to brown belt. Once I am a brown belt I will need to defeat a sufficient number of brown and/or black belts in competition in order to get enough points to qualify for my black-belt grading. (The real beasts, such as my friend and judo hero, Olympian Tim Slyfield, don't need to complete a black-belt grading because they win their black belt in competition by beating five others of the same grade or higher in a row when they are brown belts. On two separate occasions I made it to four wins and then lost on the fifth fight!)

Achievable: I was able to train regularly at a top dojo, I was a very competitive fighter and, once a brown belt, was able to attend every competition in the calendar to gain the points required for my black belt.

Relevant: This was a way in which I could feel I was striving to live up to my potential. It was also a flow activity of great enjoyment.

Time-bound: Specific New Zealand Judo timeframes for how long you had to stay in each grade before your next grading, for each belt proceeding black belt. Using this as my timeline: National black-belt grading in 2014.

WHAT IS A SMART GOAL YOU CAN SET FOR YOURSELF TO PROACTIVELY BOOST YOUR MENTAL FITNESS?

Now it's your go. Looking at your self-assessment scores across this and the preceding four PERMA-H chapters, what is a SMART goal you can set for yourself to proactively boost your mental fitness? Look at the tips and techniques in the associated chapter and choose one thing only to focus on.

Specific: What exactly do you hope to achieve? What is the specific goal?	
Measurable: How will you be able to gauge your progress and success?	
Achievable: Do you have the personal skills, time, energy, and resources to accomplish this goal? If not, what needs to happen first?	
Relevant: What does this goal mean to you? Why is it important?	
Time-bound: When do you hope to have achieved this goal? What are the smaller steps/proximate goals that will take you there? What are the timelines for these?	

Accomplishment self-assessment

This self-assessment will give you an indication of the extent to which the accomplishment domain is a priority work-on for you, or an area in which more deliberate focus will move you closer to your mental fitness potential. Answer these questions according to what is most true and accurate for you. Don't overthink them — go with the first answer that comes to mind.

Question	Very slightly or not at all (1)	A little (2)	Moderately (3)	Quite a bit (4)	Extremely (5)
To what extent have you improved yourself or your skills in some way today or within the past week?					
To what extent have you learnt something today or within the past week?					
To what extent have you maximised your time today or within the past week?					

To what extent have you progressed towards a meaningful goal today or within the past week?					
To what extent do you feel you are making progress towards accomplishing your goals?					

Total score: _____

You should get a number between 5 and 25. A higher score indicates greater levels of accomplishment.

A sense of accomplishment

A key ingredient of mental fitness is drawing upon your accomplishments — big and small.

Accomplishments often come from exercising willpower.

Willpower is like a muscle: regularly exercising it strengthens it.

The pursuit of mastery and getting better builds mental fitness.

Goals can be more readily achieved by applying the SMART framework.

12

Mental Toughness — When the Rubber Meets the Road

You lose your job. Your relationship falls apart. Someone close to you is diagnosed with a terminal illness. A loved one dies. You have an accident and lose the use of a limb, perhaps more than one. Your house burns down. Your city is devastated by an earthquake ...

One of the most glaring falsehoods in the whole notion that we ought to be in our comfort zone most, if not all of the time is that the universe has scant regard for what we want from it. Even the most blessed life is a series of ups and downs. You might think that there are people who seem to get what they want out of life without obvious effort, but it's been said many times that ducks don't see the effort other ducks are putting into swimming, because all that leg-pedalling goes on under the surface.

But in every single case, the difference between people who are flourishing and people who seem less fortunate is their ability to cope with reversals in their fortunes. It's like US motor magnate Henry Ford's observation when someone told him that he was a lucky man. 'You're right,' he is supposed to have replied. 'But, you know, the funny thing is that the harder I work, the luckier I become.' There's another saying, too (attributed to German philosopher Friedrich Nietzsche): that which doesn't kill me makes me stronger. This is only true if we have a properly adjusted attitude to setbacks and pitfalls.

As we seek to fulfil our potential, we will inevitably fail from time to time. Since avoiding failure is not an option, our task is learning to *cope* with and *grow* from failure, loss and adversity. The more mentally fit we are before we're overtaken by crisis, the better we'll cope when the shit hits the fan, and the faster and more completely we'll recover and even grow stronger from the experience.

The previous few chapters have all been about what it is to flourish and how we can proactively improve our mental fitness, because when we're flourishing (rather than floundering) and mentally fit, we can more readily absorb shocks and recover from them more quickly. That's the resilience component of mental fitness.

In this and the following chapter, we're going to look at some of the skills that you can use to cope in the heat of the moment when it's all coming crashing down. They are, if you like, the ways in which you can move to bear up under heavy pressure. And like the movements involved in getting physically strong, they're things you can practise.

Prepare, perform, recover

In the Army, it's called Stress Exposure Training — a way to make sure you can deal with whatever comes your way. The system that's used to increase this capacity is Prepare, Perform and Recover.

Preparation is all about situation, reaction and strategy. The first part of this is to identify the *situations* in which you experience stress. For the Defence Force, that's pretty easy. It's when bombs and bullets are flying. But all of us experience stress, and if we predict where it's going to come from, we'll cope with it better.

For me, sometimes it's as simple as trying to get my kids out the door. I regularly find myself asking my kids multiple times to get ready to go, without these requests having any impact on their preparedness. When this happens I find myself starting to feel a combination of high energy and unpleasantness, and run the very real risk of losing my temper, acquiring a hard tone and raising my voice. However, if I *expect* to be ignored by my kids and experience a potential loss of temper, then I stand a far better chance of controlling my reactions.

Once we have identified the situations that cause us stress, we need to gain insight into our *reactions* to this stress. Once we understand our reactions, we can use these as cues to pull the trigger on the mental skills *strategies* required to manage our emotions.

Different people react to stress in different ways. You need to study your reactions to determine your own pattern. Sometimes, it can be helpful to ask someone who knows you well for their feedback, because often you're so fused with your thoughts and emotions that you can't clearly see their impact on you.

In mental skills training in the New Zealand Army, recruits are sometimes played a scene from the movie *Sicario*, where the Special

Forces and law enforcement team is in a queue of traffic waiting to cross a border checkpoint with a high-value prisoner. They've noticed there are gangsters in some of the other cars around them: it's plain that something is going to go down. What do you notice about the new team member's reactions, the trainees are asked? Well, she is freaking out. She's looking all around her with wide eyes, her breathing has changed, she's not listening to instructions, she's closed down. We can see all that, looking on. Other members of the team are also clearly stressed, but this is not their first rodeo. For them, stress serves as a trigger for the implementation of their training. Their green brain (discussed in Chapter 11) is in action.

Once you know the situations in which you experience stress, and your reactions to the stress of such moments, you can experiment with different strategies to help remain effective and in control — to dial down the impact of the stress you experience. This chapter will outline a number of strategies you can try out as a function of the 'prepare' and 'perform' aspects of the process, before talking about the 'recover' aspect. Different strategies are more or less effective for different people and in different situations. For example, what works to keep you functioning during work stress may not be the right strategy to use during a disagreement with your partner.

The officer commanding the Conduct After Capture capability and the training exercise that I observed when writing this book was someone I will call Captain John (not his real name). He is an all-around mental toughness beast and a great trainer when it comes to helping the NZDF prepare for dealing with what must be one of the most stressful situations a person can encounter — surviving captivity. When training participants for this experience John and his team takes them though an appropriately named acronym — CALM:

Control emotions. This control focuses on the internal experience of negative thoughts and unpleasant emotions, which are completely normal and to be expected in these circumstances. It also focuses on controlling the externalisation of these emotions through actions, words, and nonverbal behaviour. The first step in assuming control is to breathe in order to get oxygenated blood back into the brain, to assist moving from a red to green brain state.

Acceptance. This involves accepting your situation and letting go of your expectations and preconceptions. A key strategy of the enemy in these situations is what John calls a 'dislocation of expectations', and the experiences of SAS soldiers such as Andy McNab who have survived torture and captivity suggest that acceptance and letting go of your expectations is key to emotional control and survival.

Listen, look, and learn from your environment. This tactic helps you take in your surroundings and formulate an effective response/course of action. It helps slow down your thinking to ensure what you do is an appropriate response for the circumstances you are in. Bowe Bergdahl was a United States solider who was held hostage by the Taliban in Afghanistan from 2009 to 2014. He told John about his own experience of applying this tactic to assess his regularly changing captors, and their habits and temperaments, to guide his responses to them and interactions with them on a day-to-day basis.

Manage your response. This goes back to the initial red to green brain transition of control emotions. It is about having the presence of mind to choose your response rather than allowing your red brain to simply react without thinking.

'Perform' is about trialling a strategy when under stress. There's only one way to figure out which of these will work best for you.

It's is also about confirming and identifying your reactions to stress and how these can be used as cues to implement a strategy. What is it that you notice about how you think, feel and respond to stress as it happens?

After the fray, there needs to be time to recoup, rebound and recover. The final component of the Prepare, Perform and Recover approach to stress-exposure training involves not only allowing yourself and your central nervous system the opportunity to return to a normal level of functioning, but also *reflecting* on your experience.

Never underestimate the importance of what happens when you're not challenged or confronted: relaxation. Put that glass down! For some of us, living stressful and demanding lives, you'll only get micro-opportunities to do this. You'll find that people who run on adrenaline — I'm thinking of the solo parent, senior leader or first responder, that kind of person — need to be extremely good at finding little moments for respite. And when these come, it's important you use them wisely.

We all know that when it comes to physical fitness, recovery is every bit as important as exertion. Mental fitness is exactly the same. We need time to recharge, to put fuel back in the tank. We also need time to reflect. I mentioned my reflective practice back in Chapter 8.

Mental toughness — the application of successful strategies for coping in times of crisis — is a learning process. You need to be constantly evaluating what you did and how effective it was, so that next time, you will know what works for you and what doesn't. Ask yourself, what worked well? What didn't? What would you do the same or differently next time? This is how we improve and prepare for the next episode of adversity coming our way or challenge we choose to step up to.

One of the core values of the SAS is the relentless pursuit of excellence. Chapter 8's section on mastery and your personal experience will confirm that you don't need to be in the Special Forces to understand the link between the feeling that you're improving and having the will and fuel to take on life's challenges.

Just the way you are

In an earlier chapter, we discussed how traditional approaches to the way in which the mind and body related to one another tended to downplay and devalue emotions and to play up the 'rational' mind instead. There was, that is, a tendency to minimise or dismiss 'negative affect'. The fact of the matter is that we *do* feel stuff, and it is better to accept what we're feeling and to explore the reasons for it than it is to try to push all that emoting to one side or try to stuff it permanently into a dark mental locker.

As previously mentioned, there are no good or bad emotions, just helpful or unhelpful ones according to the situation you find yourself in, what you do as a result of the emotions you're experiencing, and what you get as a result of this. As the saying goes, to everything there is a season. When it's the season for powerful emotional response, you'll need strategies to manage it.

A contemporary approach to psychology, often labelled Acceptance and Commitment Therapy (ACT), seeks (as the name suggests) to take a holistic view of our response to challenging situations. This aligns with the idea we discussed earlier that our feelings are as valid a part of our experience as our perceptions, beliefs and actions. In the same way it isn't helpful to dismiss and deny sensations like thirst, it isn't useful to do this with the emotional signals your body is sending you.

Everyone knows the feeling that you get when you're in crisis. You're in fight/flight/freeze mode, swamped with powerful emotions. The ACT techniques are calculated to help you get a bit of breathing space, to put your emotions at a metaphorical arm's length so that you can re-engage the rational part of your brain and achieve 'green brain' status on your way back to blue. It's all about dialling down the intensity of that emotional experience — not getting rid of it, but reducing it sufficiently so that you can respond rather than react. As soon as the needle drops from the red back into the green range, you can begin to think and plan and solve problems again.

Think of it like this. You step into quicksand. You've seen enough old cowboy movies — what's the very worst thing you can do? Struggle, right? Because your thrashing around only displaces more sand and you sink lower. So what's the *best* thing to do? Quicksand is a mixture of sand and water, so it's best to behave as you would to avoid sinking in water. Lie flat. Stay calm. Wait for the cowboy who always shows up with a rope. Or, if you choose to move towards the edge of the pit to grab that overhanging branch, make all your movements slow and steady.

This is what Acceptance and Commitment Therapy recommends to people in challenging situations. There is not necessarily a quick and easy exit from the situation you're in. Your job is to accept your situation and move through it as efficiently as you can without unnecessary wallowing about. So slow down. Differentiate between the things that you can't change (and which must be accepted) and the things that you can change (problem-solving). Look around for your options. Make your choices calm and deliberate.

Fusion/defusion

Well, that's all fine and dandy, but what about when this metaphor is translated to reality? You are faced with a challenging situation and are awash with feelings and impulses. What does 'lying flat' look like?

The technique that ACT offers for dealing with this kind of turmoil is to practise what is called 'defusion'.

Put your hands out in front of you, as though you're trying to catch a double handful of water. Imagine your hands contain all of your unpleasant emotions, negative beliefs and unhelpful perceptions of yourself.

Now bring your hands up to cover your face. What can you see? Nothing, right? Or nothing apart from the glimpses of the world you can catch between your fingers.

This is what it's like when you are confronted with a challenge and become sucked into your inner experience — you become fused. You perceive it, and your perception triggers emotions. Emotions, as their name indicates, are feelings that are designed to get you to do something: positive emotions are there to encourage you to stay in the situation you're in, negative emotions are there to get you to leave. Arousal places you in a state of physiological readiness to deal with a threat. Managing that arousal allows your systems to stay on the peak of the stress performance curve and then to return to normal, rather than bubbling over and causing more issues.

As we've discussed earlier, emotions are a combination of arousal or calm, and pleasant or unpleasant, all filtered through our cultural notions of what we're feeling means. But remember: the only way in which to determine whether your emotions can help or hinder you is to recognise them and to assess them in terms of the courses of action available to you. However, when you're in this kind of state of 'fusion' with your emotions — so beset by them that you can't see the options available — it's hard to make sensible choices at all.

Our brains tend to instinctively treat our thoughts as giving direct access to reality. Trouble is, our thoughts are *not* direct access to reality. They are heavily dependent on our beliefs and our emotions. Remember Iago, Othello and Desdemona? Our thoughts and emotions are Iago to our Othello. They mediate our experience. Once we recognise the input from our thoughts and beliefs, we can get a clearer perspective on reality and dial down the intensity of our experience of it.

So you need to 'defuse' from your thoughts and emotions. Move your hands away from your face. You can see the world around you again, clearly and without obstructions and distractions. Your hands are still at the ends of your arms, but they are no longer stopping you from engaging with life in a meaningful way. The emotions you feel don't stop happening, but they are dialled down enough to allow you to respond effectively to the challenge you are facing.

Flick that switch

When they're in the grip of powerful emotions, Army snipers and SAS soldiers are encouraged to say 'Stop!' to themselves three times. This has an immediate calming effect. They're then told to look around and notice five things in their environment. This is the conscious redirection of focus, which has the effect of wrestling your attention away from the emotional alarm signal that's sounding. This technique sits under the 'focus control' domain of the Big Four strategies we will discuss in the next chapter.

There are other things to try, too. When you're feeling challenged and your emotions are clouding your vision, ask yourself 'What am I thinking?', then say to yourself 'I notice I'm having the thought that [insert thought here].' The act of identifying your thought as a thought, rather than as direct access to reality, gives you mental distance from it and in doing so reduces its intensity.

If identifying the thought seems a little mundane, you can always try a bit of magic. If you've read Harry Potter, you'll know that there's a magical creature named a boggart. It's invisible, but it can materialise as its victim's worst fear. The spell to banish it is to yell 'Riddikulus!' and visualise something that will help you to laugh at your darkest fear.

You can try this technique with your thoughts. You can tell yourself what you're feeling in a comedy German or other accent: 'Hmmm. I seem to be feeling zer pangs of ... ANGER, ja?' Or you can tell yourself what you're feeling in the voice of your favourite cartoon character: 'Screw this anger shit! [in Eric Cartman's voice] I'm going home!' Or you can sing about your unhelpful thought to the tune of 'Happy Birthday'. Or you can imagine your thought as one of those old-fashioned screensavers that pings from top to bottom and diagonally across a blank screen. Whatever works for you ... These techniques help you to refocus your attention — like changing the focal length on a zoom lens, so that an object that may be blurring your vision of a distant object is suddenly pulled into focus.

My colleague Dr Tom Mulholland refers to techniques like this that redirect our focus as 'cognitive switches'. There are lots of examples of them. All Black and rugby league legend Brad Thorn used to splash water on his face when he felt his emotions were getting the better of him. He used to concentrate on the sensation of the water hitting his skin and running off his face, redirecting his attention away from the emotional clamour that was clouding his thought processes. It's not necessarily an approach to use in business meetings, but effective on the football pitch.

Cognitive switches don't have to be physical. They can be mental reminders that you train yourself to deploy when you're in danger of feeling overwhelmed. There might be a line from a song that you can hum (out loud, or under your breath): 'Feelings. Nothing more than feelings ...' Or you might have a store of useful phrases to repeat to yourself that change your perception and help you dial down the intensity of the emotional experience:

- what doesn't kill me makes me stronger
- this too shall pass
- inshallah
- worse things happen at sea
- shit happens
- c'est la vie
- that's the way the cookie crumbles
- the sun will rise tomorrow
- the world will keep turning
- not my circus, not my monkeys
- not today
- every cloud has a silver lining
- these things are sent to try us
- pai tū pai hinga (good to succeed, good to fail)
- pain is weakness leaving the body
- first-world problem
- #blessed
- life doesn't happen to you, it happens for you
- what is is, what isn't isn't

I'm sure you've got a few favourites, and can think of a few more. They're not magic spells to make the situation different, or even to make you feel differently: they're simply a way of dialling down the intensity of the experience and re-engaging your cognitive problem-solving capacity so that you can begin moving through the crisis.

Emotional literacy

Once you begin to study your emotions, you can begin compiling a kind of 'field guide' to them — their habits, where they are found, what they feed upon, what works to manage them. Without an understanding of the precise nature of something you're feeling, it can often be hard to know how to behave when you experience it.

Take, for example, the difference between scepticism and cynicism. They're pretty similar feelings to experience — so similar that you may not necessarily have contemplated the difference between them before. But they *are* different, and the distinction makes all the difference in how we behave based upon them.

Suppose you meet a friend for a coffee and he's telling you about his grand plans for a new business venture. You listen, feeling doubtful, both about the merits of the scheme and his ability to make a go of it. This could be scepticism — healthy doubt, that prompts you to ask penetrating questions about flaws you can see — or it could be cynicism, where your pessimistic outlook leads you to pour scorn on his idea. It's important to know where your doubts have come from in order to know how to behave. If it's scepticism, you can test the robustness of his thinking through asking questions. If it's cynicism, and your impulse is to disparage and belittle, best you just bite your tongue, right? So the same feelings (doubt), properly scrutinised and identified, can lead to two very different courses of action.

Name it to tame it

When you are experiencing an unpleasant emotion, the act of noticing it and attempting to label it dials down the intensity of it. This is because it redirects the bandwidth back towards you thinking brain and away from your emotional brain. Here's the meme — you 'name it to tame it!'. Even if you don't correctly identify what you are feeling, the act of trying will reduce the intensity of what you are experiencing. However, there are additional benefits if you're accurate in the label you affix to it. There are broad terms for categories of feelings, similar to basic colours: happy, sad, angry, afraid, disgusted and surprised. Within each category, there are shades and hues.

Take fear, for example. It can range from attentiveness (where you are a little wary of something) through unease, worry, anxiety, dread and fear to terror and panic. If I have a presentation to give and I'm a bit unprepared for it, I'm likely to feel something on this spectrum. It's important that I determine where on the spectrum I am (nervous, perhaps, which might fall between feeling uneasy and worried), and give it the appropriate label. If I say, 'I am scared about the presentation I'm giving next week', it not only overstates what I am feeling, but it actually escalates the feeling itself.

Furthermore, if we remember Lisa Feldman Barrett's finding that emotional identification is about how we interpret the combination of pleasant/unpleasant and high/low energy/arousal we are experiencing, then we can choose to reinterpret the signals we receive as more helpful alternatives. For example, if we have done something wrong, we will experience emotional unpleasantness that we might label either shame or guilt. Shame is driven by the thought that there is something wrong with us, and leads to a spiral of self-judgement and self-criticism. Guilt, on the other hand, is driven by the thought that we took the wrong actions, and leads to a desire to avoid similar future missteps. Choose guilt! As another example, let's return to the previous scenario where we are trying to differentiate between cynicism and scepticism. If you are someone who regularly demonstrates cynicism, choose to reinterpret that emotion as scepticism instead, and focus on being open to changing your mind and demonstrating sincere curiosity.

What's more, this kind of accurate identification of what we're feeling helps us identify the beliefs that were involved in synthesising the emotion. If I determine that I'm dreading giving my presentation in a week's time, I can interrogate that emotion. What underlying concerns are giving rise to the dread I'm feeling: is it a fear that my audience won't think I'm smart enough, or funny enough, or handsome enough … ? Or is it simply that this is a very important opportunity and I don't feel sufficiently prepared? If it's the former, there are things I can do to address my perceived shortcomings, even if it's just to change my *perception* of my shortcomings. Or I can simply employ some of the previously discussed techniques for dialling down the impact of these thoughts and emotions. If it is the latter, then I embrace that discomfort as motivation to prepare properly and give it heaps.

Say it to savour it

It's not just through the accurate identification and labelling of *unpleasant* emotions that we can benefit. As I mentioned earlier in the book, we can derive far more from pleasant emotions if we can accurately identify them, too.

My boys are real cheerful Charlies. Looking at them grinning and laughing, I feel good. What, I ask myself, am I feeling exactly?

I feel something like happy — that's the ballpark emotion, the primary colour. I Google some synonyms. Pleased? Too weak. Blissful? Too strong. Delighted? Delight is an emotional state characterised by a high degree of pleasure. That's it. Delight is a word I know, but I hadn't really understood the meaning of it or had recognised and labelled it in myself.

I look at my sons enjoying life and I say to myself, or to my wife, or to them, or to nobody in particular: 'That's delightful'. The effect of this is actually to deliver greater neurological activation: more oxytocin, dopamine and serotonin are released in the brain, and the positive experience just gives me a little bit more fuel in the tank of my mental fitness. If, on the other hand, I had experienced my delight as an unformed, unexamined moment of positive affect, the major part of the experience would have passed me by.

If you wish to increase your own emotional vocabulary and literacy, I recommend you use the wheel below to figure out the subtle shades of your emotional experiences. This is not by any stretch of the imagination a comprehensive set of emotion words, but it's a place to start. For a more comprehensive dive into this area, I highly recommend Tiffany Watt Smith's *The Book of Human Emotions* (2015).

A technique I encourage you to try for becoming more emotionally self-aware and literate is something I think of as the HEE-HAW approach. I call it HEE-HAW purely to make the acronym more memorable — the HAW is the relevant part. HAW stands for:

- How am I feeling?
- About what?
- Why?

Emotions wheel

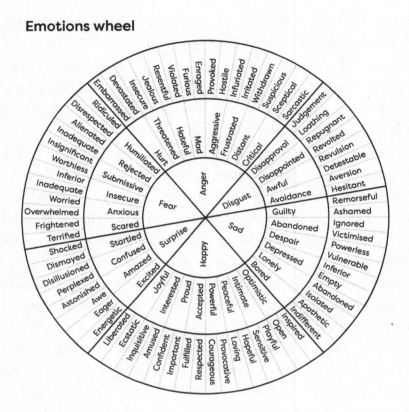

If you become practised at reflecting on these questions, you will radically transform your ability not only to dial down your unpleasant and dial up your pleasant emotional experiences, but also transform your understanding of what causes you to feel such emotions and how best to respond to them.

As if the case for increasing your emotional self-awareness and literacy wasn't already strong enough, let's briefly return to the relationships component of mental fitness. Something that will save you many thousands of dollars in relationship counselling is knowing that there is a general difference between what most men and women ultimately desire in a romantic relationship. The majority of men most desire acceptance in their relationship — feeling they are not judged and are OK just the way they are. Most women, on the other hand, desire a sense of connection and intimacy (as in into-me-you-see). They want to feel they know what their partner is thinking and feeling.

It's pretty hard to communicate to your partner if *you* don't know what you're thinking and feeling! And it doesn't need to be the heavy stuff. After doing some work together, I remember a world-champion athlete telling me how valuable it had been for his relationship to be able to respond to his wife about how his day was by reflecting positive emotions like 'uplifting'! A far cry from and greater intimacy creator than the usual 'good' that most of us resort to.

From the ashes ...

One thing to remind yourself, when you're experiencing trauma, is that you will not necessarily be permanently damaged or depleted by it. You will likely make a full recovery. You may even, as improbably as it sounds, be enriched by it.

On a dark night in February 1909, the passenger steamer *Penguin* struck a submerged object in Cook Strait and began to sink. One of the 105 people aboard was young mother Ada Hannam. Ada was put in a lifeboat with her four children; her husband was obliged to remain aboard the ship.

As the lifeboat was being lowered, it suddenly plunged end-first into the water. Ada's two-year-old was washed from her arms, but she managed to grab her again and clamber back aboard the lifeboat when it was righted. As Ada sat there, she could hear her three other children calling out to her in the darkness, but she could do nothing to save them. One by one, they fell silent. As the boat was manoeuvred away from the sinking ship, she had to call out a farewell to her husband, who had witnessed all of this from the deck.

After half an hour adrift in the boat in heavy seas, it was capsized. Ada found herself underneath it, still clutching her baby, and with at least two other people clinging to her. Soon there was only one: Ellis Matthews, a young man whom Ada managed to haul up so that he could get a hold in the air-pocket under the boat alongside her. She placed her baby on the top of the seat she was holding onto. Ellis repeatedly asked Ada if they would drown, but she replied that she was going to survive, and if he stuck with her, he would survive, too.

They were in the water for close to four hours before washing ashore. By then, Ada had realised her baby was dead, and concentrated on encouraging Matthews. True to her word, both were rescued. Ada refused offers of assistance at first, concentrating on trying to locate her husband and three children amongst the bodies washing onto the beach. When she finally allowed herself to be led up a track to a farmstead, she asked those with her to talk to her to keep her mind from what had happened. Two days later, the newspapers described her as being in 'a state of collapse'.

Who knows what Ada Hannam's life had been like before that day to prepare her for that ordeal. But Ada not only survived, she thrived. She was tracked down almost 30 years later, living in Onehunga. It turned out she had been pregnant at the time of the *Penguin* disaster: the son who was born a few months afterward grew up to become a professional mariner. Ada was happy to talk to a newspaper reporter on the thirtieth anniversary of the wreck, and to recall the details. Ellis Matthews, who had gone farming in Marlborough, never spoke of the loss of the *Penguin* and refused to go near the sea again.

Where, you wonder as you read stories like these, do people find the strength to carry on living, let alone living full, even happy, lives after such a monumentally traumatic experience? Well, we have all heard of post-traumatic stress disorder (PTSD), but fewer of us have heard of post-traumatic growth. This phenomenon was identified by a group of American researchers led by Richard Tedeschi and Lawrence Calhoun of the University of North Carolina in the mid-1990s. It's a broadly similar concept to resilience, but it goes further: some people who experience post-traumatic growth don't just 'bounce back' from trauma and return to a state similar to what they enjoyed before their experience. They are fundamentally reconfigured by their experience, and go on to live fuller and richer lives. Tedeschi and Calhoun found the following to be the top five things said by people who had experienced post-traumatic growth:

- 'My priorities have changed. I'm not afraid to do what makes me happy.'
- 'I feel closer to my friends and family.'
- 'I understand myself better. I know who I really am now.'
- 'I have a new sense of meaning and purpose in my life.'
- 'I'm better able to focus on my goals and dreams.'

Not everyone escapes post-traumatic stress disorder and experiences post-traumatic growth instead, but a surprising number do. According to Tedeschi, between a half and a third of people will. Some people suffer PTSD *and* experience post-traumatic growth. Research has so far failed to indicate exactly how and why it is that some people emerge from disaster stronger, wiser and more open to positive experience, as there doesn't seem to be a particular 'type' of person who is disposed to it.

The common factors they were able to identify were optimism (what a surprise!), openness to new experience, and extroversion (the aspect of being socially interactive is theorised as most relevant). Young children seemed to lack the cognitive ability to achieve it. Adolescents seemed more proficient than adults, presumably because their world view is already in a state of flux: they're already open to change. There's also every reason to believe that those who have made a practice of analysing and processing their emotions will be more adept at putting them into perspective once a crisis has passed — that is, those who have made an effort to become mentally fit.

For those of you thinking you need a serious trauma to get some of these benefits, relax! Researchers have found that people can experience these benefits without having a trauma, through what Dr Ann Marie Roepke calls post-ecstatic growth.

Post-ecstatic growth is what many people experience when they choose to undertake an extreme challenge, such as starting a business, becoming a parent, running a marathon, writing a book or going on a spiritual journey. According to this research, there are seven ways of thinking and acting that bring together a lot of the previously discussed areas in this book and contribute to both post-traumatic and post-ecstatic growth:

1. Adopt a challenge mindset. See obstacles and stressors as a challenge to be embraced, not a threat to be avoided.
2. Seek out what increases positive emotion and makes you stronger. When confronted by a tough challenge, look after your physical health and do the things that make you feel positive emotions (e.g., pat the dog, talk to friends, walk around the block, get into nature).

3. Strive for psychological flexibility. Be driven by curiosity, courage and the desire to learn and improve. Be open to unpleasant experiences that help you learn or get closer to your goals, such as pain and failure.

4. Take committed action. Every day, take small steps towards your most meaningful goal. Even when it's difficult to do so, take committed actions that bring you closer to where you want to be.

5. Cultivate connectedness. Strive to have at least two people you can talk honestly to about your challenges and stress, and who you can ask for help.

6. Find the heroic story. Find the heroic moments in your life story where you have been the aspirational version of yourself. Focus on the meaning and purpose behind your struggles and the strength you have shown.

7. Learn to find the benefits. Develop the skill of finding the silver lining that exists even in stress and challenge. Cultivate the attitude that life doesn't happen *to* you, but happens *for* you.

Post-ecstatic growth

The following table is designed to assist you begin your own hero's journey of post-ecstatic growth. Each of the previously outlined ingredients are listed in the left-hand column. The middle column is where you can record the opportunities you will have, how you will implement these ingredients, and any other relevant information. The final column is intended for your notes once you have begun the journey. The power to accelerate your own growth and associated mental fitness is in your hands!

Ingredients	Opportunities or implementation	Reflections
Challenge you choose to embrace		
Activities that create positive emotion or increase health		
Ways to cultivate curiosity, courage and learning		
Small daily steps that will take you to your goal		
Your support people		
A previous example of when you have shown strength and found purpose in your struggles		
The benefits of this challenge and its struggles		

13

The Special Forces Big Four

While it is possible to work out your own strategies to employ when under stress, it might just be easier to look at what the US Navy SEALs have come up with. The following 'Big Four' strategies come from extensive research by the SEALs into finding what works when shit really gets real. These strategies have since been adopted and incorporated into the training of many defence forces, Special Forces operators and elite athletes.

The Big Four are: arousal control, visualisation, self-talk and goals.

1. Arousal control

The strategy of arousal control in the Navy SEAL context focuses on the operatives' ability to control their physiological reaction to stress through breathing techniques. While this fits with the 'tactical breathing' technique outlined below, I am going to broaden the scope of this section to include techniques that more properly fall under what my friend and colleague, Defence Force psychologist Captain Drew Kingi, refers to as 'focus control'. Focus control involves a combination of arousal focus and deliberate attention (i.e. mindfulness) more generally.

Focus control is consistent with the well-established psychological phenomenon known as the spotlight theory of attention. According to this theory, your brain can only process and absorb a limited amount of new information at any given moment, and our attention is like a spotlight. We can only focus on one source of information at a time and ignore everything else. Yet there is constant competition for your brain's attention: sounds, sights, physical sensations, smells and thoughts. If you learn to control where you point your attention spotlight, you can choose to deprive the stress parts of your brain of the processing resources they need to really kick into gear. This is focus control.

There are a number of different focus-control techniques. One of them (of which we've already had a sneak preview) is called 'five things', and is recommended in the New Zealand Defence Force mental skills manual available to all Army, Navy and Air Force personnel. In this technique you focus your attention spotlight on five things you can see within your environment, but weren't previously paying attention to; then five things you can hear that you weren't previously focused on; and lastly, five physical sensations you weren't previously focused on (e.g. the weight of your arms or the sensations associated with your right big toe).

This technique focuses your attention internally, on your sensations, and externally, on what you can see and hear. A good way to think of this is 'tuning in' and 'tuning out'. Tuning in is often called 'body scanning', and tuning out 'environment scanning'.

People often find one of these areas of focus is more effective for them than the other. I really like environment scanning, and it works best if I do it through vision. To enhance its effectiveness I often take it a step further by 'gamifying' it: I pretend I need to recall every detail of my environment, as if I had a photographic memory. This is a technique I find very effective at the latter stages of long runs. Other people may find it more effective to focus on what they can hear. Experiment with your area of focus and see what most captures the beam of your attention spotlight.

Another focus-control technique is to count down in sevens from 100, or to think of as many words as you can that include your initials — the first letters of both your first and surnames. Why not try this one out right now? Firstly, think about something that causes you worry or stress. For approximately 10 seconds, focus solely on this thought and its associated sensations and emotions. Now, for approximately 60 seconds, count down from 100 in multiples of 7, or identify as many different words as you can that include your initials. (I find that my initials PW don't give me as many options as I'd like, so I often use the mental fitness initials MF instead.) See how paying deliberate attention with your attention spotlight works to manage your focus and therefore helps to control your thoughts and emotions. While such techniques are effective ways to achieve focus control, as I mentioned above the one most commonly taught within the Special Forces and broader armed services is tactical breathing. And it's not just the defence force who uses this technique: elite athletes use tactical breathing to calm themselves down and to re-engage the thinking, problem-solving part of their brains, too. In sports psychology, tactical breathing is often called 'box breathing'.

When your SNS (the fire-up side of the autonomic nervous system) is engaged, we're in fight/flight/freeze mode. But this, as we've seen, is not the body's preferred state. The PNS (parasympathetic nervous system, the calm-down side of the autonomic nervous system) is poised and waiting for a signal that it can return everything to normality again. Taking control of your breathing and tuning your attention spotlight into this process is an effective way to send this signal.

Here's how the New Zealand Defence Force manual recommends you do it. Draw in a deep breath through your nose, counting to four as you do it and allowing your stomach area (actually your diaphragm) to inflate, rather than simply expanding your ribcage or chest. Hold the breath for the count of two. Slowly exhale through your mouth, feeling your stomach deflating, for the count of six. Once you've fully breathed out, pause for a count of two before inhaling through your nose again ... Rinse and repeat, for four minutes. (While four minutes is recommended, in my experience of taking hundreds of people through this technique, most people find one minute works very well as a physiological reset.)

You'll sometimes hear people recommend breathing in for four seconds, holding for four seconds, out for four seconds, hold for four seconds (that's why it's sometimes called 'box breathing'). This is the method I personally use and take others through. I just find it simpler than changing the count for holding, exhaling, and inhaling. What the research suggests is that it doesn't matter what pattern you use: it's the rhythm and the focus control that re-establishes your capacity to manage your emotions.

When we're in a state of arousal (the SNS is engaged), our heart rate is elevated and our breathing becomes rapid and shallow, in order to ready our muscles for rapid, vigorous action. The kind of diaphragmatic breathing described above is more typical of a state of deep relaxation. Instigating diaphragmatic breathing actually sends the calm-down signal, engages the PNS and, just like that, we begin to shift from red to green and begin to calm down to blue.

2. Visualisation

This is another technique on which sports psychologists and the armed forces find a lot of common ground. There are three kinds of visualisation: motivational visualisation, instructional visualisation and what we'll call constructive visualisation.

Motivational visualisation is imagining a successful outcome to your endeavour. If you're a golfer, you'll know this one: as you get ready to hit the ball, you imagine it sailing dead straight down the centre of the fairway. A soldier will imagine emerging on the winning side of an engagement. A husband will imagine a constructive conversation with his wife. An employee will imagine walking out of the boss's office with the promise of the raise he's been seeking. A student will picture graduation.

Instructional visualisation is imagining the steps involved in getting to that successful outcome. The great soccer player Pelé used to arrive at the venue of a match hours in advance and lie in the dressing room with a towel over his eyes, visualising himself in action. Then he would go out and perform miracles on the pitch. Research has shown that exactly the same neural pathways that fire when we're in action are fired when we *visualise* ourselves in action. It's literally warming up the brain. A golfer will imagine the backswing, then the swing with the transfer of weight from foot to foot and the acceleration of the club-head through the ball. The soldier will imagine himself prioritising, executing and performing the steps that he has perfected in training. The husband will see himself sitting down comfortably with his wife, making eye contact, staying calm, exploring his wife's point of view. The employee will mentally rehearse knocking on the door, sitting down, making his case.

Constructive visualisation is designed to create a positive mood. You imagine yourself in your happy place. Maybe it's on a tropical beach, maybe it's in a forest, maybe it's less clichéd. Positivity, a lightness of mood and optimism all help you to perform under stress, and to cope with stress better.

Another very interesting example of constructive visualisation is what is known in the US Navy SEALs as 'team connectedness'. Relationships always have challenges, be they with your colleagues, family, friends or loved ones. In order to more effectively connect and work with one another, the Navy SEALs introduced a 'team connectedness' practice, which is more commonly known as love and kindness meditation.

There are lots of different ways to practise this approach, but the one used by the SEALs involves starting with imagining someone you love — a child, partner or parent, etc. You then spend three minutes wishing them loving and kind outcomes (e.g. may you be healthy, may you be safe, may you be happy, may you be free from suffering, may you be at peace). Once you have done this for three minutes, you then focus this love and kindness towards someone you feel more neutral about. Maybe it's a person on the bus or the person who serves coffee at a café you don't regularly visit. The same wishes of love and kindness are then directed at them (i.e. may you be healthy etc). You then focus for three minutes on directing those wishes to someone you find challenging to deal with. Finally, you spend three minutes directing that loving kindness towards yourself. The intention of this approach for the SEALs is that it enables them to attain a positive psychological state and extends that state to enable them to work with each other optimally.

Lieutenant-Colonel Steve Kearney of the New Zealand Defence Force refers to this as 'priming the pump'. You start with a context in which it is easy to feel what you want to feel, then gradually extend this out to harder contexts. This works in terms of both visualisation and skill development more broadly in the mental-fitness area.

Another constructive-visualisation-related way to prime this pump is to focus on a single individual whom you love but find challenging in some contexts. Maybe you want to be able to demonstrate more warmth and kindness to your partner when you are having stressful or otherwise challenging interactions. In these situations, the effective path is connection and shared resolution through love, warmth and kindness, but these don't necessarily come naturally to most people in stressful circumstances. As previously mentioned, many of us deal with high-stress and high-pressure situations caused by external challenges through emotionally disconnecting and shutting down — a kind of emotional freeze response. The problem is that when the situation *isn't* an external threat but is instead an emotionally intense interaction with someone you care about, this shutting down approach just makes you appear cold, distant and uncaring.

But you can develop a different skill set. You can practise visualising moments with your partner where it is easy to feel love for one another and to be warm, open and at ease. You can then bring to mind the feelings you have in such circumstances. Then visualise being able to experience these feelings in slightly more challenging circumstances. And finally, imagine experiencing those feelings in the situations where you are at greatest risk of shutting down.

No approach is perfect, but this mental rehearsal makes it a lot more likely that you will be able to present as a better, more effective version of yourself when it counts. You can do the same for your kids. Picturing them sleeping in bed and the warm feelings you have towards them, then attempting to mentally rehearse having these same feelings when they are tearing around the supermarket and taking things off the shelf, or refusing to pick up the Lego!

3. Self-talk

You know the little voice in your head. It has lots of tones. It can be constructive. It can be undermining and unhelpful. Controlling your self-talk can be a key component in performing successfully under stress.

Your mind is perpetually trying to make sense of what's going on around you and within you. Rationalisation can be the enemy. Let's say you're having an argument with your wife, and you're feeling bad. That's natural enough. But whoa! Here goes your mind: 'I feel like crap. It must be the relationship. We're not right for one another. It would be the best thing for both of us if we went our separate ways ...' This stuff appears like pop-up windows in an unfiltered internet session, and you need to recognise it for what it is and have strategies to reduce its impact.

I like taking an aggressive approach to challenges, so I use phrases like 'Challenge accepted', 'Come at me' or 'Is this all you got?' because that's me. You might prefer to strike a note of reassurance: 'You got this!', 'You can do this!' The key thing is that it must be constructive and motivational, not negative. You need to silence your inner critic, the voice that goes: 'Hope we don't screw this up.' Or: 'Everyone thinks you're an idiot.' I use rejoinders to this kind of self-talk like: 'Look, listen, learn' or 'Thanks inner critic, but no one else actually cares.'

You could think of the type of self-talk we've just been discussing as primarily motivational. The other kind of useful self-talk, once again, is instructional. You talk yourself through the steps you're going to take. For a soldier, it's easy: 'Ready. Aim. Fire.' For the golfer: 'Nice, easy backswing. Keep the left elbow locked and head down. Easy, relaxed downswing. Keep head down and eyes on the ball! Follow through onto the front foot …' For someone about to have a difficult conversation: 'Sit down. Pick up the phone. Punch in the numbers. Deep breath and focus on what you've prepared to say.'

My wife competes as an elite cross-country mountain bike rider and has done significant mental skills work with Jay Barrett. As a result, she uses an approach that involves reminding herself of what her 'job' is during a race if she finds her mind wandering to thoughts or concerns that don't aid her performance. She also uses a form of self-talk and visualisation that focuses on her mindset and fear management when doing scary downhills for the first time in training. She thinks of the three key words she has chosen for herself (smooth, calm, commit), focuses on a visual image that gives her confidence, then goes. When you think of your own stressful situations, what are the three words that might help you have the mindset required for success? What's your job in that situation?

Pre-eminent world mental toughness expert Dr Jim Loehr has helped more Olympic and world-title hopefuls reach the top of the podium than any other single psychologist. His primary focus is helping these elite performers harness the strength of such inner dialogue. His approach is to have his clients journal their current inner dialogue, in relevant situations if not more comprehensively.

He then has them script a *new* dialogue for themselves based on what they'd want to hear — what the best possible coaching voice would be saying to them in those situations.

Let's think about what the voice of that inner coach would say and sound like for you.

YOUR INNER COACH

On five separate occasions when you experience stress or distress, record your inner dialogue in the first column. Then, when you have recovered, write in the second column what your ideal inner coach would say to you.

	Current inner dialogue	Ideal coach dialogue
1		
2		
3		
4		
5		

4. Goals

We previously outlined the importance of making sure goals are specific, measurable, achievable, relevant, and timebound (i.e. SMART), but that's the *how* of goals. When it comes to the actual perseverance to complete real challenges when the heat is on, we need the *why* of goals.

If you Google 'motivation', you'll find a vast number of theories on what it is that makes people do things, and how it is you can get people to do what you want them to do. Sports coaches, the boss, parents — knowing how to get people to do stuff willingly is the holy grail for all of them. Accordingly, teams of psychologists have devoted their entire careers to devising theories of motivation with such picturesque names as Maslow's hierarchy of needs, Ouchi's Theory Y, Vroom's expectancy theory, Alderfer's ERG theory and more. You can group them into categories such as content theories (what motivation is), process theories (how motivation works) or cognitive theories (how our relationship to the world affects our motivation). Or you can just cut to the chase, which is what I now propose to do!

The biggest motivational factor at work in practically every situation is the human fear of loss. When considering an action (or the decision not to act), the thing that most commonly influences us is the answer to the question: what do I stand to lose?

There are two ways of conceptualising loss: you can lose something you already have, or you can lose what you might otherwise stand to gain. The fear of losing what you already have can be regarded as the conservative conceptualisation ('conservative' literally means keeping what you have). If you apply this physical fitness, when you're asking yourself what the hell you're doing out in the rain with your lungs burning and your legs hurting, running to the top of an apparently endless hill, the answer is something like: 'I'm doing this because I want to stay healthy, so that I can stay mobile and be able to do things with my family and feel good about myself.'

Everyone is different and, let's face it, your answers to a lot of life's big questions will change as you get older or your situation changes. But I regard myself as what you might call potential-focused. I'm not so much concerned about losing what I already have (although that's the baseline from which many normally functioning individuals operate); I'm more concerned about what it is that I might yet have if I work for it — my potential. Why am I running up this hill? Not merely because I am fit enough — just — to run up it now, and I want to stay that way. It's because if I run up it enough times between now and race day, I'll get fitter. I'll be able to run a marathon, maybe even an ultramarathon, and be better prepared for whatever else life might lob my way.

As discussed in Chapter 5, if you really think about what makes us 'happy' (if you choose to use that term) or fulfilled (if you prefer to be realistic about what a good life is), then you will be at least in part focused on what it is you might achieve in the future if you put the effort in now. And, of course, I'm not just talking about physical fitness. I'm talking about all of your potential — physical, mental and moral. If you acknowledge that a well-lived life is one in which you are physically fit, mentally tough and resilient, and strive to live your values, then you're talking about a whole lot of human potential just sitting there waiting to be developed. But unless you actively set about developing it, that's all that potential will ever do: sit there, unrealised. It's a bit like investment. You can stuff your money under the mattress, whereupon inflation will steadily erode its value. Or you can invest it, which entails a bit of risk, but which also stands to deliver rewards. Choosing to realise your potential is just like investing money: it's a case of use it or lose it.

Don't forget — *never* forget — that time is your enemy. Perhaps I feel this more acutely than most people my age, because I spent so much of my time as a young man either out of it on drugs or languishing in a prison cell, or both. I literally wasted so much time that, as seventeenth-century poet Andrew Marvell put it, 'at my back I always hear / Time's wingèd chariot hurrying near.' Time is running out!

The average lifespan in New Zealand is a whisker over 81 years. That's 29,565 days from go to whoa. That's 709,560 hours.

It might sound like a lot, but if you're 30, you've already used up over a third of that time. You've only got 446,760 hours left, and you'll be spending nearly a third of that time asleep. There is quite literally no time to waste!

That is what motivates me. That's what should motivate you.

We've touched on the importance of 'why' several times already. We've talked about the difference between 'push' and 'pull' factors. You couldn't just order someone, or pay someone, or promise someone good things to put themselves through the SAS selection process or training cycle. Even people who think the life of a Special Forces soldier will be better than what they currently have tend not to make the grade: these 'push' factors don't cut it. You need to be 'pulled'. You need to see yourself as an SAS soldier and to burn with the desire to settle for nothing less. As one of the successful recruits in the documentary *First Among Equals*, about the New Zealand SAS selection process, puts it, 'I would have walked through a brick wall to get there.' He was willing to attempt the impossible to realise his dream. I recently spoke to another successfully badged officer who made it into the SAS. He said it was never a question for him. His father had been in the SAS, and he was certain that The Regiment was where he belonged.

As you prepare for a crisis, as you pre-expose yourself to stress, you'll experience unpleasant emotions. You'll want to give up. You won't persist just because you've bought a book that tells you to keep going. You'll need a pull factor to get you through. Get that why sorted!

Picture yourself coping in a crisis. Ask yourself 'What would the person I want to be do in this situation?' and do it. There's your why. You're putting in the hard yards now so that, cometh the hour, you will be the one who steps up.

MINI-GOALS

Yet sometimes when the struggle is real and goals are big, you need to bring those goals right back down to size. Sometimes it means shrinking your focus down to what are called mini-goals.

Remember my SAS mate and his tiny chunks of muesli bar? In the Navy SEALs they talk about what's going to get you to your next meal during Hell Week. Hell Week isn't a misnomer — as I said in Chapter 11, it's five and a half days of the most intense physical training possible. The only thing that they can count on, other than misery, is getting to eat. So rather than focus on getting through the whole, hellish week, the candidates who are most likely to succeed focus only on getting to the next meal. Likewise, when I ran my first marathon, I didn't focus on getting through the whole 42.2 kilometres. Instead, I focused on getting to each drink station (approximately 3 kilometres apart).

To remain mentally tough and effective, identify and focus on the next small goal. It might be the next lamppost during a run, it might be your lunch break during a tough day. It might be some other small marker that helps you shrink the goal to bite-sized chunks and stay focused.

14

Fighting Fit

Special Forces trainers talk about producing 'pre-combat veterans' — people who are already equipped with the skills they'll need so that when the shit hits the fan, they can apply them unthinkingly. Mental toughness is the same deal. If you've put in the work to acquire the tools and a working knowledge of using them before you need them, you'll be equipped to cope when the heat is on. As noted in Chapter 12, this requires preparation — getting in the habit of exposing yourself to stress, so that when life presents you with the opportunity to deploy your coping skills, you'll do it pretty much instinctively. It's taking the Special Forces combat mindset and applying it to everyday life.

It's like physical training. I'm not naturally a runner, but when I first started marathon training I would (obviously) go running. I wouldn't go for long runs, but they were tough, because where I live, distance isn't the major challenge — it's the hills. My route took me up some steep tracks, down some steep tracks and then up even more and steeper tracks. I knew it would hurt. I knew there would be moments — probably quite a few moments —

when I would ask myself: why the hell am I doing this? And my brain would nonchalantly suggest I should stop running and walk.

We all know what you need to do to get physically fit. You need to do physical exercise. You need to do it regularly — it's an often overlooked fact that consistency is more important than anything else, including level of effort. This might seem counterintuitive to those of us who think that each time you exercise, you need to do it to the point where it challenges your resources. No pain, no gain, right? This is true in that if you stop short of the point at which your resources are stretched, your body isn't going to get the message that it needs to improve its capacity. But often developing the habit of physical (or mental) exercise is actually the hardest part. Until that's done, the only focus should be on getting out and doing it, not making it hurt.

Once you're in the habit, there will be joy and satisfaction in making it hurt. But you need to increase your level of exercise by increments. Of course, the point at which it begins to hurt will be different for different people, and for each individual, it will change as you get fitter. When you first begin, you might feel that you're surely going to die around the 2 kilometre mark on your 3 kilometre run. But after a month or two, you'll feel as though you're only warming up after 3 kilometres. By now, the pain will be setting in at 5, 6, maybe even 10 kilometres.

Without a valid reason to be subjecting myself to the discomfort of training for a marathon, I wouldn't have been able to make myself do it. And this has been proven in study after study to be, for most people, the main barrier to improving their physical fitness: they might know *how* to do it, but they can't convince themselves of the *need* to do it today. They can't say *why* they're doing it and why today rather than tomorrow.

The same is true of mental toughness. I can show you how to become mentally tougher and more resilient (i.e. mentally fitter). But there's literally no point at all in doing so if you can't see *why* you should subject yourself to the discomfort involved.

I went running each day because I had a marathon coming up. I'm fairly fit, but I knew for a fact that I wouldn't be able to just show up on the day and run 42.2 kilometres. So I had to prepare, to do the hard yards — ever wonder where that expression came from? — so that, come race day, I had the physical resources to do it.

Preparing for life's mental and emotional demands is just the same. Mental fitness determines our ability to remain effective and flourish for longer under stressful circumstances, and to recover faster from crises. There is no point in waiting until you're challenged, until you're in the thick of it: you need to proactively develop your mental resources now so that when things get tough, you have those resources to call upon.

Getting in the habit

By now, you'll already have worked out that the method of becoming mentally fit is exactly what your personal trainer would recommend as the method for becoming physically stronger and fitter. I am encouraging you to make working on your mental fitness a habit — what psychologists call 'habitual behaviours'.

Just like pretty much all human behavioural tendencies, habits are good and necessary things — until they're not. They can be counterproductive, like the bad habits we use as mental crutches in times of stress. But just as habits can be bad because they exert a powerful force on our behaviour, they can be highly useful, too, for the same reason.

Habits are essentially behaviours that we perform without having to put too much conscious thought into them. Think of what happens when someone tosses you a tennis ball: if you've ever learned to catch, you simply reach up a hand and close it around the moving object. You don't think about distance from source, relative velocities, the effect of gravity, the size and weight of the object, or the motions required to lift your arm, open your hand and then close your fingers around the ball. There is actually an astonishing array of variables to consider, and this is how it seems to a child who is learning how to do it. Most of us couldn't do the maths involved even if we got an Excellence in NCEA Calculus. But once you've mastered catching a tennis ball, you just do it automatically.

We call this kind of automatic behaviour 'muscle memory'. And this is a characteristic of habits: automaticity. We generally develop habits by repetition, by performing the tasks involved over and over again. Think of the hundreds, even thousands, of hours that an All Blacks goal-kicker will have spent kicking the ball through the posts. He goes through all that tedious repetition to develop this muscle memory — basically a set of physical and mental habits — so that he doesn't have to invent a way of kicking the ball through the posts every time he lines up a shot at goal in a test match.

Habitual behaviours are like putting the plane on autopilot: it flies itself, leaving the pilot free to do other things. You can see their evolutionary usefulness immediately. There are a whole range of actions that must have been useful to our early ancestors to perform without having to devote a moment's conscious thought to them: throwing a spear, lighting a fire, dodging sabre-toothed cats and so on. Mental processes are highly demanding, and take a toll on our physical and emotional resources (anyone who has ever sat an exam will know how drained you feel afterwards, even though to all appearances you've done nothing but sit in a room). Any useful task that can be performed without calling the higher functions of your brain in on the job is a win for your inner bean-counter.

And that's the usefulness of forming habits. Special Forces soldiers spend so much time training so that when the moment comes to act, most of their behaviours are automatic and their mind is free to concentrate on other things. As I mentioned before, the mantra taught to Navy SEALs by SEAL legend Jocko Willink is 'Prioritise and execute.' If they had to think about execution, they would have less and less bandwidth to spare for prioritisation.

It's surprising how much of our everyday behaviour is automatic. How often have you had the experience of leaving the house and getting halfway across town before wondering, with a sick jolt, whether you left the iron on the ironing board, or a pot bubbling on the stove? Eek! Did I close the garage door? I have no memory whatsoever of closing the garage door! You make panicked phone calls, or turn around and drive home, only to find that your good old subconscious was on the job: the garage door is securely closed, the element under the pot is off and the iron is not only cold, but in its place in the laundry cupboard. Because we performed the tasks of unplugging and putting away the iron, turning off the stove, closing the garage door subconsciously (sub means 'underneath' in Latin) we didn't do them consciously and thus didn't form a memory of doing them.

If we can make the tasks required to become mentally fit habitual, it will be less burdensome for us to perform them, less difficult to motivate ourselves to do them, and easier to employ them when under stress and pressure.

Building Rome

Like lots of good things, developing good habits takes time. Incremental steps, right? You build, brick by brick, and then, one day: Rome!

In fact, it's been shown that it takes at least 21 days for human beings to get used to a change. This timeframe was first noticed (or at least, reported) by a plastic surgeon by the name of Maxwell Maltz, who found that his patients tended to take three weeks or so to get used to the changes he was performing upon their bodies — be it a nose-job or an amputation. You've probably found much the same thing when you've bought a new piece of furniture. For the first little while, it sticks out and you can't for the life of you see how it's ever going to seem right for the room. But then, after some magical interval — almost certainly no less than 21 days — you find you can't remember what things were like before that new armchair was there.

You may have noticed that I was cautious to state that 21 days was a *minimum*, not a fixed and firm number. Subsequent research into Maltz's fascinating hypothesis has shown that it can take anything from 18 to over 250 days for a new behaviour to become habitual. What we know from the research out of Harvard's happiness lab is that it takes on average 21 days to notice the impact of a new activity on our mental fitness. We also know from research into habit formation that an impact is often felt before a habit is consolidated. So I recommend applying what I'll call the 21/90 day rule. Experiment for 21 days to see if you get a desired impact from an activity in this book. If you do, commit to carrying on for 90 days to consolidate the habit.

Give it a try. Choose something to build into your daily routine. It could be something easy (like drinking a glass of water at lunchtime) or something harder (like going for a run just before your evening meal). Try to perform it every day. You'll probably forget here and there. Instead of fretting over a lapse, try to devise ways to reinforce the behaviour. An example: in recent times, I found I had acquired a habit (not a good one) of having a little extra meal after the children had gone to bed. It didn't help that the extra meal was usually ice cream. So I decided to try to get out of the habit of eating that extra meal. I found it helped if I put a sticker chart with 30 empty squares on it on the kitchen wall, and put a tick there every day that I stayed on the path and didn't have an extra meal. I could keep track of my progress, and so could everyone else in the house. It worked — or at least, it worked for me. I broke the habit, and seeing that sheet full of ticks was truly satisfying. I recommend giving it a go.

Another method, and one that the best writer on this subject, James Clear (author of *Atomic Habits: An Easy and Proven Way to Build Good Habits and Break Bad Ones*), advocates, is to keep a habits journal. You need to approach the formation of a habit like a scientist, Clear reckons, experimenting with ways of making it easier to perform and recording the effects of each method. Just as a scientist will record the positive outcome of an experiment — glass of water drunk, 15-minute run achieved, ice cream refused — a scientist will also record a failure, and try to imagine ways in which failure might be avoided in the future.

Focus on the repetition, and the fact that what you're asking of yourself on any given day is a small, incremental change. You can imagine it would be pretty daunting to rock up to a hilly site on the Tiber River and decide to build a city there. Impossible, you would think! But if you decided instead to lay ten bricks every hour in your eight-hour working day, you'd soon find you were making progress. Habits are just like that. Your ultimate goal might seem impossible from your baseline, and you might baulk at the scale of the commitment. It's like running a marathon — hugely daunting for most people. But going for a little run? That we can handle. Start so small it feels too small, and then slowly build over time.

And another thing — don't worry about how long it will take. The actual time it takes to bed in a new habit will vary from person to person, and it will depend upon how ambitious the target and the incremental steps towards it are. There will also be any number of other factors in play, because life is messy. In the end, it doesn't matter how long it will take. What's important is that you make a start. As Clear puts it: 'The only way to get to day 500 is to start with day 1. So forget about the number and focus on doing the work.'

Charles Duhigg's book *The Power of Habit* recommends focusing on the '3 Rs' of habit-building: a *reminder* (the trigger for your new behaviour), the *routine* (the behaviour itself) and the *reward* (which is usually a sense that you are making progress towards your goal).

This is all fine and dandy when it comes to eating (or not eating) ice cream, building cities and getting physically fit, but what has all this to do with mental fitness? Well, the process — and Clear and Duhigg are both clear about this, too: habit-building is a process, not an event — is exactly the same when it comes to building mental fitness. Willpower and moral fortitude are like muscles: the more you use them, the stronger they become and the easier it is to use them. In order to harness habit-building in your quest for mental toughness and resilience, you could do what the Stoic philosophers recommended and set a goal of trying something difficult every day, even if it's something small:

- Doing the dishes when you would rather sit down and watch TV.

- Picking clothes up off the floor rather than walking past them.
- Maintaining good posture.
- Always taking the stairs instead of the escalator or lift.
- Making your bed.

Until the behaviours and tactics associated with mental fitness become a habit, they can remain stressors that consume our psychological and emotional energy, much as exercise can play on our mind. It requires effort to start — until it becomes a habitual part of our day that we look forward to and would miss if we didn't do it. Once behaviours related to mental fitness become habits, they are easier to employ in the heat of the moment. They will proactively prompt us to take the breaks required for recovery, even as we continue to build our mental fitness.

We all face fire-fights in our lives. If we take a combat mindset to preparing for those, we'll perform better when our version of bullets and bombs are flying.

Combat mindset: a summary

Preparation for performing under pressure entails making habits of coping strategies before you need them (just like training for combat).

Habits are formed over time through the consistent application of effort.

There is no time like the present for beginning the process of acquiring a habit.

Small daily steps make big differences over time.

15

Your Mission

So here we are. We've arrived at the most important part of the book. Because now it's not about what I have to say. It's all about what you are going to do. It's all about you. I'm about to put down my pen, and it's time for you to pick yours up. You're going to write down one thing that you're going to start working on to get you closer to your goal of being a better person. Someone who's more effective in a crisis, who feels like they are flourishing on a day-to-day basis, and who not only bounces back from adversity, but grows as a result. In other words, someone who likes themselves and feels proud of the path they are on.

By now, you know all about the why. This book began by seeking to give you insights into the difference between the popular desire to be happy *in* your life — with all the unrealistic expectations it produces that you'll be stress-free and experiencing pleasant emotions all the time — and the more realistic and useful notion of being happy *with* your life. Being happy with your life leaves room for the slings and arrows that life itself will lob your way. Be assured that life will do this — adversity is part of the human experience. But you can choose to perceive such stress as a challenge to be embraced, not a threat to be avoided. You won't feel like a failure, because you realise that stress is what we're *supposed* to feel when we rise to the occasion. Stress is a sign that we are living a meaningful life and pursuing our potential. Perhaps the single, simplest way to feel happier with your life is to accept stress and then use tools such as the flourishing versus fatigued continuum (discussed in Chapter 4) to get more effective at proactively managing it.

The middle part of the book gave you the PERMA-H framework to ensure you pay attention to the mental fitness foundations of sleep, exercise, and nutrition. It also invited you to look at how *positive* you are about your approach to life and its challenges. It asked you to look at how *engaged* you are — how much of your life you spend attempting tasks that make demands on your resources, and deliver in turn the fulfilling experience of living in the moment with complete focus. It suggested you cast a ruler over your *relationships*, to identify what kinds of relationships you have with others, the ways in which they fall short of what you'd like them to be, and how you can do your bit to make them better. We're social animals, right? Meaningful connections with others are a big part of what makes us thrive. Human beings flourish when they feel their lives have *meaning* — a sense that we're part of something bigger and more important than ourselves. I gave you a list of values to help guide you to a better sense of what gives your life meaning. You're a lucky person if you can write a list of the things that you most want to be and tick them all off: values are, by nature, aspirational. They're the qualities that the better version of yourself will display at times when we're under the hammer. And better never stops. Lastly, we looked at the way in which *accomplishments* put fuel in our emotional tank and can be reflected on to give us a boost when times are tough. Each of us has a cookie jar, to use David Goggins's term. Recalling the moments when we succeeded under pressure assures us of our ability to do just that again — to make our actions count when the rubber hits the road. To be the hero rather than the coward or the villain.

Exploring the PERMA-H model may have identified gaps in your own mental fitness regime, which when plugged will ensure you can get more from life when the going is good. When we're flourishing, we're doing more than just feeling empowered and strong on a daily basis, we are putting fuel in the tank of our emotional and mental resources, which in turn helps us to bounce back more quickly and completely after reverses. Or even accelerate our growth as people.

What you've just been reading about in the last section of this book was you in a crisis. We looked at the value of stress exposure training, and how you can employ tools like the Big Four used by the Special Forces to cope when the pressure is really on. You may not actually be contemplating rappelling out of a helicopter to perform a covert op 100 kilometres behind enemy lines in a war zone, but you can learn plenty from the people who are. Preparing for a crisis is all about familiarising yourself with the tools you'll need to get you through, so that when the moment is upon you, you can use them with competence and confidence to deal with it. You'll be a pre-combat veteran. You'll know what to expect, because you'll have thought about the kind of situations that cause the walls to close in on you and your red brain, fight/flight/freeze suite of responses to kick in. You'll know what to do, because you'll have experimented with various ways in which you can defuse from your emotions and hit upon the ones that are most effective for you. You'll have practised them by using them in stressful situations, even if those stressful situations are only simulations — instructive visualisations — of the situations you know you'll one day confront. If you follow the advice in the previous chapter, you'll have practised them until they're habitual behaviours, and don't require any thought or deliberation to deploy.

Sound like a lot of work? Too much work? Too hard? Mini-goals! Take it one small step at a time. The biggest mistake most people make when deciding they want to get physically fit is to go out too hard and too fast. Don't make the same mistake with your mental fitness. Start with one commitment from this book and then build in others slowly over time. You are playing the long game here.

Write an action plan for your priority focus. If it helps, use the SMART framework, or think about this acronym: WOOP.

WOOP

WOOP is an evidence-based motivation tool that makes it significantly more likely that you will take the small steps required to achieve your goals. WOOP does this by getting you to identify an important wish/goal, imagine the desired outcomes and the obstacles, and making a plan for overcoming them. (Visit www.woopmylife.org to learn more about WOOP.)

_____

_____

_____

_____

_____

W = WISH

Based on this book, what is a mental-fitness exercise you will experiment with over the next 21 days? What is the first thing you must do to make a start? When, where, what time, and with whom, etc, will you practise this?

_____

_____

_____

_____

_____

O = OUTCOME

What will be the best result from accomplishing your goal? How will you feel if you accomplish it? What is the cost to you of not achieving this goal? Answer as fully as possible.

_____

_____

_____

_____

_____

O = OBSTACLE

What are the main obstacles that might prevent you from accomplishing your goal? Include any self-defeating thoughts/beliefs and associated emotions. Answer as fully as possible.

_____

_____

_____

_____

_____

P = PLAN

What can you do to overcome your obstacles? Name one action you can take or thought you can have. Make it an If/then plan: If [obstacle], then I will [effective action or thought].

_____

_____

_____

_____

_____

*

Well, what are you waiting for? You've got your pen in your hand. Write down that first, small step you're going to take towards improving your mental fitness. Over the next 21 days, journalise your efforts and experiences in making it stick. Treat it like an experiment and record your results. Tweak and tinker with the technique to find what works. Replace it with another technique if it's not had the desired effect after 21 days. Then keep doing it for 90 days, until it becomes a routine part of your life. This is how you strive for your potential. This is how you build the mental fitness to be happier with your life and become the person you really want to be.

LIST OF REFERENCES

Ben-Shahar, T. (2017). *Happier: Learn the Secrets to Daily Joy and Lasting Fulfillment*. McGraw-Hill Professional.

Brickman, P., & Campbell, D.T. (1971). 'Hedonic relativism and planning the good society', in M.H. Apley (ed.), *Adaptation Level Theory: A Symposium*. Academic Press.

Brickman, P., Coates, D., & Janoff-Bulman, R. (1978). 'Lottery winners and accident victims: is happiness relative?'. *Journal of Personality and Social Psychology*, 36 (8): 917–927.

Burton, R. (1621). *The Anatomy of Melancholy*.

Buss, D.M. (2019). *Evolutionary Psychology: The New Science of the Mind* (6th edn). Routledge.

Carnegie, D. ([1936] 1998). *How to Win Friends and Influence People*. Pocket Books.

Charles River Editors (2016). *The Space Shuttle Challenger Disaster: The History and Legacy of NASA's Most Notorious Tragedy*.

Clear, J. (2018). *Atomic Habits: An Easy and Proven Way to Build Good Habits & Break Bad Ones*. Penguin.

Conrad, C.D. (2011). *The Handbook of Stress: Neuropsychological Effects on the Brain*. Blackwell Publishing Ltd.

Covey, S.R. (2020). *The 7 Habits of Highly Effective People* (30th anniversary edition). Simon & Schuster.

Csikszentmihalyi, M. (2008). *Flow: The Psychology of Optimal Experience*. Harper Perennial.

Defence Health Directorate (2020). *Staying at the Top of Your Game: A Guide for Maintaining Health for the Defence Community*. New Zealand Defence Force.

Diamond, J. (1977). *Guns, Germs, and Steel: The Fates of Human Societies*. W.W. Norton.

Druett, J. (2007). *Island of the Lost: Shipwrecked at the Edge of the World*. Algonquin Books.

Duhigg, C. (2014). *The Power of Habit: Why We Do What We Do in Life and Business*. Random House.

Dunmont, F. (2010). *A History of Personality Psychology: Theory, Science, and Research from Hellenism to the Twenty-First Century*. Cambridge University Press.

Englert, P. (2021). *Futureselves: Free Will and the Science of Living Well*. In press.

Epictetus ([1st century] 2008). *Discourses and Selected Writings*. Translated by R.F. Dobbin. Penguin Classics.

Evans, C. (2019). *Perform Under Pressure*. HarperCollins.

Feldman Barrett, L. (2017). *How Emotions Are Made: The Secret Life of the Brain*. Houghton Mifflin Harcourt.

Fredrickson, B.L. (2004). 'The broaden-and-build theory of positive emotions'. *Philosophical Transactions of the Royal Society of Biological Sciences*, 359 (1449): 1367–1378.

Gilbert, D. (2007). *Stumbling on Happiness*. Vintage.

Gilmartin, K.M. (2002). *Emotional Survival for Law Enforcement: A Guide for Officers and their Families*. E-S Press.

Goggins, D. (2018). *Can't Hurt Me: Master Your Mind and Defy the Odds*. Lioncrest Publishing.

Gottman, J.M. (2015). *The Relationship Cure: A 5 Step Guide to Strengthening Your Marriage, Family, and Friendships*. Crown Publications.

Gruber, J. (2019). *The Oxford Handbook of Positive Emotion and Psychopathology*. Oxford Library of Psychology.

Hamilton, E. (1961). *The Collected Dialogues of Plato*. Translated by Lane Cooper. Princeton University Press.

Harari, Y.N. (2018). *Sapiens: A Brief History of Humankind*. HarperCollins.

Harris, R. (2007). *The Happiness Trap: Stop Struggling, Start Living*. Exisle Publishing.

Hecht, D. (2013). 'The neural basis of optimism and pessimism'. PubMed, 173–199.

Holmes, T.H., & Rahe, R.H. (1967). 'The social readjustment rating scale'. *Journal of Psychosomatic Research*, 11 (1): 213–218.

Holtz, L. (1998). *Winning Every Day: The Game Plan for Success*. Harper Business.

Johnson, A., & Protor, R. (2004). *Attention: Theory and Practice*. SAGE Publications.

Joseph, S. (2013). *What Doesn't Kill Us: The New Psychology of Posttraumatic Growth*. Cambridge University Press.

Kahneman, D. (2011). *Thinking, Fast and Slow*. Farrar, Straus and Giroux.

Kashdan, T., & Rottenberg, J. (2010). 'Psychological flexibility as a fundamental aspect of health'. *Clinical Psychology Review*, 30 (7): 865–878.

Kotler, S. (2014). *The Rise of Superman: Decoding the Science of Ultimate Human Performance*. New Harvest.

Leary, M.R. (2013). *Understanding the Mysteries of Human Behavior*. The Teaching Company.

Loehr, J.E. (2007). *The Power of Story: Rewrite Your Destiny in Business and in Life*. Free Press.

Maltz, M. (2017). *Psycho-Cybernetics*. Penguin Putnam.

McEwen, B.S., & Stellar, E. (1993). 'Stress and the individual: mechanisms leading to disease'. *Archives of Internal Medicine*, 27 September, 153(18): 2093–2101.

McGonigal, J. (2015). *SuperBetter: A Revolutionary Approach to Getting Stronger, Happier, Braver and More Resilient, Powered by the Science of Games*. Penguin Books.

Middleton, A. (2018). *First Man In: Leading from the Front*. HarperCollins.

Mulholland, T. (2004). *Healthy Thinking: How to Turn Life's Lemons into Lemonade*. Reed.

Neubauer, S., Hublin, J.J., & Gunz, G. (2018). 'The evolution of modern human brain shape'. *Science Advances*, 4 (1).

Pink, D.H. (2018). *Drive: The Surprising Truth About What Motivates Us*. Canongate Books.

Rahe R.H., & Arthur, R.J. (1978). 'Life change and illness studies: past history and future directions'. *Journal of Human Stress*. 4 (1): 3–5.

Rahe, R.H. et al. (2000). 'The stress and coping inventory: an educational and research instrument'. *Stress Medicine*, 16: 199–208.

Rahe, R.H., Mahan, J.L., & Arthur, R.J. (1970). 'Prediction of near-future health change from subjects' preceding life changes'. *Journal of Psychosomatic Research*. 14 (4): 401–406.

Roberts, A. (2011). *Evolution: The Human Story*. Dorling Kindersley.

Rock, D. (2009). *Your Brain at Work: Strategies for Overcoming Distraction, Regaining Focus, and Working Smarter All Day Long.* Harper Business.

Sawyer, K.R. (2007). *Group Genius: The Creative Power of Collaboration.* Penguin Professional.

Seligman, M. (2011). *Learned Optimism.* William Heinemann Australia.

Seligman, M. (2012). *Flourish.* William Heinemann Australia.

Selye, H. (1956). *The Stress of Life.* McGraw-Hill.

Steger, M.F., Dik, B.J., & Byrne, Z. (2013). *Purpose and Meaning in the Workplace.* American Psychological Association.

Stockdale, J.B. (1995). *Thoughts of a Philosophical Fighter Pilot.* Hoover Institution Press.

Stover, D. (2000). *Beyond a World Divided: Human Values in the Brain-Mind Science of Roger Sperry.* iUniverse.

Tedeschi, R.G., & Moore, B.A. (2016). *The Posttraumatic Growth Workbook: Coming Through Trauma Wiser, Stronger, and More Resilient.* New Harbinger Publications.

Walker, M. (2018). *Why We Sleep: The New Science of Sleep and Dreams.* Penguin Press.

Watt Smith, T. (2017). *The Book of Human Emotions.* Profile Books.

Williams, R.B., & Williams, V.P. (2003). *The Type E Personality: 10 Steps to Emotional Excellence in Love, Work, and Life.* Rodale Press.

Wood, P. (2019). *How to Escape from Prison.* HarperCollins.

Yerkes, R.M., & Dodson, J.D. (1908). 'The relationship of strength of stimulus to rapidity of habit formation'. *Journal of Comparative Neurology and Psychology,* 18: 459–482.

ACKNOWLEDGEMENTS

The first person I would like to thank and acknowledge is my wife, Mary-Ann Moller. Not only is she the love of my life and mother of my boys, but she is a genuine bad-ass and one of the mentally toughest people I know. I am constantly inspired by her work ethic, willingness to take on big challenges, commitment to excellence, and courage when the tracks get gnarly and the heat is on. I would also like to thank the Conduct after Capture team and the SAS for allowing me to observe some seriously impressive stress exposure training in action! Furthermore, a heartfelt thanks to Captain Paul 'Stevo' Stevens, Lieutenant Colonel Stephen Kearny, Captain Drew Kingi, Flight Lieutenant Frances Gedye Smith, and the rest of the Defence Force psychologists who were so generous with their time, insights, and knowledge in the preparation of this book. Thanks also to the friends and colleagues who acted as sources, sounding boards, and inspiration; including Dr Paul Englert, Captain Tony Williams, Dr Elliot Bell, Dr Tom Mulholland, Dr Ben Palmer, Sam Farmer, Gary Moller, Jay Barrett, and Big Al (your stories are better than your chess mate). I also want to acknowledge my father, Brian Wood, who survived the Blitz and has never uttered a word of complaint about a hardship or challenge. Finally, a special thanks to the HarperCollins team and John McCrystal who not only believed in this book but were great collaborators along the way.